T0342081

In Dependence

In Dependence

Women and the Patriarchal State
in Revolutionary America

Jacqueline Beatty

New York University Press
NEW YORK

NEW YORK UNIVERSITY PRESS
New York
www.nyupress.org
© 2023 by New York University
All rights reserved

Library of Congress Cataloging-in-Publication Data

Names: Beatty, Jacqueline, author.
Title: In dependence : women and the patriarchal state in revolutionary
    America / Jacqueline Beatty.
Description: New York : New York University Press, [2023] | Series: Early
    American places | Includes bibliographical references and index.
Identifiers: LCCN 2022036507 | ISBN 9781479812127 (hardback) |
    ISBN 9781479812134 (ebook other) | ISBN 9781479812158 (ebook)
Subjects: LCSH: Women—United States—History—18th century. |
    Women—United States—Social conditions—18th century. |
    Women—Legal status, laws, etc.—United States—History—18th century. |
    United States—History—Revolution, 1775–1783.
Classification: LCC HQ1418 .B39 2023 | DDC 305.420973/09033—dc23/eng/20220825
LC record available at https://lccn.loc.gov/2022036507

New York University Press books are printed on acid-free paper, and their binding materials
are chosen for strength and durability. We strive to use environmentally responsible
suppliers and materials to the greatest extent possible in publishing our books.
Manufactured in the United States of America
10 9 8 7 6 5 4 3 2 1
Also available as an ebook

CONTENTS

Introduction

Elizabeth Graeme Fergusson was among the "most learned" of eighteenth-century American women. She was well known among Philadelphia society for her thoughtful prose, her graceful poetry—in essence, for her pen. The circumstances of her life, however, compelled her to take up her pen for nonliterary purposes. Fergusson petitioned Pennsylvania's state officials on a number of occasions in an attempt to protect from confiscation the property left to her by her late father. The trouble started when she courted a man very briefly before the two rushed into a clandestine marriage and fled the country. Henry Hugh Fergusson, a devoted loyalist twelve years Elizabeth's junior, left Philadelphia with the British. Under the laws of coverture and the revolutionary government of Pennsylvania's property confiscation policies, the late Thomas Graeme's property left (he thought) to his unmarried daughter instead belonged to the state. The property transferred to Henry Fergusson after the marriage; because Elizabeth had kept the union secret from her father, he did not make legal provision for her to own the property in her own right, separate from Henry, so when Henry left Philadelphia, the property reverted to the state. After her father's death and her husband's absconding, Elizabeth fell into great debt, receiving loans from friends that she had no hope of repaying.[1]

In her desperation, Elizabeth petitioned Pennsylvania's Supreme Executive Council in 1781, after a years-long back and forth with the body.[2] She claimed that the state's sale of Graeme Park, her late father's estate, would serve "at once to destroy the sole Support of One who (must

FIGURE I.1. Graeme Park, Horsham, Pennsylvania, 2022. Photo by Jeffrey Beatty.

she repeat it) will not be found to have deserved Evil at their Hands"—namely, herself.[3] Elizabeth implored the council to "relieve her" of her insurmountable burdens, and "benevolently" return Graeme Park to her so that she might "make such Disposition of it as may be necessary for her future Support." In closing, she reached out to the council members' sense of obligation to citizens (and particularly dependents) in her situation, imploring that they consider her own innocence in the matter of her husband's behavior and forgive her association with him: "She flatters herself their own Feeling's will never reproach them for the Act and Neither Heaven nor Man 'grieve at the Mercy.'" As an addendum, Elizabeth included a list of forty-one men who could attest both to the legitimacy of her claims and to her position as an object worthy of the council's compassion.[4]

Significantly, evidence suggests that Elizabeth played a critical role in the drafting of her several petitions, and that she purposely and thoughtfully crafted a narrative that employed tropes of feminine helplessness and vulnerability. Elizabeth's 1781 petition, the product of several years of edits and amendments, is cluttered with strikeouts, crammed with commentary in the margins, supplementing and at times contradicting the original text. Letters from Andrew Robeson, an attorney and friend of Elizabeth's, reveal whose hand drafted the markups. Robeson wrote to Elizabeth, assuring her that "Mr. Matlack has been waited on and the alterations made agreeably *to your Desire*."[5] Elizabeth's plea, replete with tropes of feminine dependence, was a clear product of her own pen and mind, and engaged an artful strategy designed to evoke the sympathy of the legislative body.

Early American women like Elizabeth Graeme Fergusson understood the power inherent in their performance of, and acquiescence to, expectations of feminine comportment. When deployed judiciously, this language convinced men in positions of authority to provide aid, assistance, and especially financial relief to women in distressed situations. Joseph Reed, a delegate in the Continental Congress and president of Pennsylvania, wrote to Elizabeth's friend Annis Stockton suggesting that Elizabeth was wise to target the fellow feeling of these elite men: "As to the Lady who is the Subject of our Concern I hope she & you will do me the Justice to believe I sincerely pity & sympathize with her in the Misfortunes which have clouded her Prospects & embittered her Life . . . My Wishes & Intentions ever were to soften her Calamities to the utmost of my Power." Further, Reed insisted that Elizabeth should consider herself fortunate that the power and ability to relieve her of her distresses were "lodged in the Hands of Gentlemen of Tenderness & Consideration" who had a record of showing "the most favorable Attention to Distress like hers."[6] Elizabeth, in other words, was utilizing the most powerful political weapon at her disposal—the petition—and put pen to paper in deploying the most effective language she could muster.

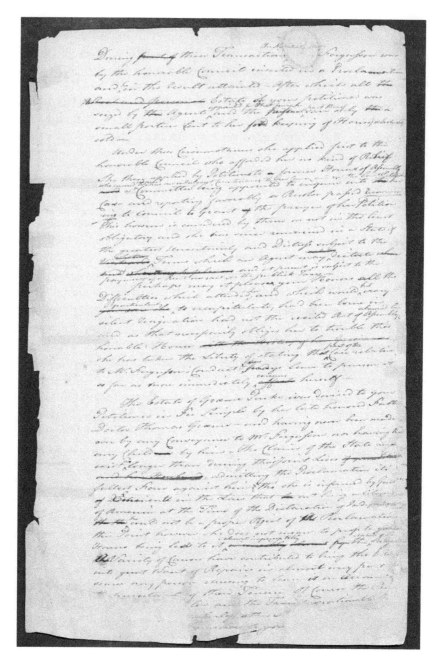

FIGURE I.2. Evidence of Elizabeth Graeme Fergusson's suggestions and edits are clear in this petition, with a number of deletions and marginal notes. Source: "Petition of Elizabeth Graeme Fergusson to the Supreme Executive Council of Pennsylvania, 20 February 1781." Simon Gratz autograph collection [0250B], case 14, box 16, folder 9. Reproduced with permission from the Historical Society of Pennsylvania.

American women in the revolutionary era like Elizabeth Graeme Fergusson knew well the terms of their multifaceted dependencies. Despite enormous legal, social, and economic restrictions, however, early American women were far from powerless. How is it, then, that these women with few rights under the law (and restricted access to the political sphere) were able to express power? During and after the Revolution, women's petitions to the patriarchal state—the colonial, revolutionary, and early national institutions, organizations, and spaces governed and controlled by elite white men—increased exponentially. The consequences of war provided both the impetus and the opportunity for women to seek intervention from male authorities in their communities and at the state level. In their increased interactions with the patriarchal state, women employed the very terms of their intersectional dependencies as a strategy to exert agency over their own lives. Significantly, too, the American Revolution provided some women with the language and opportunities with which to claim old rights—the rights of dependents—in new ways. Paradoxically, then, early American women were able to negotiate and argue for a relative degree of power, independence, and rights from the patriarchal state because of, and while they existed firmly within, this state of dependence.

Historians have spent decades investigating whether the American Revolution benefited women or provoked changes in women's status.[7] By and large, white women's traditional political rights and legal status remained relatively stagnant in the wake of the American Revolution.[8] In some ways, women's legal status declined over the course of the long eighteenth century.[9] Certain women's private lives, however, did see some important shifts, especially in regards to family limitation and motherhood.[10] Importantly, the Revolution politicized some women who participated in boycotts, contributed to and consumed Tory and Whig literature, and even acted as spies or soldiers themselves during the war.[11] Women also carefully negotiated their political positions to manage the survival and safety of their families.[12] In the postwar period, elite white women gained greater access to education, though ultimately in service of raising respectable republican sons and their worthy wives.[13] In many ways, however, the lives of American women looked much the same in the postrevolutionary period as they had prior to the war. Despite Abigail Adams's threat to "foment a rebellion" if women were not included formally in the new American body politic, there would be no great women's revolution in the late eighteenth and early nineteenth centuries.[14]

Asking whether the Revolution benefited women or brought meaningful changes in their social, legal, and economic statuses, however, cannot fully illuminate the war's impact on women's lives. In some ways, this framework is both anachronistic and problematic. Constructing our queries in this way asks too much from a historical period in which inequality and unfreedom were so deeply embedded in patriarchal law, culture, and society as to render such a sea change unlikely at best.[15] Likewise, this line of inquiry presumes that revolutionary-era women collectively desired what first- and second-wave feminists sought for themselves.[16] It also judges the consequences of the Revolution for women from a set of expectations codified as masculine.[17] Certainly, there were a few noteworthy women who sought rights and freedoms for which liberal feminists of the nineteenth and twentieth century fought, but the Abigail Adamses, Mercy Otis Warrens, and Judith Sargent Murrays of the American revolutionary era were few and far between.[18]

This long scholarly conversation about whether the American Revolution was centrally a moment of change, stagnation, or decline in women's lives has framed many historical investigations from the wrong perspective. Ironically, we have been studying patriarchal oppression, resistance to it, and attempts to overcome it from a patriarchal standard all along.[19] We must seek to understand the impact of the American Revolution on women's lives by framing our inquisition around women's *own* worldview, their *own* needs, aspirations, and desires, even when doing so is uncomfortable to our modern sensibilities. What function did the Revolution serve in women's lives? How did women interpret the rhetoric of the Revolution? How did they make the disruption and upheaval of this historical moment work to their advantage, with the tools already at their disposal? How did they use the apparatus of patriarchal oppression—namely, assumptions of their subordination and powerlessness—to their advantage? What did they want for themselves in this period, and were they able to achieve it? When the impact of the Revolution is investigated with this shift in perspective, we are able to observe the ways in which women's individual and collective consciousness changed, even if the Revolution was not radical enough to propel them from their unequal station in American society.

In Dependence asks these questions from a regionally comparative and chronologically wide-ranging perspective, focusing on three vibrant urban areas—Boston, Massachusetts; Philadelphia, Pennsylvania; and Charleston, South Carolina—between 1750 and 1820, or what I refer to broadly as the "revolutionary era." These three cities serve as ideal locations for a study of early American women's experiences as their laws, social customs, and cultures varied significantly. Boston, Philadelphia, and Charleston were three of the most populous cities in the American colonies and, later, the early republic, which provided inhabitants with access to burgeoning communities as well as the growing marketplaces of goods, printed materials, and ideas.[20] Massachusetts's, Pennsylvania's, and South Carolina's laws regarding marriage, divorce, and property ownership (and thus their demarcation of women's rights and legal status) all differed a great deal during this period. I chose to focus my study on urban as opposed to rural areas so as to include in this work impoverished communities, whose members often turned for assistance to city almshouses and other local organizations. Women in each of these three cities had the opportunity to petition their state legislatures for redress, yet because of their varying experiences and racial and class identities, they did so for different reasons, with different access to seats of patriarchal power, and certainly with different outcomes.

The revolutionary era was a period in which ideas about the meanings of independence, freedom, and individual rights were undergoing dynamic changes.[21] Dependence was a fact of life in colonial British America, defining relationships ranging from colonial subjects' connections to the king to wives' unions with their husbands. Both parties in these relationships had power—even dependents—and these relationships required a set of mutual obligations. Thus, dependence was not an inherently impotent status.[22] The meaning of dependence shifted, however, with the adoption of the Declaration of Independence. Dependence ceased to be a construct with positive connotations in the American imagination, and likewise became imbued with a sense of powerlessness.[23] The newly independent United States required the allegiance of its people, and adopted the concept of voluntary citizenship rather than involuntary subjectship.[24] Accordingly, the law recognized women's personhood and, to a certain degree, their citizenship, but it also presumed their dependence, which codified them as legally vulnerable and passive. Dependence, then, became highly gendered, and feminized.[25] Women's dependent status was likewise contingent on their socioeconomic status, their race, the legal jurisdiction in which they resided, and their relationship to men in power.

Importantly, dependence must not be observed as the ultimate foil to independence. These terms are not abjectly dichotomous to one another, but exist on a fluid spectrum.[26] Situated on this continuum, women firmly asserted their dependence while expressing the "powers of the weak." While a traditional understanding of "power" implies some form of domination of one party over another through possession, control, command, or authority, this conception obscures the meaning of the word itself while also negating the exercises and expressions of power that do not conform to these standards.[27] If power is also understood as existing on a fluid spectrum, then, an analysis of women's invocation of the language of dependence in their petitions to state legislatures, courts, local aid societies, and their communities becomes much different.

Notions of power and freedom in early America were contingent upon a person's intersectional identities.[28] Wealthy, white male enslavers, for example, had different understandings and experiences of freedom than did the Black women they enslaved, and because of the legal structure of the patriarchal state, these white male enslavers held a great deal of power over unfree, enslaved Black women. Like dependence and independence, freedom and unfreedom existed on different ends of the same spectrum.[29] Race, gender, class, religion, region, status of apprenticeship, servitude, or enslavement, and other elements of an early American's identity shaped their relationship to freedom and unfreedom. Notably, this continuum was deeply hierarchical. Even if enslaved women earned or purchased their legal freedom from the institution of slavery, that free status was still tenuous, as was the free status of any children they bore.

Likewise, enslaved women would have viewed freedom differently than their white counterparts. Black women in particular often defined freedom as self-ownership, the ability to own property, to profess their faith freely, and to ensure freedom for their families.[30] Freedom for many enslaved people was a matter of degrees, a game of inches, a process of constant negotiation for small margins of autonomy and independence in an otherwise deeply oppressive system. Even if they obtained documentation that declared them legally free from the institution of slavery, that did not guarantee their perpetual freedom, and it certainly did not grant them equality under the law; that freedom—even if it existed on paper—was tenuous. Additionally, American freedom did not evolve and expand in a teleological manner; in many cases, even in the revolutionary era, freedoms *de*volved and disappeared for certain marginalized groups of Americans.[31] We must always consider the ways in which Americans' experiences of their freedoms were not (and in many ways, still are not) equal.

Black women experienced multiple, layered dependencies that were compounded by their race and gender, and especially by the existence of the race-based system of chattel slavery that relied on Black women's reproductive capacity to enhance the power of white patriarchs.[32] Black women, therefore, were not endowed with the same legal protections, rights, and privileges as their white contemporaries were. Engaging with the sympathies of white patriarchs, for example, was not a functional or effective strategy for Black women, as it was for white women.[33] In order to fully understand how Black women exploited the terms of their intersectional dependencies, then, we must examine the unique experiences of Black women from within these interlocking systems of oppression.[34]

The notion that women could—and can still—express power because of their subordinate status and the protection it offers indicates that women have never been completely powerless. Like other historically marginalized groups or individuals, women have been able to express a degree of power, autonomy, and agency over their own lives while still being overtly suppressed by a controlling authority.[35] Thus, dependents expressed power in a variety of ways, including more subtle means such as claiming a public voice or becoming politically active via the submission of petitions.[36] What is especially significant, however, is not that women found power through petitioning various authorities but that they found power in this way through public declarations of their dependent, unequal, and subordinate status.

The legal structure was integral in framing women's dependence and their ability to express power over their own lives. The law must also be understood as an outline for how members of society viewed themselves in relationship to one another. Laws are "the aspiration of lawmakers, the vision of the kind of society they wanted to create, the social order they wished to enforce."[37] But laws are also what people make them.[38] Petitions as sources provide clues of women's lived experience when the historical record is otherwise silent; they show us the ways in which women conformed to the law and social custom, but also the ways in which they made the law their own. Rather than seeing the law's power as absolute or rendering women's resistance exceptional, this study endeavors, more broadly, to recognize women's power through their exploitation of this confining system.

While women's dependent status was well defined under the law, it also permeated Anglo-American society and culture in the revolutionary era in the form of conduct literature. Pamphlets, novels, magazines, essays, and poems all established separate standards of behavior for women and men, especially in regard to their marital roles. The "good wife," for example, was charged with the task of upholding the "solemn contract" of marriage by remaining "virtuous, constant, and faithful to her husband; chaste, pure, and unblemished, in every thought, word, and deed." She was to be submissive to her husband's authority, and she was to *desire* and *strive* to obey him by her own inclination.[39] Women, though, were not the only ones called to perform certain standards of comportment in this mutual relationship. Just as wives owed a certain amount of deference to their husbands' authority, so too were husbands expected to behave in a certain way.[40] Men were specifically entrusted with the duty of providing financially for their wives, protecting women under their "covered" status.

These "recipricol" duties found their roots in Blackstone's *Commentaries on the Laws of England* and his discussions of the common law practice of coverture.[41] At the time of her marriage, a woman became a *feme covert*, "under the protection and influence of her husband," and as a result, she was to "depend almost all the legal rights, duties, and disabilities, that either of them acquire by the marriage." In exchange, "the husband is bound to provide his wife with necessaries by law, as much as himself . . . for he has adopted her and her sircumstances together." Blackstone acknowledged that these "disabilities, which the wife lies under, are for the most part intended for her protection and benefit." He even went so far as to describe women's legal situation as making them "a favourite . . . of the laws of England."[42]

With this understanding of revolutionary-era law and culture in mind, this work employs evidence derived from extensive research in legislative petitions, divorce cases, marriage settlements, equity cases, probate records, manumission deeds, almshouse records, and charitable institutional files. For the most part, I have chosen to focus on formal petitions to the state legislature or county courts submitted by women individually or collectively, to which they signed their own names or left their own mark, in advocacy for themselves. Because few Black women submitted petitions directly to patriarchal state authorities in the ways outlined above, I have expanded my conception of the archive of petitions to include manumission deeds and other legal records to which Black women were party.

Petitioning was a right of subjects of the British Crown and, later, of citizens of the United States, even (and perhaps especially) for dependents. The petition was both a personal and a political outlet that allowed supplicants to request or demand certain things from the state. Many scholars who study eighteenth- and early-nineteenth-century women's petitions have demonstrated that these documents illustrate the ways in which women entered into the public, political sphere.[43] While these claims are well documented, this is not the only conclusion that can be drawn from these rich sources. These petitions reveal the inherent and deeply rooted influence of the discourse of dependence on revolutionary-era women's lives. While the rhetoric and narratives that permeate these petitions appear reflexive, and perhaps a formality, deeper analysis reveals that women made a purposeful choice in how they presented their own stories to the patriarchal state. Thus, petitions can be viewed as an expression of women's agency through the exploitation of their subordinate status in a way that inherently and ironically rejects this status.

In Dependence is organized thematically, and each chapter considers its respective theme from a comparative geographical perspective. Legislative and judicial petitions were an outlet in which early Americans solicited assistance from the state. The language of women's petitions analyzed in chapter 1 closely mirrors the gendered expectations of white femininity in the Anglo-American Atlantic world. Women deployed tropes of helplessness and vulnerability in order to elicit the sympathies of elite, white patriarchs in power. Particularly as the war provoked untold disruption and devastation in women's lives, they used the outlet of the petition to implore the patriarchal state to care and provide for them in accordance with their obligation to social, legal, and economic dependents. Walking a careful tightrope, women's petitions provided the space in which to critique one form of patriarchal authority—either their husbands or the state itself—while demonstrating proper deference to the other. The deployment of such language and the performance of feminine dependence was an effective strategy for surviving some of the most brutal consequences of the American Revolution, and paradoxically empowered women as they explicitly emphasized their powerlessness.

Dependence also governed women's positions in the legal institution of marriage, examined in chapter 2. In seeking to extricate themselves from these unions, women deployed similarly gendered language in their suits to county courts. Women's petitions for divorce reveal the ways in which they exploited the legal and social obligations of the marital contract in order to break themselves free from it. Women insisted in their petitions for marital separation that their husbands had failed in their responsibility to provide financial support, physical protection, or fidelity to their wives, all the while insisting that they had impeccably performed their duties as wives. In so doing, women entered the masculine space of the courtroom to argue for freedom from one patriarchal authority—their husbands—by invoking their own compliance with the expectations of marriage as defined by the patriarchal state.

Not all women, however, were legally able to divorce their husbands. Regional contingency becomes especially evident in chapter 3, which describes how women in jurisdictions such as South Carolina had to employ other means to earn a degree of independence from the confines of marriage and coverture. Certain women were able to negotiate a variety of marital settlements due to specific protections of property ownership provided in South Carolina law. Because of long-standing protections for white, patriarchal rule under colonial and, later, state law, South Carolina women possessed particular property rights that women in other regions did not enjoy. These women could obtain *feme sole* trader status and sue their husbands in equity courts to gain financial security and, in some cases, independence from their husbands. In some ways, then, these women were freer than those women in other jurisdictions who could obtain legal divorces from their husbands (who, in many cases, did not have much if any financial power), yet they employed the same framework of dependence and the language of the contractual obligations of marriage that those who petitioned for divorce utilized. These women thus claimed financial acuity and, in certain cases, greater fiscal proficiency than their husbands, but ironically, presented these skills as an extension of their dependent, feminine roles: as wives, mothers, and daughters.

Despite legal, social, and economic expectations that men protect and care for women in their subordinate status, many women found that this patriarchal structure was inadequate in ensuring their safety and survival. Chapter 4 explores how women built, sustained, and depended upon female networks of interdependence when their mechanisms of protection within the patriarchal state failed them. Women relied on female family members and friends across North America and throughout the Atlantic world, but also in their neighborhoods, often bypassing or explicitly challenging male authority in the process. Women's communal and familial networks enabled them to critique men and the patriarchal state in an effort to protect the women in their lives, in some ways usurping the role of the male protector and expressly undermining women's dependence. Paradoxically, however, by challenging domestic and state patriarchs on an individual level, these female networks bolstered the legitimacy of women's collective dependence on men by reinforcing patriarchal standards of protection and women's subordination.

While women could exploit and perform feminine dependence to gain advantages from the patriarchal state, the power white women exercised in doing so was contingent upon class as well as their willingness to buy into patriarchal assumptions about gender. These strategies were limited for poor white women and women who did not conform to the social expectations of white femininity, as presented in chapter 5. The latter expressly chose to employ language that was overtly critical of political or household patriarchs or overstepped the boundaries of feminine comportment. In so doing, they demonstrated that although the performance of gender was somewhat fluid during wartime, the patriarchal hierarchy remained the powerful framework from within which women's lives were ultimately governed. Poor white women faced a dilemma brought on by their doubled dependencies: poverty and womanhood. Poor women could not properly perform feminine dependence, as they were often required to work to support their families, but they likewise could not meet early American society's developing standards of the "worthy poor" who were required to work to earn relief, due to expectations that a patriarchal figure should provide for his financial dependents. The expectations of white femininity, then, acted as a blockade for poor women on multiple fronts. For poor women and for women who overstepped the increasingly indurate boundaries of gender comportment in the revolutionary era, the framework of dependence was a problem, not a solution.

Importantly, women's dependence was also contingent upon race and racial privilege. Black women were not endowed with the same legal, social, and economic protections that dependence afforded white women, and thus could not employ the same strategies in their interactions with the patriarchal state. Black women's formal petitions to the patriarchal state were few, but that does not mean that they did not seek redress from the state in other ways. By expanding the concept of petitioning, chapter 6 takes seriously Black women's efforts in forcing the various mechanisms of the patriarchal state to recognize their humanity and their womanhood. This requires the historian to broaden her source base beyond the traditional legal archive. Redefining what constituted a petition and investigating the lived experience of Black women on their own terms reveals that free and enslaved Black women advocated for themselves and their families in important ways. Free and enslaved Black men and women deployed their marital unions to claim legal protections for themselves and their children, particularly as free Black women's bodies birthed legal freedom to their descendants. Black women resisted the patriarchal state's authority by using its own bulwarks of intersectional oppression against them.

For the most part, women's rhetorical strategies of exploiting their dependent status remained consistent from the late colonial period through the years of the early republic. Overall, the frequency and quantity of women's petitions ballooned over the course of the revolutionary era due to the consequences of the war in women's lives; this politicized a number of women, but simultaneously fueled the expectation that the state fill a patriarchal, paternalistic role in women's lives, ultimately reinforcing their subordination in this hierarchical system. The evidence suggests one notable, and significant, shift in women's status, argued in chapter 7. In legislative petitions and divorce cases, women declared that they were endowed with rights contingent upon and particular to their status as dependents. The American Revolution, then, did affect women's understanding of their dependence in one significant way: in the language and declaration of their rights. The rhetoric of the revolution and the "rights talk" surrounding the conflict provided them with a new framework through which to argue for these old, well-established rights. Early American women, then, emerged from the revolutionary era with a new consciousness as rights-bearing individuals because of their experiences in dependence.

* * *

Elizabeth Graeme Fergusson's 1781 petition mirrored, in many ways, pleas submitted by women in comparably devastating circumstances wrought by the American Revolution. With her husband in England and without any ability to support herself, she turned to the state to act as a surrogate patriarch to protect her and relieve her distress. She highlighted her detachment from the political upheavals of the war, insisting that her actions reflected those of a wife, dutifully obeying her husband. Like other women, Elizabeth stressed her own dependence on various male authorities in an attempt to earn relief from the state. In other ways, however, her situation was exceptional. She enjoyed both economic and racial privilege; she stood to inherit property (coverture issues notwithstanding) and therefore managed to live on her own without her husband's support. Additionally, she was well educated and well respected for her mind. Notably, too, the extant manuscript sources make clear that her rhetorical strategy was a deliberate choice, and that she understood the inherent efficacy of these constructs. But most women who petitioned the patriarchal state did not leave such copious correspondence (if any), and not all women had access to powerful men who could intervene on their behalf. Women in the revolutionary era existed on a spectrum of dependence that influenced the ways in which they could interact with the patriarchal state—the degree to which they could utilize the language of feminine dependence and subordination in their appeals to male authorities, and the extent to which they could claim various forms of assistance, freedom, and independence in the process. Using this framework, many women in the revolutionary era effectively exploited the limitations constructed by the patriarchal state by expressing power through the deliberate accentuation of their powerlessness.

1 / Sympathy and the State

When the British evacuated Boston in 1776, Samuel Tarbell, a loyalist sympathizer, fled with them. For three years, he remained in Newport, Rhode Island, while his wife and children stayed home.[1] Seeking to reunite her family amid the violence and upheaval of war, Rebecca Tarbell filed a petition with the Massachusetts General Assembly in which she requested to leave the city and live with her husband once again.[2] Rebecca's plea detailed the "very disagreeable situation" in which she found herself in Samuel's absence. "Her prospects for support for herself, and her two children," she offered to the legislators, "are very gloomy and distressing." Rebecca foresaw no way out of her predicament, save for joining her husband in Newport. There, "by his assistance," she could "find means to lighten the burdens and avoid some of the evils in which she must otherwise be subjected." She asked only that she be able to carry with her "the pitiable pittance of bedding, and other furniture . . . which she apprehends will be necessary for the present subsistence of herself and family."[3] Her situation was dire, and she asked for the bare minimum in order to survive.

Rebecca's narrative was replete with humility, feminine deference, and—importantly—a heartbreaking portrait of a wife and mother devastated by the political choices of men. Women like Rebecca Tarbell wisely framed their pleas in such a way as to provoke the fellow feeling of state legislators and court authorities.[4] In so doing, they exploited the terms of their feminine dependence to gain relief, assistance, and intervention from the patriarchal state; in other words, they crafted a narrative attuned to what their audience wanted to hear. Notably, too, Rebecca made no attempts to distance herself from her husband's political choices. Knowing full well that the state harbored resentment towards men in her husband's position, Rebecca sought to use her own performance of wifely duty to soften her husband's image: "She confesses also that she feels a degree of affection to the man with whom she is connected by the strongest and most tender bonds: and who to other faults has never added that of unkindness to his wife and children."[5] Assenting to Samuel's unfortunate role in the war—his "other faults," as she obliquely wrote—Rebecca nevertheless sought to focus instead on Samuel's fulfillment of his domestic duties. In this case, he benefited from his association with such a dutiful wife who was willing to advocate for him in this way.

Rebecca's petition is emblematic of hundreds of pleas submitted by women to the patriarchal state in the revolutionary era. Her story was the essence of dependent womanhood, of vulnerable white femininity—in short, a precise match for what the patriarchal state dictated she be. She portrayed herself as the helpless victim of a flawed and failed patriarch, yet she reinforced her own dependence on and need for her husband. In so doing, she sought the assistance of the state. Her own sympathetic narrative was critical in detracting from her husband's politics and securing a pass for herself and her children to once again be reunited with their source of financial and emotional support.[6] Rebecca's petition was an explicit display of a helpless, vulnerable female citizen in need of patriarchal authorities to intervene on her behalf. It was an adept employment of women's ostensible distance from politics to achieve a political solution to her family's problems. It was a gendered performance designed to provoke empathy from these legislators. "Performance," in this case, is the operative word.

Although gender is a sociocultural construct, it had concrete meanings and consequences for men and women in the Anglo-American world of the revolutionary era. Both men and women were subject to social, cultural, political, and economic standards of comportment according to their gender as well as their race, class, and region. While white men assumed the roles of heads of household and heads of state, they were likewise tasked with the defense and protection of their dependents—namely, their wives and children. White women, on the other hand, were expected to submit to male authority, and in exchange were entitled to certain protections and benefits from their fathers and husbands. In eighteenth-century Anglo-America, examples of these gendered identities were propagated widely throughout contemporary conduct literature in its various forms. Women who submitted petitions to various colonial and state legislatures and county courts played on and performed these expectations by invoking their dependence and subordination as a justification for their pleas for relief. But women's legislative and judicial petitions in this period did not unthinkingly parrot the language they learned from prescriptive literature. Instead, these sources reveal women's deep comprehension of the power of the gendered construct of their femininity as well as their adept practice of exploiting these tropes to their advantage.

It is critical to see women's petitions—their narratives replete with the rhetoric of feminine helplessness and dependence—as performative. While these documents often had an instinctively supplicating tone, this was not always the case. To dismiss this rhetoric as automatic and a necessary component of the medium is to undermine the significance of the choices women made in presenting their cases to the patriarchal state.[7] Instead, these sources make evident the fact that women were proficient at "troubling" the expectations of their gender in a number of ways.[8] In some regard, the question of whether women themselves accepted these notions of their subordination is immaterial, insofar as the effectiveness of their strategy is concerned.[9] Women understood the power of these gendered constructs and used them in such a way as to work to their individual advantage. Though ostensibly consenting to women's dependence and subordination, these petitions tested the boundaries of late-eighteenth- and early-nineteenth-century gender roles during and in the wake of the war, thus demonstrating the "contingency and mutability" of gender in the late eighteenth and early nineteenth centuries.[10]

Performing Dependence

Women's petitions focused broadly on their helplessness, their vulnerability, and, in some cases, their inability to care for themselves in the absence of their husbands. Some, for example, exploited assumptions of their financial ineptitude to successfully plead for the return of banished men in their lives who had been punished for their politics, thus restoring these women's support system. Mary Peronneau, widow to the late Arthur, sought mercy for her brother-in-law, Robert, whom the legislature had banished and whose property was seized as a result of South Carolina's 1782 Confiscation Act. Robert had been "warmly attached to the Cause of his Country," Peronneau argued. So "eager" was he "to take an active part in it" that Robert traveled from Britain to the United States in 1778, "through numberless appeasing difficulties." He served nobly, she insisted, until Charleston fell into British hands.[11]

Like many others in her situation, Mary argued that the circumstances of the war coerced Robert to sign the Congratulatory Address to Lord Cornwallis upon the general's victory at Camden. It was in "an unguarded moment," she insisted, and at the urging of friends, that he acquiesced to the British loyalty oath. Robert's health was subsequently in decline, and Mary was convinced that the stress of this ordeal had been the provocation. Likewise, his poor health caused trouble for herself and her children. With her husband, Arthur, deceased, Mary and her children found themselves wanting and "in a great measure" still "dependent on [her brother-in-law] for support."[12] Without Robert, Mary and her children had nowhere to turn; she insisted that she was incapable of providing for her family without his assistance, painting herself as the consummate pitiable figure.

It was in this emphasis on her dependence and helplessness—particularly in financial matters—that Mary found a legitimate reason to petition her government for leniency in Robert's case. In the end, the legislature granted her petition, earning Robert clemency for his ostensible disloyalty.[13] Mary's situation, though, was not unique. A number of women faced similar hardships in the wake of the British retreat from Charleston, and the majority repeated gendered tropes of female helplessness and vulnerability. In so doing, they managed to reassert a bit of power and agency over their lives, through ironically emphasizing this very powerlessness.

Mary's petition also highlights the ways in which women's language emasculated men and undermined their patriarchal authority while elevating women's roles in the family and potentially in the eyes of the state. Mary crafted an image of her brother-in-law, Robert, as her sole source of financial support, but also as a powerless stooge who bowed to the whims of Tory authorities and peer pressure, abandoning his political convictions when they became inconvenient or threatened his status. The Robert of 1782 was not the man of principle of 1778. His declining health also seemed to speak to the weakness of his constitution in coping with the consequences of his actions. Mary's request for "compassion to her & a large family, who have suffered much in these calamitous times" met the gendered expectations of white femininity, though Robert failed to hold fast to his convictions, failing his family in the process. In similar cases, women's language implicitly illustrated that they had the strength to hold fast to expectations of gendered comportment in wartime, even when the men around them did not.

Women likewise demonstrated their adherence to standards of feminine comportment by including the legitimating force of male voices in their petitions. A young woman from Philadelphia named Ann Sutter had been convicted of larceny, of stealing "sundry sums of Money the Property of Jonathan Price," for which she was sentenced to receive corporal punishment. Although Sutter's petition to have her punishment remitted was rather brief and nondescript, the letter accompanying it was an in-depth defense of her character, signed by thirty-nine men from her Philadelphia community. By their signatures, these men legitimated Sutter's case, even though she did little to defend herself in her own words. Significantly, the reason these men provided as to why Sutter was deserving of leniency was that she was "seduced" to commit the crime. Sutter, the "unfortunate" girl of fourteen or fifteen years of age, was allegedly influenced by others to commit theft. The men insisted, too, that punishing Sutter would only "harden" her, rather than reform her. Sutter's helplessness was reinforced by her silence.[14] Pennsylvania's Supreme Executive Council was convinced of Sutter's relative innocence because of both her dependence upon men in her community and their explicit classification of her as a defenseless young woman; the body remitted both her fine and corporal punishment.[15]

Margaret Baker, like Ann Sutter, attempted to mitigate her circumstances by calling upon local men to attest to her suffering and thus strengthen her appeal for mercy. Baker requested clemency from the same body because she had two young children to support by herself, and threatened that they would starve without her.[16] Her cosignatories described Baker as an "honest, sober, industrious woman" who supported herself and two children, having married a man "who neither performs the part of a Husband, a Father, or a good member of Society." They accused him of irresponsibly spending all of the money *she* had earned, so much so that she had to take in boarders to earn money. One of these boarders, Robert Waterman, swindled her and convinced the authorities that she had been involved in the theft of a watch, which the subscribers were thoroughly convinced she was not guilty of doing.[17] Baker was thus the victim of both her husband's profligacy and Waterman's deceit; these men portrayed her as an innocent, hapless victim who had fallen prey to the manipulations of men. With these seventeen community patriarchs as her legitimating force, Baker's second-hand sympathetic narrative successfully convinced the council that she deserved to have both her fine and her year of hard labor remitted.[18]

Women often claimed ignorance in their petitions—ignorance of the law in particular—and thus took advantage of well-established assumptions about women's intellectual capacity.[19] Ann Cannon, for instance, had received an annual pension after her veteran husband, William, died in 1781. In May of 1794, Ann petitioned the Commission on Pensions requesting that her annuities be repaid because "for several years past from her ignorance of the mode of application she has not received the annual allowance." She requested that the committee grant her "whatever Arrears may be found due her," which would "make her old age happy & Comfortable."[20] Ann's petition emphasized her "ignorance" of the laws and also of the exact sum due to her. She knew enough to recognize this language as an effective mode of petitioning; a woman ignorant of the law and her own financial status could not be to blame for inadequacies in her pension application. She was a widow; her husband was not alive to provide this guidance. So, the state should do so in his stead. Ann received fifteen pounds' compensation from the body in response to her petition.[21]

Elizabeth Toussiger likewise framed her plea around feminine ignorance, but in a more assertive fashion. A "widow destitute of subsistence for herself and four young children," Toussiger claimed that her late husband had never been paid for his service to his country. "Through Ignorance," she claimed, she and her children had "been deprived of the beneficence of the State" owed to the "Widows and Orphans of those that have fallen in the cause of America." Importantly, Toussiger positioned the state, and its "beneficence," as being responsible for the maintenance of herself and her children.[22] It was the state, after all, for whom Toussinger's husband gave his life; it was the "cause of America" that left her widowed and her children orphaned. Toussinger was careful that her diction was not critical of the legislature's failure to pay her late husband for his service, the sympathetic language of her petition serving more as a gentle reminder of the patriarchal state's responsibility to its dependents. The commission assigned to consider Toussinger's case obliged.[23]

Troubling Gender

Other women engaged these tropes in a more subtle, subversive way. A number of petitioners, particularly those thrust into difficult circumstances during and after the war, insinuated that they were inhibited from following the standards of gender comportment because of the challenges of their individual situations. These women insisted that they *desired* and *attempted* to perform the consummate feminine roles of wife and mother, and went to great lengths to do so—and to describe their efforts to state legislators. Yet, these petitioners argued that they were impeded from fulfilling their prescribed roles by a number of obstacles, including the war, financial difficulties, or a husband's absence. All presented their narratives within a sympathetic framework that, combined with portrayals of themselves as dutiful wives and mothers, often secured them the aid, relief, or compensation they sought from the patriarchal state.

In offering their willingness to argue for the release of their husbands from British prisons, for example, some women demonstrated the extraordinary lengths to which they were willing to go to fulfill their duties as wives. They requested passes from their legislators in order to depart the state during wartime and negotiate in person the release of their husbands or sons from imprisonment. These women believed— and in some cases said as much to their legislators—that they could parley with British officials by using sympathetic language to secure these men's freedom. Mary Dunton, for instance, declared that she had "no support but what arose from the labor of her Husband," who had been imprisoned in New York. With "no hopes of relief," Dunton surmised that if she were granted a pass to go to New York, "she could effect his exchange or Liberty" from captivity.[24] Sarah White's husband, William, was "the only prop and support of his wife and Children"; Sarah therefore requested a pass to travel to New York in an attempt to liberate her husband and restore him to his role of family provider.[25] Catherine Richards declared that her "Sole dependence" was contingent upon her husband Robert's "success"; with three "helpless" children at home and Richard in prison in New York, Catherine pled with the Executive Council to permit her to travel to New York in an attempt to negotiate for his freedom.[26] Mary Dunton, Sarah White, and Catherine Richards demonstrated their inability to act as dutiful wives and mothers in their husbands' absence, and used this premise to argue for a pass to attempt to free their husbands.

These wives' narratives, however, went beyond a simple acknowledgment of their helplessness related to their husbands' actions. Implicit in their petitions for passage to New York was their insistence that they—as wives, as women—would be best positioned to argue for their husbands' freedom. These women presumed that British authorities, similarly moved to compassion for the fair sex, would release these men so as to alleviate the distresses of their families. Notably, too, these petitions served as an implicit critique of the revolutionary government, which was so weak in arguing for the release of its most patriotic citizens—those who put their lives on the line for the cause of America—that women were deployed to save their husbands when the state could not. All of this—the intended manipulation of British officials, the faint yet sophisticated judgment of the patriarchal state's impotence—was cloaked in the veil of feminine helplessness.

In the same way, women also played with tropes of masculinity in their petitions to state legislatures, highlighting husbands' duty to care for their wives and children. Some women used these assumptions to leave the state entirely and move behind enemy lines in British-occupied territory. Anna Roberts, for example, stated very clearly her reason for petitioning for a pass to see her imprisoned husband in New York: "Your Petitioner has a large family to Maintain which depended on [her husband's] Industry. His Absence distresses them."[27] Mary Badger held that "unless she can obtain leave to go to her husband, where she is very desirous of going," she surely would be forced into destitution with her two small children. Badger compelled the legislature to bestow their "Compassionate consideration" on her situation, and allow her to join her banished husband in New York.[28] Abigail Gallop described being backed into a corner, her husband having left Boston before the British evacuation. She requested leave to go to Halifax only after she had "expended all she had for [her family's] support" and no longer had any way of maintaining them.[29] Mary Anderson complained that the only way of "saving her self and poor Infants from perishing for want of the Common necessarys" would be if the Executive Council were to grant her a pass to go to New York, where her husband could provide for his family.[30] The veiled threat of further becoming dependent on the state itself combined with the promise that husbands would dutifully provide for their families once these women left the state convinced officials to grant their requests for passes.

In their petitions, women who argued that they were unable to perform their wifely duties situated themselves as victims, although their husbands, in some cases, would be the ultimate benefactors of the patriarchal state's intervention. In her petition for her husband's clemency, Mary Smith painted a picture of a distraught, helpless mother who could do nothing to support her family without her (admittedly criminal) husband. Smith's husband was confined in a Philadelphia jail, leaving her without her main source of support. Smith characterized herself as "friendless—poor and distressed," eight months pregnant and in desperation. She attempted to support her husband and work to reduce his fine, but failed in her attempt to do so. She was forced to sell her clothes, which was made more troubling with the winter approaching. "She wants to be not on the Public" dole, she insisted, but with "her Support"—her husband—confined in jail, she surely would have had no other choice but to become fully dependent upon the patriarchal state. In her plea, Smith requested that the council "Extend your Compassion" to "Help her & relieve her." Perhaps because Smith requested that the council release her husband from confinement not for his own sake but to help her and her soon-to-be-born child, they found her a worthy object of their sympathy and decided to release her husband from confinement.[31]

Some women performed their wifely devotion by advocating for husbands who, according to these petitioners, had only acted against the American cause in order to protect their families. In these cases, women petitioners supplemented their own victimhood with narratives of their husbands' devotion to family as ultimately fulfilling their domestic patriarchal duties. These women implicitly took the fall for their husbands' loyalism. Female petitioners argued that it was because of their dependence, their helplessness, and their need for protection that their husbands had ostensibly abandoned their political duties. Thus, in so doing, they successfully repatriated their husbands through their petitions to the legislature. In their public declarations of dependence, many women described their husbands' actions in terms of their dedication to family and their performance of duty to their communities. Women's politically ambiguous positions allowed them to employ their dependence as a mechanism to bring their banished husbands home to their families.

By performing the role of vulnerable, defenseless wives, women could justify their husbands' behavior and see these banished men (and their property) returned to their company. Sarah Scott, for example, attempted to account for her husband John's alleged disloyalty to the American cause. She noted that John had served in the militia in Charleston, but the British imprisoned him once they captured the city. They subsequently forced John, in her view, to sign a congratulatory address applauding General Cornwallis's victory at Camden. Sarah insisted that John felt compelled to do so or he would risk losing the home in which she and her child lived. This was "the effect of necessity, not of choice"; knowing "the distresses of his family being then exceedingly great," she insisted, John signed the address, as doing so was, in her view, the only means of "alleviating the wants of his family."[32] Moreover, Sarah maintained that the American General Woodford would vouch for her husband's kindness and patriotism during the conflict. In closing, Sarah beseeched the General Assembly of South Carolina to "relieve the misery and distress in which she and her innocent child are involved."[33] If the assembly did not heed Scott's plea, both she and her child would be innocent victims of the destruction wrought by a war begun and waged by men.

Scott's expressions of dependence on her husband were both implicit and explicit in her plea. She suggested that her family's survival was contingent upon John's safe return and the return of his property, subtly yet deftly demonstrating her reliance on him. In justifying her husband's seemingly treasonous actions as valiant acts of a devoted spouse and father, however, she signaled her own dependence on him. It was Sarah's and her child's dependence on John that forced the man's hand, compelling him to acquiesce to British demands, and subsequently necessitating his violation of the Confiscation Act of 1782. The power of Sarah's language was in her exploitation of the tropes of femininity but also of husbandly duty to wife and child; a husband, after all, was socially and legally obligated to care and provide for the dependents under his care. Sarah's narrative was evidently persuasive to the committee charged with considering her petition despite John's ostensible disloyalty; Scott achieved her goal, though her husband was politically neutered in the process.[34]

Other women were able to explain their husbands' shifting political allegiances in a way that at least attempted to retain the veneer of masculine honor. Mary Brown suggested that prior to the occupation of Charleston, her husband, Archibald, "was amongst the foremost at the Post of Danger," acting as "a zealous and active Friend in the Cause of his Country." He fought for the British only after the fall of the city, when he believed the cause had been lost. When he took command of the Goose Creek Company, he did so out of a sense of "Duty, to keep the Peace of the Town as he had formerly done under the American Government." Mary linked his allegedly treacherous behavior with that of "a Multitude of other Inhabitants."[35] Archibald abandoned his political principles, in this instance, to protect the people of Charleston, to act as a community patriarch.

Importantly, women's position as apolitical actors allowed them (and their narratives) to soften the effect that such a rebuke of Whig leadership might have had were the critique to have come from men.[36] Mary's implicit suggestion that she understood the political machinations of men, too, was couched in terms of her role as a wife, and was therefore more palatable to the assembly. Throughout her petition, Mary continued to cite the numerous ways in which her husband had been an advocate for American interests. She cited Archibald's record as a member of the American militia and as an agent to France, and reminded the assembly of his injuries at Port Royal and Savannah, which he had sustained "in the Cause of his Country."[37] He had established a long history of active military service, having sacrificed his body for political principles, and only abdicated his position when the war and his ideals seemed lost.

But Mary could not ignore the specter of the loyalty oath Archibald had signed. The only "excuse" she could offer was that her husband was taken by "that kind of Contagion which spreads on such occasions, from the force of Examples set before him." Up to this point, Mary had portrayed her husband as a strong man, one willing to put his life on the line for his beliefs. The only way she could explain away his behavior, though, was to describe this moment of weakness as his having succumbed to a "Contagion," a disease of the mind, having capitulated to public pressure, in this case, which compelled him to waver. Yielding to this metaphorical weakness, he signed the oath because it was his only option, according to Mary, and was the only way to protect his "many near Connexions who have much dependence on him."[38]

Though she presented a snapshot of a moment of weakness for her husband, Mary's humility and powerlessness were the focal point of her narrative. She admitted her own discomfort in inserting herself into the political and military affairs of men. She was "loath to bear testimonies" of her husband's conduct, yet felt compelled to do so out of her love for him and the well-being of her family.[39] Mary's petition had wandered into the affairs of men, but only insofar as doing so was an extension of proper feminine comportment—or so she presented her case. She was justified in challenging the legislature's decision to banish her husband because she did so as a wife and mother. Like Sarah Scott, Mary Brown was successful in exploiting her own dependence and need in order to exonerate her husband. The committee assigned to her case decided to grant her petition.[40] Knowing that society presumed them to be apolitical, women positioned themselves as *objects* of men's battles, rather than as political actors in their own right, though the act of petitioning belied that very rhetorical strategy.

Women countered the state's accusations of men's misplaced political loyalties by insisting that their husbands merely prioritized their duty to family over that of country. Eliza Clitherall, for instance, framed her request that both her husband and his property be returned to her family by emphasizing his dedication to his wife and children. Eliza held that her husband, James, only accepted the office of commissioner of claims for the British government "for the support of a large Family . . . and whilst he held it acquitted himself with great Justice & Integrity." While simultaneously defending her husband's actions as necessary for the survival of his family, Eliza similarly focused the General Assembly of South Carolina's attention on her own dependence. Eliza also named ten men—avowed Whigs—who could vouch for James's valiant efforts to "render every service in his power to the Citizens of this State."[41] This tactic proved effective, as the committee assigned to consider her petition permitted James to return to his family as a result of Eliza's petition.[42]

Effectively, women explained that because they had performed their feminine role as dependent spouses, their husbands were compelled to protect them, as was their masculine duty. In highlighting their husbands' dedication to family, especially as the primary cause for their ostensibly loyalist sympathies, women essentially took the blame for this treasonous behavior. Susannah Smyth, for instance, claimed that her husband, John, had only taken a commission with the British because he did not want to lose "his whole fortune on which his Family altogether depended for Support." If not for her needs and the needs of her children, she held, he never would have made such a decision.

Because of the contested nature of women's political agency, Susannah could openly admit that her dependence fueled her husband's loyalism, and she could do so with little fear of any political repercussions for herself. The implication, then, was that John certainly would have joined the American militia (or at least refused to join its British counterpart) had he not been hindered by the need to support and protect his family. By simultaneously positioning herself as a weak, sympathetic figure while insisting that her husband had only forsaken his country to ensure the safety of his family, Susannah played with traditional notions of feminine *and* masculine comportment to successfully bring her husband home to South Carolina.[43] Women's petitions, though often formulaic, display a great adroitness of language and understanding, their rhetoric recognizing the potency of gendered norms while also exploiting upheavals of war to allow for a more malleable interpretation of the expectations of femininity and masculinity.

Motherhood—an identity steeped not only in the dependence of women on men but also in the dependence of children on their mothers—also gave these women a powerful bargaining tool to wield in their petitions. Women could easily and convincingly portray their children as objects of the state's sympathies. Many women's petitions mentioned their dependent children who, without the support of a father in their lives—especially financially—would certainly find their survival under threat. Mary Inglis requested, for instance, that her husband, Alexander, be allowed to return to South Carolina on account of his "disconsolate" family, which included not only her own four children but also several of Alexander's uncle's children and the orphans of his late business partner.[44] Having been "deprived of her Husband's Estate," Sarah Capers contended that she had "Nothing to Maintain [her children] with."[45] With her husband in New York, Mary Crippe found herself unable to support her family, offering that her children "depend on [her husband's] Industry for Support" as leverage in her request to receive a pass to travel to New York.[46] Mary Johnson begged the Pennsylvania council to "have Compassion on her and her poor innocent babes" who suffered with her in Philadelphia in her husbands' absence, living "without any Means for their Support." She contended that "the most extreme poverty and distress" awaited her family were the council to ignore her request.[47] Revealing the desperate situation of fatherless children in these cases, these women utilized the presumption that they were not able to care for their children—certainly financially, but perhaps also emotionally, as some petitions would suggest—without their husbands' presence (and property).

Women were even able to invoke their attempts at performing their feminine roles as mothers to free them from punishments related to crimes they committed. Mary Yard's petition for a remission of her fine essentially freed her from any disciplinary action after she was convicted of assault. After she was sentenced to pay the state twenty shillings, the county held Yard in custody until she paid the fine. Yard insisted, however, that she would never be able to pay the full amount. She was "poor and friendless"; she had "four helpless children to Support," not to mention a husband who had, according to Yard, been sick and unable to work for quite some time. On top of all of these financial obstacles, Yard was "so very pregnant" and evidently could have delivered her child at any moment. In this "miserable" state, Yard requested that the Pennsylvania Supreme Executive Council consider the difficulties she faced and remit her fine.[48] It is notable that the crime for which Yard was convicted was assault, certainly a breach of feminine comportment. Yet Yard's performance of helplessness, of utter destitution, convinced the council that her fine should be remitted.[49] Ultimately, Yard engaged the sympathy of the state to be absolved of a violent crime, and held out her children as potential casualties of her situation.

Women's use of their children as objects of sympathy in their petitions was especially effective, because it at once highlighted women's attempts to fulfill their duties as mothers while emphasizing their own gendered incapacity to attenuate the circumstances of these innocent children's lives. Mary Lincoln, for example, requested the interest payments on the patrimony due to her late mother after her father's death. In her widowhood, Lincoln struggled to provide for her two sons, hoping for years that her share would be distributed to her for that purpose. When submitting a petition to the Massachusetts legislature, she made her children the primary focus of her request: "The time is now come that the minds of her Children must be formed by a proper Education upon principles which will make them good & . . . full members . . . of society."[50] It was in her desperation to provide an adequate education for her sons—so that they might be upstanding American citizens in the new republic—that Mary Lincoln employed her destitute situation to present her case to the legislature. She couched her dependence and declarations of helplessness within the framework of republican motherhood, staking the very future of the newly independent United States on her sons' situation.[51] This was, evidently, a shrewd strategy: the Massachusetts General Assembly awarded her 1,116 pounds, along with the promise of any future annual interest that should become due to her.[52] Mary Lincoln tied her sons' futures to the future of the American republic, engaging not just the sympathies of the state but their deep-seated anxieties, too.

Women effectively called on the state to intervene as a surrogate patriarch in situations in which they could not support their children in their husbands' absence. Sarah Lewis's plea provided a litany of reasons why the Massachusetts legislature should find her case particularly difficult, while simultaneously asserting that she was only turning to the body for assistance because she could think of no other outlet for relief for herself and her children. She requested "Compassion & Benevolence to the Widdow & fatherless who has none other to help." Lewis's husband left his family to fight in the Revolutionary War, yet not having heard from him for some time, she assumed he had been lost at sea. She offered that "this grievous affliction was most severely felt by your petitioner," who by the gift of "providence" survived by the assistance of her son, who was "exceedingly kind and tender of his Widdow Mother."[53]

This second source of male support on whom she could depend, however, had also recently been lost to her. Lewis knew only that her son had last sailed out of Maryland, but had not heard from him for some time. In the absence of her husband and son who had previously supported her, Lewis had to care for six other children, all of whom were under the age of fourteen, and three of whom were under the age of four. Adding to her struggles, Lewis claimed, was a "bleeding sore in my hand" that prevented her from working. It was in her utter desperation and sense of helplessness that she turned to the state for assistance: "Your petitioner feels grieved to trouble your Honors with her Case, but great & pressing necessity urges me, and I would not apply did I know of any other way in the world where to get relief in an *honest way.*"[54] Here, Lewis knowingly triggered an alarm; she backed the legislature into a corner by indicating in no uncertain terms that she might be forced to turn to a life of theft or even prostitution to support herself and her children. Lewis's threat—and her adept usage of the sympathetic narrative—worked to great success; the Massachusetts legislature granted her relief in the form of two hundred pounds.[55]

In emphasizing their "orphaned" or "fatherless" children, women hinted at the expectation that the state was responsible for fulfilling the role of surrogate patriarch under these circumstances.[56] Women even used the threat of dependence on the patriarchal state to their advantage.[57] Sarah Bonsall, who resided in Philadelphia, requested a pass to travel to New York, where she could live under the protection and support of her husband. She demonstrated that her advanced pregnancy made her separation from her husband, "from whom alone She can expect any support," all the more difficult. If the state did not permit Bonsall to join her husband, "of course" she would "be reduced to great distress and Misery." Insinuating that the state would be responsible for her torment and that of her unborn child, Sarah Bonsall called upon the compassion of Pennsylvania's council, which allowed her to leave the state and join her husband in New York.[58] These effective gendered performances of feminine dependence often elicited the sympathy of patriarchal state authorities and provoked intervention that benefited not just these women petitioners but their families as well.

Active Dependents

While some women sought to mitigate their situations by emphasizing their own devotion to wifely and motherly duty, others made the choice to actively distance themselves from their husbands' politics, and in so doing made a political choice themselves. Many of these women employed the presumption of female innocence or ignorance in political affairs. Dorcas Hutchins claimed to have been blindsided by her husband's actions. Having encountered the "inhumanity of the unnatural enemy," she escaped from the city of Boston in 1775. Later, she discovered that her husband "had been so far prevailed on by the enemy as to go off with them," leaving her to her own devices, devoid of any property or real estate for a suitable financial maintenance in his absence. Having four small children under the age of five, Dorcas found herself "destitute of every necessaries of life, & unable to procure any." As a result, she cast herself into her mother's care. Her mother, being an old and infirm widow, though, had little means to support Dorcas and her young children. Having positioned her husband as an "enemy" to his country, Dorcas identified herself as a person who "has ever manifested the same regard for the cause of America *as far as her situation would admit*."[59] Here, Dorcas presented her efforts as being confined by the limits of women's political expressions. Dorcas considered herself an American patriot so far as society and the state would allow her to be, and for expressing this behavior in light of her husband's loyalism, she believed, she deserved relief from the legislature. Dorcas successfully received portions of her husband's property that she could use to sell—and thereby subsist—in her husband's absence.[60]

Some women rejected their husbands' political ties rather expertly. Ruth Gay conceded that her husband, Martin, had "render'd himself obnoxious to the good people of this State." He had departed for Nova Scotia, leaving his family in Boston, yet she did not condemn his actions outright. Unlike a number of her peers, she expressed no desire to leave to join him in Halifax and thereby receive support from him there; instead, she requested support out of his estate, which he had left in Boston. Ruth employed the traditional tropes of feminine dependence in her plea: "Your petitioner has with her two children who entirely depend on her for support—she has no way of obtaining even a subsistence for herself but by the work of her own hands." Of course, this was not necessarily true; like other women in similar situations, Ruth could have requested a pass to travel to Halifax, where her husband theoretically would have provided their family with the necessary support. Instead, she made the choice to stay in Boston, attempting to acquire a suitable maintenance for her family in her husband's absence; the only solution she offered the state was her acquisition of the third of Martin's estate reserved to Ruth for her dower.[61] The legislature granted her request to "consider & commiserate her hard & unfortunate situation," thereby relieving her of the need to "support herself" and her two children, and providing her with her dower as if she were a widow.[62]

This is an interesting case for a number of reasons. First, and perhaps most notably, Ruth indicated no clear intention to be reunited with her husband, Martin, in Halifax; in this instance, therefore, she was *not* fulfilling the consummate role of wife and mother. Similarly, the state did not seem to take any issue with Ruth's apparent feminine transgressions. Rather, they granted her dower rights as if her husband were legally dead. What seems to have been most effective here was Ruth's employment of the sympathetic narrative and her reluctance to attach herself to an accused loyalist, all while failing to condemn him directly.

Women positioned themselves as victims of political circumstances brought on by the decisions of men. Wives of absentee husbands portrayed themselves as casualties in these scenarios, betrayed, in some cases, by husbands who had no regard for their family's well-being, thus exhorting state legislatures to have mercy on their pitiable situations. They therefore needed to demonstrate their worthiness for aid despite their husband's political blunders. Freelove Scott employed this strategy on multiple occasions, gaining additional relief and control over property over time, the more she demonstrated helplessness and dependence to the Massachusetts General Assembly. Joseph Scott, Freelove's husband, left Boston when the British evacuated the city. Because of his absence, Freelove found herself compelled to request the "Compassion of your honors please for the distresses of an unfortunate Mother who has the care of five Children without Money to support them or the means of procuring it." These children, she argued, should not be forced to "Suffer for the faults of their Father," but should instead be rescued from certain "Poverty and destitution," which would befall them were they to be neglected by the state.[63] Scott requested that she and her children be permitted to live in their home rent free until the legislature rectified the unfortunate confiscation of her absentee husband's property in her favor. The legislature granted her request, but insisted that no other action be taken until the General Court decreed any further resolves.[64]

Freelove Scott's second petition indicates that she expected a certain amount of protection from the state in her husband's absence, insinuating that the state should fill in as surrogate provider for herself and her children. Again insisting that her husband's absconding "reduced your Petitioner with five Children to" a "helpless Situation," Scott reinforced her powerless position and implored the legislature to have sympathy on her plight. Indeed, she *expected* it: "She Presumed [her situation] would have intitled her to such a share of Commiseration as to have Produced a suitable support for herself and Family out of her Husbands Effects." Significantly, it was not just a legal claim that Scott made to the Massachusetts General Court but a social and cultural claim to an expression of "Commiseration" for a destitute woman in a troubling situation. Here, Scott called on the state to fill in as husband to her and father to her children, compelling it to provide for herself and her family in her husband's stead. By her very act of petitioning, then, Scott expressed agency and undermined her own dependence, all the while asserting her "helpless Situation."

Scott's pleas, however, were imbued with subtle accusations of the legislature's lack of sympathy toward her plight. She accused the body of "only" granting her 150 pounds. Scott observed that this sum was insufficient to maintain herself and her family "at a time Distressfull as the present." Having accrued a number of debts in her husband's absence, she argued that 150 pounds was not enough to properly care for her family.[65] In response, the legislature granted her possession of one-third of her husband's estate, supplying Freelove Scott with her dower on the spot.[66] Scott's insistence that she was entitled to more protection on the basis of her dependent status convinced the legislature to act on a matter that they had resolved not to revisit until a later date.[67] The General Court seemed to waver a number of times regarding Joseph's estate, but ultimately decided to grant Freelove her dower, as "she and her children are now suffering for the necessarys of life."[68] Perhaps most importantly, Scott's petition provided a precedent for other women in similar situations; the Committee of Sequestration in Massachusetts became "impower'd to settle with any of the Absentees Wives remaining in this State & who have not quitted it to join the Enemies of the United States of America," thus granting dependent wives just cause to defy their husbands' political authority.[69]

A few years later, Scott petitioned the body a third time. On this occasion, she turned away from focusing on her husband's absconding as the impetus that forced her into destitution. Instead, she accused the General Court itself of putting her in such a perilous situation, having neglected its patriarchal duty to protect and support her in her husband's absence. This time, she actively accused the state of failing to fulfill its obligation as a substitute patriarch in her husband's absence. When Freelove Scott received her dower, the legislature seems to have suspended her ability to live rent free in her husband's home. In response, Scott petitioned the legislature again in 1779, citing "the most distressing & humiliating expedients" that inhibited her from obtaining even "a procarious support for herself and five children." Although she consented that she received "some temporary relief" from the body, this was evidently "very inadequate to her maintenance."

In the same way that she indirectly chastised her husband for failing to provide for his family, Freelove now explicitly rebuked the legislature for foundering in its duty to fulfill the role of surrogate husband and father. Because Joseph had fled the country—perhaps because she had exhausted her ability to cite his absence as a reason for her distress, it now having been several years removed from his absconding—Freelove Scott declared her dependence instead on the state, which she believed owed her protection and support because she no longer had a husband to provide for her: "She is therefore now constrained to ask a permanent & regular support from your Honors out of the estate left by her husband, nor can she think this request extravagant." In such instances, Freelove Scott and others turned to the state to provide "public Money if not public Justice" to "rescue . . . unoffending [families] from ruin."[70] Her husband may have been guilty of harboring loyalist sentiments, but in her dependent state, Freelove suggested, she should not be held accountable for his actions, nor receive comparable punishment for his crimes. In addition to the dower she received from her absentee husband's estate, Freelove continued to live rent free in Joseph's home, despite his continued absence from the state.[71] Her relentless petitions and multifaceted manipulations of feminine dependence and masculine duty found continued success in Massachusetts's General Court.

As Scott's set of pleas demonstrates, women who petitioned state legislatures were forced to mind the fine line between expressing individual autonomy and declaring dependence. When they distanced themselves from their husbands or openly criticized or rebuked these men, women were compelled to reassert their position as dependents in the patriarchal hierarchy in order to gain the sympathy of the legislatures and courts. On a number of occasions, women succeeded where their husbands had failed. Elizabeth Pierpont, for example, was able to gain relief from the Massachusetts state legislature when her husband had failed to acquire any aid on several occasions. Nathaniel Pierpont provided materials and labor to make bread for the Continental troops in 1775, and by 1810 had received no compensation for his supplies and work. He petitioned the legislature unsuccessfully a number of times, despite his having sufficient evidence to prove that the state owed him money for his goods and services. Nathaniel died before ever receiving remuneration from the state.

His wife, Elizabeth, used her widowhood and her pitiable situation to receive three hundred dollars in compensation from the state of Massachusetts.[72] By emphasizing her difficult situation as a widow with several children "who look to her for aid," Elizabeth Pierpont received support from the state not once but twice.[73] After receiving the sum of three hundred dollars in 1810, Elizabeth petitioned the Massachusetts legislature again in 1812, providing more details of her difficult situation and accusing the government of not providing her with the financial support she believed she deserved and desperately needed. The "denyal of justice" to which Elizabeth referred was both not providing the Pierponts with their due and also failing to effectively take pity on weak dependents in a deplorable situation.[74]

Elizabeth used both her helpless situation and her accusation of a denial of justice to gain additional relief from the state legislature. Not only did she believe that the amount of three hundred dollars was an amount insufficient to account for her difficult situation ("your memorialist being poor and having a family to provide for was compelled to receive what she believed by no means a compensation"), but she also claimed that the legislature failed to provide her with the full amount that it originally promised.[75] Still, she continued to be deferential to the legislature's authority; she feared that her assertion "might bar any further attempt at obtaining justice" for her family. But she remained resolute, insisting that her family's situation was desperate enough to warrant her defensive petition.[76] Despite her firm tone, her pitiable circumstances were enough to attract the attention of the legislature; the body recalculated what the state owed her husband (including interest), with the new amount coming to 535 dollars. Because of her employment of the sympathetic narrative and her insistence that justice be served to her husband's dependents, Elizabeth Pierpont received an additional 235 dollars from the state of Massachusetts following her second petition.[77] Elizabeth was able to present her husband's story within a sympathetic framework to provide her family with 535 dollars that her husband had never been able to acquire. In this way, women like Elizabeth Pierpont were active dependents—advocating for themselves and their families while presenting behavior and language that both transgressed and followed standards of traditional feminine comportment.

Active dependence facilitated women's political agency by creating a permission structure by which women could express political power while still performing subordinate femininity. Through distancing themselves from or outright rejecting their husbands' political ties, women exposed the fiction of their political powerlessness and lack of independent political identities. Patience Capen distinguished her own political opinions from those of her husband and used this technique to defend him against what she (and he) perceived as unjust persecution. Patience's husband, Hopestill, was jailed for refusing to sign a loyalty oath for religious reasons. He was also, however, a member of the Boston Association of Loyalists, which condemned the violence perpetrated by the Sons of Liberty, believing their actions to be treasonous.[78] In 1776, Hopestill published a broadside from prison in which he attempted to defend his actions and seemed to have little interest in denouncing his political sentiments.[79] He only received clemency when his wife, Patience, petitioned the Massachusetts General Court. She accused the state of persecuting her husband, while simultaneously describing her own clear attachment to her "Native Country," so strong that she "cannot think of leaving it." Forced to confront the fact that her husband might be banished from the state, she likened the prospect to "plucking out a right eye or cutting off a right hand."[80] To Patience, her husband was literally a physical part of her, from whom she could not bear to part. Her choice of words—her emphasis on her closeness to her husband and her deep need of him—played right into the expectations that the legislature had for women's behavior.

Patience, however, adeptly manipulated the tension between her independent political identity and her dependence on her husband. By portraying herself as a woman with deeply held patriotic sentiments for her country, but also one who could not bear to be without her husband, who harbored loyalist sympathies, she compelled the legislature to reconsider Hopestill's confinement. She claimed that hers was indeed a "distress'd case" that presented the potential for great suffering: "If the desire of my eyes, and the fruit of my body" was "away from me, what good will my life do?" From her position of dependence, she implored the legislature to "grant relief" to *her* by freeing her husband from jail.[81] The body "carefully enquired into the Character & Conduct" of her husband, and found that he was indeed *not* guilty of "being inimical to this & the United States."[82] Hopestill himself had called for such an examination two years prior to his wife's petition, but it was not until Patience implored the General Court to investigate her husband's political sentiments that they actually took action, having heard her desperate plea for sympathy based on her devotion to and dependence on her jailed husband.

Like Patience Capen, other women had to come to terms with the conflicts between their own political beliefs and those of their husbands, especially when their husbands were punished for theirs. The political convulsions that arose during and as a result of the American Revolution put women in particularly difficult positions: politically, socially, and, often, practically. Challenges arose when women became objects in the fight over men's political loyalties. Wives of purported loyalists were often not directly punished themselves but rather suffered as a result of the penalties that befell their husbands, such as banishment or the confiscation of property. Without their husbands working to provide a living for their families, and without homes to live in or property to sustain them, women faced the harsh realities of their ambiguous citizenship under the law. Likewise, women found themselves objects of men's political battles, becoming victims of the war that destroyed their homes and tore apart their families. Women continued to play into the notion that their citizenship was "filtered through their husbands' civic identity" while simultaneously distancing themselves from these men.[83]

Women, by their obligations of obedience to their husbands, could thus more easily argue for their political impotence and innocence in these petitions than could men. Certainly, this frustrating and humiliating legal structure undermined the notion of women's political agency. At the same time, however, it provided a loophole of sorts through which women could argue their innocence in their husbands' political crimes, while railing against these men and the actions of the state that ultimately caused them harm. Martha Moore's husband, James, was a "Briton" who evacuated Philadelphia with the British and traveled with them to New York. Martha insisted that she was "willing and desirous to follow the Fate of her Husband"; because she did not deny her husband's political loyalties, however, Martha attached a recommendation from John Gibson, a Philadelphia lawyer, in order to deflect attention away from her husband's political leanings, and instead draw the focus to her own helplessness and political impotence. Gibson insisted that "her Behavior has been altogether inoffensive, and I believe *perfectly devoid of Politicks*."[84] Here, Martha employed a legitimating male voice to assert her own compliance with stereotypical notions of women's political disinterestedness. Not only did Gibson confirm her lack of any political opinions or affiliations; he emphasized that she was poor and found it "difficult to support herself and Child." Gibson insisted that "she would be relieved in this Respect if she was with her Husband."[85] Because of Gibson's verification of Moore's apolitical beliefs and dependence on her husband, Pennsylvania's Supreme Executive Council permitted Martha to move to New York with her child and thus be reunited with her husband and source of support.[86]

Due to their relatively ambiguous political status, women could criticize (however slightly) both their husbands and the state by emphasizing their own helplessness and destitute situations. Mary Weeks was able to subtly inveigh against the Revolutionary War by highlighting the detrimental effects it had on innocent women and children. Her husband, a clergyman, left her and their eight children with "means very inadequate," and she blamed the "national convulsion" for forcing him to go abroad. Similarly, she pointed to the war as the cause of her husband's halted communications, which inhibited her from obtaining "even those necessary supplies which her husband might have remitted her" had he been given the chance. The war forced Mary and her daughter to become "objects of charity," which she detested; her need to turn to the public for assistance rendered her situation "irksome and pitiable." She loathed having to constantly request assistance from her friends, whom she likely considered of equal station and rank. The only thing that would free her from the confines of her "absolute dependency"—a situation into which she was propelled by the Revolution—would be joining her husband in Halifax, where he could provide for her as he had done before war broke out. There, she could return to her wifely dependence, an altogether different and preferable form of dependence than what she was then experiencing.[87]

Mary's deft use of language justified her delicate condemnation of her husband's failure to leave her family with funds for support and of the state's role in provoking devastating consequences for the families of alleged loyalists. She wisely packaged her disparaging language in the trappings of traditional expectations of feminine behavior, stressing her inability to provide for her family in her husband's absence and her helplessness in this state of "absolute dependency." In so doing, however, she also demonstrated that she was not the incapable woman that she made herself out to be. Through her delicate castigation of American authorities for failing to properly protect her family and their property, Weeks asserted her defiance of norms that dictated women's political disinterestedness. Yet at the same time, she adroitly used the language of dependence to temper her censorious language. Mary Weeks's petition highlights the inherent irony of women's declarations of dependence through petitioning—that by actively declaring dependence and making claims for assistance in individual petitions, they were indeed empowered in advocating for themselves and their families.

* * *

Women played with social and cultural expectations of masculinity and femininity in significant ways in order to affect change in their own lives, all the while expressing power through the use of linguistic tropes of feminine powerlessness. In the revolutionary era, women used this tactic with relative consistency across time and space, though the war itself provoked an increase in petitions overall. Women activated the language of dependence as a strategy for survival, portraying themselves as helpless, financially dependent, apolitical, ignorant, and in need of the legitimation of male voices. All the while, the very act of petitioning stood at odds with these claims, undermining the linguistic performance of this behavior in their pleas. Their performance of helplessness and vulnerability belied the goals and outcomes of their petitions to colonial and state legislatures in this period: they were able to gain a measure of power over their own lives by explicitly emphasizing feminine impotence.

Significantly, other women transgressed socially accepted expectations of women's behavior in their accusations by distancing themselves from their husbands' political identities and by castigating their husbands as failed patriarchs. All the while, however, they contextualized these critiques of their husbands' authority within the framework of wifely duty and feminine dependence. This strategy of transgressing helpless femininity while simultaneously performing it provided women with an outlet to critique and challenge their husbands' authority while still existing within the realm of proper feminine comportment. Through employing these strategies of "troubling gender," women in the revolutionary era were able to gain a measure of power over their own lives by explicitly engaging with the sympathetic language of dependence and female helplessness and soliciting the protective powers of the patriarchal state.

This was an individualized power, however, and applied in a very limited fashion. The law still confined women's agency in countless ways. Importantly, too, the fact that women actively employed this rhetoric of feminine dependence and subordination may have served to bolster its staying power in the early republic. The patriarchal state desired and expected to hear the language of women's helplessness. When women's petitions met those expectations, their doing so was, in a way, a form of tacit consent to the terms of their unequal status. By deploying their dependence as a tool of empowerment, they simultaneously assented to it, and perhaps legitimated it in the eyes of the patriarchal state.

Independence in Dependence

Jane Houston had been married to her husband, Samuel, since July of 1792. From that time until she submitted a petition for divorce in March of 1805, she "continued to live & cohabit" with Samuel "as his lawfull wife." During the course of their marriage, however, Samuel had been unfaithful. In fact, he was a bigamist. Jane learned from an acquaintance that Samuel's *other* wife resided in the West Indies, and he had actually been married to this woman prior to having met Jane. This fact, along with evidence to support it, was sufficient to justify Jane's legal cause for separation from Samuel. Yet, her petition did not merely consist of this startling revelation.

The bulk of Jane's plea highlighted the extensive and varied abuses she suffered while married to Samuel Houston. Her marriage had been, in her words, "one continued scene of vexation & distress." Samuel was a drunkard, one who regularly neglected his work in favor of regular presence at the local tavern. Likewise, he frequented "Lewd houses," imbibing in spirits and cavorting with sex workers. Armed with the knowledge of Samuel's regular trips to the neighborhood brothel, Jane accused her husband of adultery with "sundry lewd women whose Company & Society he constantly frequents." As early as 1796, Jane even cited an incident in which Samuel brought one of these women into their home, where he was "detected" by an unnamed witness "in the Act of Adultery." From his escapades Samuel would return to his wife "intoxicated with strong liquor," and in such a state would regularly beat Jane "in the most cruel & barbarous Manner." These abuses often prohibited Jane from "attend[ing] to her family concerns" as she "languished under her bruises for several days in bed."[1]

Jane's petition accused her husband of violating their marital vows in virtually every way. Because of their legal dependence, Philadelphia wives petitioning for divorce required the assistance of two other individuals—their lawyer and their "next friend," who was often identified within the petition, and who was almost always male.[2] Jane's next

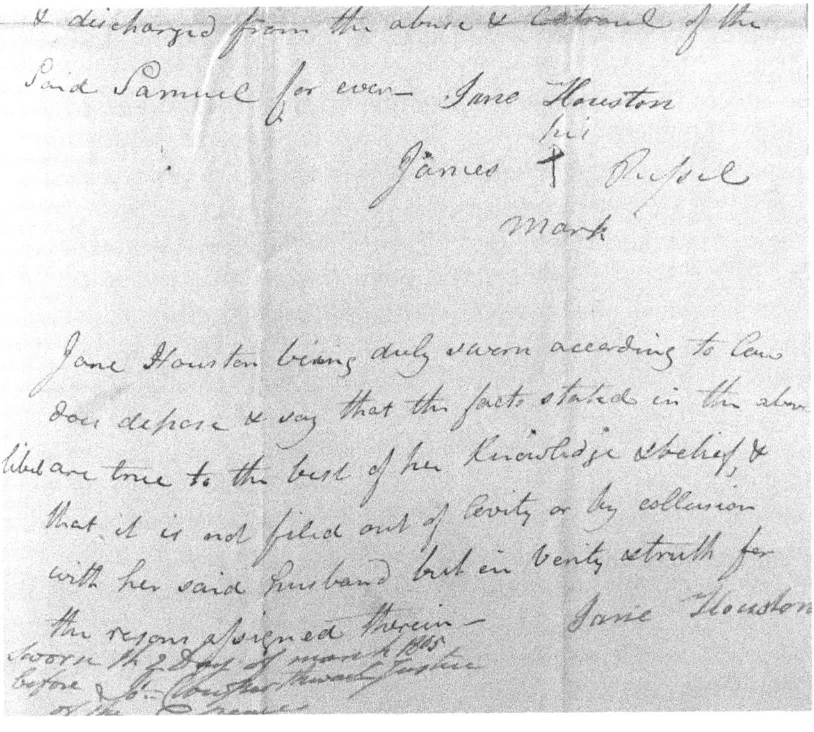
& discharged from the abuse & controul of the
Said Samuel for ever— Jane Houston
his
James + Russell
mark

Jane Houston being duly sworn according to Law
does depose & say that the facts stated in the above
libel are true to the best of her knowledge & belief, &
that it is not filed out of levity or by collusion
with her said husband but in verity & truth for
the reasons assigned therein— Jane Houston
Sworn the 2 Day of March 1805
before

FIGURE 2.1. Jane Houston's signature. The name "Jane Houston" appears at the bottom of the page of Jane Houston's libel, and the penmanship, particularly the way in which the writer crafted her capital "J," is markedly different from the way in which the name "Jane Houston" was repeatedly crafted throughout the petition. Likewise, if Jane had not penned the signature herself, she would have simply made her mark—an "X"—in the same way that her next friend, James Russell, did. Source: Libel of Jane Houston, 5 March 1805, Houston divorce, Record Group 33 Supreme Court of Pennsylvania, A Eastern District, 41 Divorce Papers, 1786–1815, Pennsylvania State Archives, Harrisburg, PA.

friend, James Russell, merely made his mark at the bottom of the petition: an "X" indicating his confirmation of Jane's story. Jane's petition was in her voice, from her perspective, but likely not written by her hand. Through an examination of the handwriting of Jane's petition, one line stands out as having been penned by another: her signature, the result of her *own* hand pressing her own name to the page.[3] In this way, Jane Houston claimed ownership over her story and her attempt to free herself from the confines of an abusive marriage.

Jane Houston's case, while perhaps extreme and extensive, was not unique. Women in certain colonies and, later, states were able to win divorce suits from their husbands under particular circumstances. Significantly, they presented arguments for legal separation explicitly from their position of dependence, deploying the rhetorical framework of wifely duty and subordination while emphasizing the legal protections owed to them as dependent wives. Women entered the male sphere of the courtroom, and were thus obligated to pander to their audience—the patriarchal state—in their petitions. They dutifully performed their roles as devoted and obedient wives while portraying their husbands as having broken the marriage contract and thus transgressing their obligations as household patriarchs. They bought into certain standards of the patriarchal system, including their subordination to male authority in word and in deed, in order to free themselves from oppressive marriages. Certainly, divorce was not a perfect solution for women, nor did it solve all of their problems or grant them complete independence within the patriarchal system. Yet while the law restricted women's freedom in many ways, it also facilitated its expression and expansion in others. By engaging with expectations of submissive, dependent wifely duty in their petitions, though, women were thus able to secure a measure of independence from their husbands.

Baron and Femme in Law and Society

Differences in marital law across colonial and state jurisdictions governed the ways in which revolutionary-era American women could seek marital separations from their spouses.[4] Marital laws varied widely during the period, and in some cases, changed during the course of the Revolution. Through the study of two cities in two different jurisdictions in which divorce was legal—Boston and Philadelphia—we can observe the ways in which these legal constrictions, though divergent in a number of ways, did not necessarily produce marked differences in women's petitions. Although both Massachusetts and Pennsylvania allowed for divorce during this period, the two states approached marriage, and marital separation, differently.[5] While Massachusetts inherited its tradition of divorce from the Puritan understanding of marriage as a civil contract, Pennsylvania's 1785 divorce law was influenced by republican rhetoric and the American Revolution.[6]

As Boston and Philadelphia women's capacity to seek legal divorce differed, so too did some of the language they used to argue for these separations. Boston women explicitly emphasized that marriage was a civil contract, and when their husbands broke the terms of this contract, they used these conditions as leverage to argue for their freedom from their husbands and their marital unions. The vast majority of Boston women petitioning for divorce between 1750 and 1820 referred to the marital contract in some way, whether they noted the date when the marriage was "contracted," insisted that they had fulfilled their end of the bargain, or argued that husbands had betrayed the agreement.[7] Philadelphia women, on the other hand, rarely referred to marriage as a "contract," and instead complained of their husbands eschewing their marital "vows" or the "mutual faith plighted" to one another.[8]

This distinction may seem tedious, but it is crucial. Because Massachusetts law, from its early Puritan influences, observed marriage primarily as a civil contract, Boston wives almost always stressed their dependence on men who failed to abide by the terms of this contract. Likewise, Boston women were more likely to highlight specific ways in which their husbands violated their marital contracts and spurned their husbandly duties in their petitions than were Philadelphia women. In so doing, Boston women exploited the idea of the civil contract of marriage, which included their dependence on and submission to their husbands, in order to gain freedom from the institution of marriage. Philadelphia women, however, in emphasizing their marital vows, still held their husbands accountable for their spousal obligations, yet not in such precise and targeted language. Women in both cities conformed their performance of femininity to the expectations laid out in the law.

Philadelphia women's divorce cases differed from those of their counterparts in Boston in other ways, too. Pennsylvania demanded several additional requirements for women who sought divorces, such as the cosignatory of a "next friend" and an oath swearing that their decision to apply for a marital separation was "not made out of levity."[9] These supplementary stipulations placed on Philadelphia women underscored their dependence on men and on other forms of patriarchal authority imposed by the state, especially when compared to Boston women's petitions. The extant divorce files submitted to the Philadelphia County Supreme Court by women seeking to end their marriages highlight the extensive and multifaceted declarations of dependence required of Philadelphia women. While many of these women's petitions are brief and extraordinarily formulaic—a characteristic of this medium—a majority of these files include comprehensive depositions from family members, neighbors, and friends—often men—marking another important distinction from those petitions filed in Boston.[10]

Despite these myriad differences in form and structure, women's petitions filed in Boston and Philadelphia do underscore commonalities in rhetorical strategies, even though the confines of the law differed. Women in both cities emphasized their performance of wifely dependence, of submission and obedience to their husbands' authority, and of their husbands' failures to live up to the social and legal expectations set to them. The patriarchal state may have dictated the terms and logistics of women's pleas, but women's strategies at their core remained constant: they used the very terms of their dependence to undermine that notion and gain a degree of freedom from their spouses and their marriages.

Equally powerful a force over women's lives—and thus the language of their petitions—were the social prescriptions of marital duties for both husbands and wives in the revolutionary era. Because of the widespread norms in literature, culture, and social custom in Anglo-American society, patterns existed across divorce petitions in this period, despite the varying stipulations in marital law across jurisdictions.[11] While women were obligated to be obedient and faithful to their husbands, their spouses in return were tasked with their protection—both financial and emotional. In exchange for their submission to their husbands' authority, women were promised their husbands' fidelity, affection, and financial support according to the terms of their marriage; husbands who broke their vows by committing adultery, abusing their wives, deserting them, and failing to provide an adequate maintenance for them could be taken to court over their crimes in colonies and, later, states in which divorce was legal.[12] These mutual, reciprocal duties were understood, in theory, to create a symbiotic relationship of sorts, with husbands remaining in a position of authority over wives, who were dependent upon their husbands' support.[13]

In order to obtain a legal divorce or separation, women directly engaged the terms of these marital obligations—both the social and legal confines governing their behavior—citing the mutual duties of a husband and wife, and in particular their husband's failure to perform these responsibilities, as just cause for their divorces. Many claimed to have been "dutiful," "prudent," "virtuous," "affectionate," or "loving" wives to their husbands.[14] They frequently cited the "mutual vows and faith plighted" to each other in matrimony, while occasionally referencing the "strict adherence to each other and to that constancy and Chastity which ought to be inseparable from the Marriage State."[15] Others invoked the ways in which husbands' behavior threatened feminine virtue by the use of "indecent Language" and "improper Discourse" that was offensive to women "of Modesty."[16] Women understood the power inherent in these legal and social obligations of marriage and held their husbands accountable for the mutual, if uneven, performative duties that spouses owed each other.

In order to effectively argue for a divorce from their husbands, Boston women demonstrated how their husbands had broken the terms of their marital contract. Nearly every Boston petitioner addressed the ways in which her husband violated his marriage "covenant," "contract," "vows," or "duties" by his behavior. This required them to demonstrate that they had acted as good female dependents: dutiful, obedient, and submissive wives despite their husbands' wrongdoings. Catherine Rogers, for example, "ever behaved towards [her husband] as a dutiful wife, and discharged all the duties incumbent on her as such."[17] Mary Hamilton behaved "with the utmost Fidelity of Submission" and "discharged the Duty's incumbent on her as his Wife."[18] Susanna Moses even explicitly argued that she "in no instance violated her marriage duties towards her said husband."[19] Each woman portrayed herself in this light, but the language each chose varied. Some wives described themselves as "faithful," "dutiful," and "obedient," emphasizing their acquiescence to their husband's authority, dependent on his judgment and control. Others focused on their "chaste," "prudent," and "affectionate" qualities becoming of a virtuous, submissive wife—characteristic of the ideals of companionate marriage.[20] These women described their marriages less in terms of affection and love, and instead presented their role in the institution as one of duty, obligation, and performative behavior.

Despite the fact that Philadelphia women did not consistently refer to marriage as a "contract," they understood the institution to have certain mutual and reciprocal duties in the way that many other early American women did, and their petitions reflected this larger social pattern. Jane Everly, for example, referenced the "mutual good offices" by which she and her husband were bound by their marital vows.[21] Other women cited their husbands' duty to treat them with "tenderness" and "decency"; they were "bound to protect and comfort" their wives, and to "render her life happy," they were to guarantee their "fidelity" to their wives.[22] Women also emphasized the reciprocal nature of this kindness, asserting that if they acted with consideration and affection towards their husbands, they deserved this treatment in return. Sarah Lloyd accused her husband of withholding the "kindness & tenderness of a husband" during their marriage.[23] In addition to kind treatment and affection, a husband was "bound" by "conjugal vows" and the law to "protect & provide for his wife."[24]

When one reads through dozens of divorce petitions, it is difficult to look beyond the rote and repetitive language women employed. The seemingly perfunctory nature of women's claims and accusations in divorce petitions, however, should not be dismissed or overlooked. Instead, their often clinical and dispassionate language emphasized both the highly established nature of the expectations of spousal behavior and the serious legal and contractual nature of marriage in revolutionary America. The fact that women emphasized their compliance to the expectations of obedience and submission in marriage in nearly every divorce petition illustrates the strength of prescribed customary gender norms and the power of conduct literature in the popular consciousness. In order to obtain divorces, women used commonly understood constructions of gender comportment for both sexes that were encoded in the language of the law. To successfully argue for a divorce from their husbands, many women who petitioned the court to end their marriages employed the rhetorical framework of dutiful dependence in order to gain the trust and sympathy of the court, and eventually, to obtain their independence from their husbands.

Divorce, Dependence, and Marital Duty

Women's declarations of dependence in divorce petitions ultimately found their greatest success when wives accused their husbands of infidelity. Adultery violated the marital contract when perpetrated both by men and by women. While women's sexuality was policed more heavily than men's in early America, the duties of a husband also encompassed the performance of "proper sexual expression" toward their wives.[25] Women whose husbands committed adultery might bring suit against them in court, maintaining that their husbands violated the terms of their marriage. Eunice Shed claimed that her husband, "regardless of his marriage vows and the duty and fidelity, thereby owing to his wife," committed adultery with a number of unknown women. In the process, he "wholly destroyed" her "domestic peace and comfort," violating the "obligations of a true and lawful husband."[26] Similarly, Lucy Bates accused her husband, Luke, of having "wholly abandoned his duty" while living "in gross lewdness and wickedness."[27] Catharine Ober accused her husband, Joseph, a mariner, of having committed adultery with four different women, after having abandoned her and their children for these "wicked and debauched" women.[28] Despite— and sometimes because of—women's continued adherence to their dependent, submissive roles, their husbands' actions made it possible for women to argue for divorce and, likewise, a relative degree of independence from their husbands.

Wives' accusations of adultery also undermined their husbands' honor and manhood.[29] A number of women provided evidence that their husbands had contracted—and transmitted to them—a venereal disease, the "somatic mark of a man's profligate character" underscoring their husbands' "lack of manly vigor and fortitude."[30] Adultery undermined a husband's authority in the home and his position as leader of his family.[31] Women's accusations of adultery had the twofold effect of holding their husbands accountable for their contractual obligation of fidelity as well as empowering women to attack their husbands' masculinity without fear of reproach. Ultimately, then, adultery was dangerous to the social order, to the very power inherent in the patriarchal state, and thus women's complaints of their husbands' infidelity often met with success in court.

In addition to adultery, many women cited their husbands' abandonment as the central reason for their desire for a separation. Implicit in women's accusations of their husbands' absconding was these men's unwillingness, inability, or failure to provide financially for their wives and children—a particular threat to women and the patriarchal state alike. In cases of husbands deserting their wives, it was the state to whom it would likely fall to care for those dependents forced into destitution. Despite the fact that adultery provided the legal grounds for divorce, many women's petitions put less emphasis on their husbands' infidelity than on their desertion and failure to provide financially for their families. Certainly, this makes sense on a practical level. Relatively few women in early America petitioned for divorce; those who did take this step did so out of pure desperation, finding no feasible way out of their situations.[32] It was their financial dependence and the destitution resulting from their husbands' desertion that they identified as the clearest justification for their deserving freedom from the bonds of matrimony.

As with other justifications for divorce petitions, women needed to prove that their husbands had "willfully" and "maliciously" deserted them.[33] Many likewise asserted that their husbands had left them "without provocation" or "without a reasonable cause."[34] Abandoned women often spoke of their husbands' abandonment and their inability to provide for them as a dereliction of the husband's duty. Mary Simmons accused her husband, Stephen, of being "unmindful of his marriage vow" and abandoning her "wholly regardless of the duties incumbent upon him as a husband."[35] For this reason, deserted wives chose to emphasize their husbands' inability or refusal to provide for their families, clearly demonstrating their failures as provider and protector of their dependent family members, thus undermining husbands' household patriarchal authority. Mary Murphy, for example, accused her husband, Henry, of continuing to "neglect & refuse to provide suitable maintenance for her the said Mary."[36] Jeremiah Beals had "entirely with drawn himself from the company & support of" his wife, Ruth.[37] Henry Murphy and Jeremiah Beals both committed the crime of adultery, but their wives' central concern was these men's failures to provide for their wives and children in their dependent state. Abandonment often left wives "to want and misery," struggling to find an outlet with which they could care for themselves and their children without their husbands' financial assistance.[38]

Women who highlighted husbands' failures to provide for their dependents undermined their authority, and likewise their masculinity.[39] Especially when wives' petitions accused husbands of shirking their duty to provide for their families, women undermined their husbands' power and in turn, strengthened their own, all while affirming their own dependence on patriarchal authority. Mary Foot deplored her husband's drunkenness, which "squander'd away and destroyed all the fruits of *her* honest Industry."[40] Rosanna McKanacker's petition for alimony argued against the claim of her husband, Daniel, that he could not support his family. Despite the fact that Rosanna had been supporting herself and her children without any help from Daniel, she found that "her own exertions" were "inadequate" if she were to continue in the same vein in the future. She also added that she knew Daniel had recently come into a significant amount of property in Philadelphia, and despite their recent decree of divorce, Rosanna believed that a portion of this estate was rightfully due to herself and her children.[41]

Wives argued that this duty of their husbands to provide financially for their families extended into and during their marital separation. Ann Holland argued that her husband James's position as a house carpenter made it so that he was fully capable of contributing to his family's support, "as by his marriage vow he is bound to do." Ann invoked her husband's obligations to provide financially for her family, and undercut James's authority by berating his apparent heartlessness.[42] Significantly, Ann and James had lived separately from each other on account of his violence and short temper.[43] Ann evidently did not feel compelled to petition the court for a divorce, however, until James failed to provide the necessary maintenance for herself and her children, as he was obligated to do. Ann Holland found success in her divorce petition by accusing her husband of deserting his family, behaving with extreme cruelty, and failing to provide for his wife and children.[44]

Importantly, deserted wives often remained in a state of legal limbo. Circumstances forced them into the double bind of legally depending on an absentee husband for financial support while in reality having to provide for themselves and their children with few options for recourse. Despite the challenges that divorced women faced, including poverty and potential homelessness, many women argued that legal separation was preferable to existing in a state of dependence with no real protector or provider on whom they could depend. Wives often cited that their husbands left them "without any provision" or "manner of support."[45] Others divulged that their husbands "refused" outright to provide them with suitable maintenance or support.[46]

In certain cases, husbands' failure to provide financially for their families could be presented as cruelty. Frederick Goodenow's behavior, according to his spouse, extended beyond mere neglect and instead took the form of cruel interference. Frederick treated his wife, Sarah, "with great cruelty," and had subsequently abandoned his wife and children several years prior to Sarah's petition. As a result, Sarah was forced to support her children and herself "by her labor"—a duty legally incumbent upon her husband—in Frederick's absence. Despite her efforts to provide financially for her family after Frederick's desertion, he actively prevented her "from recovering the wages of her labor, . . . thereby throw[ing] her and her children into distress."[47] Not only was Frederick a negligent provider; he was an idler who attempted to usurp his wife's earnings while she desperately tried to ensure her family's survival.

Sarah Goodenow's petition highlights one of the major problems inherent in coverture. When a husband failed to live up to his duty as a provider, he had the potential to endanger the life of his wife and his children. Even if a wife worked for wages, that money was not her own while she remained legally married. In Sarah Goodenow's case, the most effective way for her to argue for a divorce was to claim her dependence on a man who could not and would not provide for her. She simultaneously painted him in an unflattering light and demonstrated his failure to fulfill the role of provider in order to obtain a divorce from her husband. Only then could she and her children truly survive—legally, financially, and physically separated from the cad whom she had unfortunately married.

Sarah clearly did not *want* to remain dependent on her husband, but she carefully and meticulously used the framework of her dependence in coverture to undermine it, tailoring the language of her petition to suit the expectations of her audience—the patriarchal state. She portrayed herself as mired in this dependence, wherein her husband left her and did not provide for the family. Remaining a dutiful wife in his absence, she had not attempted to divorce him, and worked to support herself and her children in his stead. She did this until he tried to claim the wages that she earned (to which he had a legitimate legal claim), and ultimately gave her no choice but to file for divorce. The crippling state of dependence in which she found herself provided the just cause for her to petition the Massachusetts Supreme Judicial Court for a divorce, which they willingly granted her on the grounds of "extreme cruelty."[48] Paradoxically, then, women's declarations of dependence in divorce petitions simultaneously undermined their subordinate legal positions.

In some ways, it was more difficult for women to justify their need for a divorce on the grounds of cruel treatment, negligent protection, or a lack of care than it was in cases of adultery or abandonment. As part of their wifely duty, early American women were required to endure more in the way of bad treatment from their husbands than their husbands were expected to tolerate from them. Some literature suggested that a wife make every effort to reform a profligate or adulterous husband, and even intimated that her husband's misdeeds might have been her own fault. A short essay entitled "On Conjugal Affection," for example, mused that "a husband may, possibly, in his daily excursions, see many women whom he thinks handsomer than his wife; but it is generally her fault if he meets with one that he thinks more amiable." The author also suggests that if a husband were to go so far as to stray from his wife's affections in favor of another woman, the wife should conduct "a serious, strict, and impartial review of her own conduct, even to the minutiae of her dress, and the expressions of her looks, from the first of her acquaintance with her husband."[49] Accordingly, in their petitions, women sometimes highlighted their redoubled efforts at reconciliation with negligent husbands to reinforce their sustained performance of their wifely duties.

Elizabeth Stevens's divorce petition demonstrates the lived experience of these expectations. She accused her husband, John, of diminished "conjugal Affection" as a result of his having "habituated himself to strong liquors & frequent intoxication." As a result, he "hath almost wholly neglected to provide for ye support and maintenance of his said wife & their Child." Instead of the love, affection, and support John owed Elizabeth according to their marital contract, Elizabeth was forced to live with a frequently drunk and idle husband, and provide financially for herself and their child. Her husband also physically and verbally abused her; he used "scandalous expressions," offered "terrifying threats," and abused her with "actual & severe blows." Despite his behavior, Elizabeth attempted "to preserve as long as possible their sacred connection" by forgiving him and "endeavour[ing] to reclaim him." In the end, she found these attempts "fruitless." Her life and the life of her child surpassed the importance of her vows to a man who clearly disregarded them.[50] Here, Elizabeth, like other abused wives, demonstrated her repeated attempts to persevere through violent beatings, prioritizing her marriage and family—ultimately telling a story the patriarchal state expected to hear.

Women, then, were compelled to counter the notion that they somehow deserved the abuse they received at the hands of their husbands, their patriarchal protectors. In their divorce petitions, wives who accused their husbands of cruelty often claimed that their husbands' actions occurred "for no reason" or "without justification," stressing that they had not acted in such a way as to provoke the physical violence of their abusive husbands. In cases of extreme cruelty, the law permitted women to live separately from their husbands; husbands were then required to provide for their support.[51] The legal understanding of husband as "protector" of dependents, then, was a crucial component of women seeking divorces on the grounds of cruelty.[52] Especially in the early years of the new republic, the rising importance of "companionate marriage" gave women a reasonable expectation for affection in these unions.[53] When men failed to live up to this role of "protector" of their dependent wives, women could justifiably argue for a divorce, provided their husbands' cruelty fell outside the realm of "reasonable bounds." Wives used their position as defenseless dependents subject to husbands' cruelty to justify their petitions for divorce.

Plaintiffs and witnesses alike often deemed this behavior unacceptable, and evidence like this was frequently included in the litany of justifications provided for divorce. For example, rather than the "tenderness and humanity" that George Shipley was "bound" to provide his wife, he instead acted as a "Tyrant and Tormentor," behaving with extreme cruelty and barbarity.[54] Ann Gardner held that her behavior as an "affectionate and obedient wife" was returned with "no affection" but instead a "Savage" disposition that "manifests itself in the most Violent acts of Cruelty & destroys all those happy purposes which are the natural & legal objects of the marriage state."[55] Although Helena Bayard acted "as a dutiful tender & affectionate wife careful of [her husband's] interests & assiduously attentive to his happiness & welfare," her husband, James, "utterly ceased to love neglected to cherish and support her and in the stead of tenderness and affection has substituted a fixed and inveterate hatred to your unhappy memorialist." His "inveterate enmity and hatred" later turned to violence; James beat his wife on several occasions and often threatened her life.[56] Bayard's and Gardner's pleas demonstrate the dangers of such emotional neglect turning to abject cruelty and abuse.

Women's petitions reveal the sordid private lives of revolutionary-era Americans and illustrate the ways in which the patriarchal ideal of protection of dependents was often, in practicality, a flimsy farce. Margaret Knodle's husband, Frederick, shirked his husbandly duties from the start. Margaret's plea for divorce called into question her husband Frederick's original motives in marrying her. Far from expressing love and devotion toward her, Frederick seems to have entrapped her and gotten her pregnant, seducing her for her late parents' money. Margaret claimed that only a few days after their marriage, Frederick "began to quarrel with & very much abuse" her and just a fortnight after their wedding began to "cruelly beat her." When she attempted to escape from her husband and instead live with her sister in Albany, Frederick stalked his family, and had his wife put in jail for allegedly stealing from him. (She claimed to have only taken a few dollars and clothes for herself and children.) He eventually dropped the charges because he wanted to "avoid being chargeable for her maintenance" in jail.

After Frederick brought his wife home, he continued to abuse Margaret. He was often drunk and "treated her with inexpressible barbarity," so much so that their neighbors worried for her life. She left him some three weeks prior to filing a divorce petition with the court in order to protect her estate and support herself and her children. Frederick later posted a notice of her desertion in the local papers, requesting that the public not honor any requests for credit made by her on his accounts.[57] As a result, Margaret was forced to rely on "the Charity of some good people for her support," rather than the money left to her by her parents. Here, the restrictions of coverture put her in a double bind: her husband's cruelty and abuse forced her out of their home, for she believed her "Life can not be safe while under his power," but at the same time, her late parents' property remained under his control. Margaret requested that as Frederick had an estate worth at least thirteen hundred pounds (and likely more), her "distressing Circumstances" could only be relieved by allocating that money for her support and maintenance. In her telling, not only was Frederick guilty of cruelty nearly from the moment he married Margaret, but he also wed her only for the wealth she had accumulated from her parents. He had no real desire or capacity to support her or their children.[58] The patriarchal ideal had failed to protect Margaret Knodle.

As in Margaret Knodle's case, wives' divorce petitions provide extensive evidence of physical abuse occurring in revolutionary-era marriages. This physical abuse, however, was not universally tabooed, or even illegal in all cases. Although Blackstone's *Commentaries* argued that men were permitted to give their wives "moderate correction," this was to be "confined within reasonable bounds."[59] Despite the fact that Blackstone's conception of "reasonable bounds" was in reference to older laws, the notion that a husband might have a rational justification for abusing his wife was widely accepted.[60] Husbands thus acted as if there were certain circumstances in which their wives deserved physical abuse. Jacob Burkhart, for instance, claimed that it was his wife's "Lewd Conduct" that provoked him to slap her "in such a manner as to hurt her but very little."[61] Andrew McBride said that he only abused his wife if he "was occasioned by the violation of her temper and Disposition and by . . . [her] indifferent and provoking conduct."[62] Daniel McKanacker believed himself fully justified in his foul treatment of his wife. "She rightly deserved it," he insisted, because "she was so provoking in her Tongue he could not keep his hands off her."[63] Wives' petitions for divorce thus had to address the generally accepted social conventions that spousal abuse of wives by husbands was permissible under certain circumstances, and as a result, often painted desperate pictures of husbands' brutality that far exceeded that norm.

Divorcing the Patriarch, Bolstering the Patriarchy

Women's divorce petitions challenged and reinforced patriarchal authority simultaneously. On one hand, divorce petitions inherently undermined husbands' patriarchal authority. Women's pleas for divorce, by their very existence, eroded any notion of absolute authority of men over women in patriarchal society. Women consistently demonstrated the ways in which their husbands were abusive, adulterous, and absconding spouses. Taking up the pen and giving voice to their complaints served to subvert the household authority of men in individual marriages in these two cities.

But, at the same time, women's petitions had to pass through the masculine realms of the courtroom and the law while being convincing to patriarchal state officials. Male judges and lawyers, clerks and officers of the court, and legislators themselves governed the legal terms through which women could be granted divorces from men. The patriarchal state—its various levers and mechanisms of power—defined the scope of women's abilities to be free from their husbands. Women therefore employed the very language of these mechanisms of power in their attempts to liberate themselves from their marriages. In other words, women acquiesced to the larger confines of the patriarchal state in order to challenge patriarchal authority on a local and household level, which may have had the effect of bolstering and legitimating these confines in the process.

Because women's petitions for divorce challenged their husbands' patriarchal authority, the language of their pleas carefully vacillated between undermining these men and simultaneously emphasizing their own submission to male authority writ large. In these ways, women played with expectations of both feminine *and* masculine comportment. Their disputations against patriarchal authority in the form of their individual husbands were permissible in certain cases in which they highlighted how these men failed to protect and provide for their wives—in effect, demonstrating that their husbands were failed patriarchs—despite their wives' continued performance of wifely duty. This careful strategy provided them the opportunity to critique and challenge their husbands while still performing traditional expressions of feminine behavior.

In toeing the line between undermining individual patriarchal authority—in the form of their husbands—and acquiescing to the larger structural power of the patriarchal state, women seeking divorces employed sympathetic narratives much in the same way as women who petitioned state legislatures for relief. Tales of cruelty and violence filled the parchment submitted by wives in an attempt to free themselves from abusive husbands, yet all the while these were couched in expectations of feminine submission to patriarchal authority. Tabetha Hearsey, for example, first demonstrated that on her part, she behaved as society and the law expected her to in her marriage: "The petitioner ever endeavoured to fulfill all the duties of a good wife to her said husband." Despite her role as a "good wife," her husband provided her with "nothing but injuries and abuses."

What was unique about divorce files relative to legislative petitions, however, was the contractual framework of marriage. Tabetha thus identified Israel's wrongdoings in terms of his violations against the laws of coverture. It was "during the coverture" when he "assaulted and cruelly beat the petitioner, at other times thrown fire upon her with intent to burn & destroy her, at other times in winter where she lay taken all the bedcloaths off her and thrown the windows open with intent to expose her to perish in the cold, and . . . injuries and abuses of one or other of these kinds were extreamly frequent with him." The clear implication was that Israel's actions breached the terms of Tabetha's marital contract in which she exchanged her relative freedom for obedience and dutiful submission to her husband in order to gain his protection, love, and support. In fact, her plea offered evidence of his active attempts to harm her. In her petition, Tabetha effectively claimed her dependence, and used this as a device to leverage for a divorce.

Tabetha also provided evidence of her husband's failure to protect her feminine virtue as a viable reason for divorce. While the expectations of female chastity were often constrictive, here Tabetha used this conception as a weapon against her husband, accusing Israel of violating her in a number of ways and therefore providing a justification for their divorce. During their marriage, Tabetha "suffered to an incredible degree from the wicked and unnatural lust of her said husband attempting things too shocking to utter with her." Implying a socially inappropriate sexual desire in her husband, Tabetha insisted that her resolve to preserve her feminine virtue remained strong, despite Israel's near constant attempts to thwart her efforts. "For her refusal to comply with such demands," Tabetha continued, Israel "inflict[ed] the most grievous pains & tortures on her, and threaten[ed] [her] Life." Israel also tried to trick her into sleeping with other men, which he would later employ in a blackmail scheme against her: "In defiance of his marriage covenant," Israel "persuaded other men to go to bed to the petitioner, hoping thereby to have a handle against her in which wicked attempts he has been unsuccessful." Despite the aggressive efforts of her husband, Tabetha remained resolute in defense of her feminine virtue. Her descriptions of her steadfastness amid Israel's failure to live up to the role of protector painted a powerful picture for the courts. Describing herself as the victim of unseemly husbandly lust, Tabetha traded her shame and fear for her life with a divorce, precipitated by the especially upsetting narrative she presented to the courts. When her husband refused to protect her virtue or her reputation—a critical currency for women, who had few legal and economic protections—she looked to the patriarchal state to do so.

Despite women's use of the terms of their dependence in these petitions, there were instances in which they carefully constructed narratives that undermined the assumptions undergirding that dependence. Tabetha first presented her husband's crimes specifically as violations of his spousal obligations. His assault and abuses ran counter to his commitment to protect her from harm. Next, she highlighted his failures to respect her chastity; he frequently forced himself on her, demanding that she do things with which she was not comfortable, and on at least one occasion, attempted to entrap her into adultery by convincing other men to seduce her. For these reasons, she thought that death "wou'd appear more eligible to her than to live again subjected to the will of one so monstrous in his affections and so inhuman in his disposition."[64] That she was "subjected" to the will of this monster was part and parcel of her coverture; her dependence on his authority was a central component of her marriage. Her submission put her in such a position that her happiness and her survival were at stake. Through identifying Israel's abuses and lustfulness, Tabetha manipulated both masculine and feminine expectations of marital behavior to gain freedom from her husband. Women like Tabetha Hearsey could present justifiable critiques of the traditional expectations of husband and wife if they simultaneously presented themselves as dutiful spouses who complied with these roles.

Portraying a husband's violation of his marital duties through a narrative structure was key to an effective petition. This strategy could mask a woman's challenge to her husband's authority and instead shift the focus of her petition to these men's abhorrent, abusive behavior, all the while highlighting her need for the patriarchal state to intervene on her behalf. After enduring significant violence and hardships at the hands of her husband, Mary Pedley presented perhaps one of the most effective petitions that illustrated her own strength of character and virtue juxtaposed with her husband's wanton cruelty and failures to live up to his obligations as her spouse. Mary opened her petition, as did other women seeking divorce, with a description of her attempts to remain faithful and obedient to her husband, despite his deficiencies: "Ever desirous for the preservation of her marriage Vow, & knowing that the foibles of human Nature claim continual forbearance & forgiveness," she "endeavoured to soften him by gentleness from the Course of Vice to which he had abandoned himself." Mary demonstrated her attempts to "soften" and reform her violent husband with her feminine virtue, though this tactic proved unsuccessful. Having laid out her dutiful, wifely behavior, she delineated her husband's crimes to the court. He "struck your Proponent a number of Blows"; he removed "the Cloths from off her while in bed & there beating her in the face & upon the Body in a cruel manner"; he "kicked and beat your Proponent" in front of two of their friends "in so outrageous a manner as obliged her & keep her in Bed for two days after." But her depiction of his cruelty did not end there.

Before describing her husband's most egregious violation, she mindfully set up the climax of her narrative "to close the Scene of his Cruelty." That she was aware of the power of her story and adeptly placed her readers at the "Scene" of her husband's crimes confirms that women did, in fact, understand the power of their narrativity, and the way it swayed jurists to their side. Pedley described her husband stabbing her in an attempt to kill her. He took a pen knife and jabbed her on her right side, an injury that "tho fortunately not mortal, confined your Proponent to a Bed of Languishing and Sickness for six week's afterwards." Four women and one man corroborated her story, adding credence and legitimacy to her narrative.[65] Like Mary Pedley, women in similar situations could only protect themselves from their violent husbands by demonstrating that in hurting their wives, husbands failed to fulfill their duties to be faithful, caring, supportive protectors of the purportedly weaker sex. By challenging her husband's patriarchal authority within the effective device of the sympathetic narrative, Mary Pedley successfully escaped the clutches of her violent husband.

Effectively, women's divorce petitions used patriarchal standards of women's dependence to undermine that status, while simultaneously turning to the patriarchal state to legitimate their claims. Mary Arthur's narrative presented an extremely sympathetic account while simultaneously portraying herself as the dutiful, submissive wife, despite her husband's myriad misdeeds. Her petition for divorce chronicled George's abuse in great detail. She described him "frequently from time to time without any Provocation Beating, Pinching, and Horse whipping her in a Barbarous and inhuman Manner so as to leave painfull and lasting Bruises on her Body, with Fury and Violence throwing her down and casting anything that comes to his hands at her to her grievous hurt great Terror and danger of her Life." She endured such beatings over nine years and was constantly covered in bruises, so much so that her body was never free of these marks for more than a fortnight. In combination with these physical abuses, Mary endured verbal attacks, as well as George's having squandered away the money she had brought to their marriage. Mary Arthur presented numerous justifications for divorce from her husband, providing a plethora of details that should have convinced the most hardened of jurists to grant her a divorce.

Despite presenting a chronicle of near continuous physical abuse, Mary knew that the success of her petition—the very vehicle to free herself from these abuses—was contingent on her ability to demonstrate that she had done nothing to deserve this violence. In fact, social custom and the common law of coverture dictated that she was obligated to demonstrate her continued fidelity and obedience despite this abuse. She had "borne with Patience" his cruelty, both physical and verbal. She endured "great Bodily Pain" all the while "in her expressable grief of mind hoping he would relent and cease to treat her in this Merciless manner." She suffered in silence, braving life with a violent husband who was supposed to be her protector. It was only when she found herself with nowhere to turn, "utterly despair[ing] of all relief," finding no hope in her husband's reformation, that she relented and petitioned for a divorce.[66]

Not only did Mary Arthur illustrate in great detail the various ways in which her husband abused her for nearly a decade, but she also presented herself as the consummate wife, dutifully remaining by her husband's side despite his violent nature and his near-constant abuses. It was only when she found no other recourse for her situation that she laid claim to her victimhood, actively asserting her dependence both on an abusive husband and on the mercy of the court. In one regard, Mary Arthur transformed this victimhood into self-empowerment, using her dependent status to gain a divorce from a hateful, abusive husband. In another, she was compelled to supplicate herself to state officials and assent to the very strictures of the patriarchal system that compelled her to suffer in this violent marriage, which she endured for years before seeking to be free of it.

There were other ways in which wives challenged one form of patriarchal authority—their husbands—through their dependence on others.

Women often relied on patriarchs in their communities, such as men in their families and neighborhoods, to act as a mouthpiece for their critiques of their husbands.[67] In soliciting depositions from other male figures in their lives, wives could pass their potentially problematic challenges to household patriarchal authority on to another. These male witnesses legitimated women's claims against their husbands to state officials. They effectively reinforced women's accusations of their husbands' failures and abuses, providing evidence of a wife's dependence on a negligent husband, which in turn assisted in her ability to obtain a divorce. Women thus used individual men to push back against the patriarchal system in their own homes. Yet testimonies provided by men tended to reinforce women's positions of subordination within the larger patriarchal system. In this way, then, women's institutionalized, legal dependence on men intensified.

The divorce case of Lucy and Luke Bates demonstrates the ways in which women seeking divorce employed certain patriarchal voices to challenge the authority of another. Henry Parker, Lucy Bates's brother, lambasted his brother-in-law, Luke, for his licentious behavior. He maintained that he saw Luke "in bed with a woman, other than his wife" with only "his shirt & drawers on," and the woman down to her shift. Parker was one of the few men deposed in this case who castigated another man's behavior. Parker had "known [Luke] in various places & in various ports of the United States, to be a man of loose life & conversation." Because of his sense of brotherly duty, he had "taken some care to see what his conduct and behavior has been when he was in ports & places, where I could have an opportunity to see him."

Parker expressed familial obligation to his sister but also had the professional opportunity as a shipmate of Bates's to follow Luke and eventually present witness testimony against him. Parker even provided details of Luke's regular salary, presumably to be used as evidence when the court decided the amount of alimony that should be allowed to Lucy. He described the destitute situation in which Luke left his poor wife: "When he parted from her, he took away all her household furniture, her bed & bedding, & left her nothing but her own clothing."[68] While most men did not present such censorious testimony against other men, Henry Parker, because of his close familial ties with the plaintiff, came to his sister's aid and demonstrated how Luke had failed to protect and provide for his wife. Lucy, in this case, remained dependent upon the legitimating force of her brother's words in her quest for a measure of independence from her husband.

The testimony of male family members in particular often enhanced the legitimacy of women's divorce petitions, as they had private, intimate knowledge of these women's lives. While Hannah Coombs's son, John L. Taylor, was the fourth to testify against his stepfather, William Coombs, his testimony went well beyond those made by others who simply claimed that William often used abusive language towards his wife. In addition to the use of profane language, Taylor also asserted that William threatened Hannah with a knife after she claimed her son would come to her defense against William. Taylor also presented evidence of his having committed adultery with a woman named Jemima, the family's Black servant, who was also deposed in the case.[69] As William's stepson, Taylor would have had access to their home; interestingly, Taylor chose to undermine William's household authority in court in defense of his mother's plea.

Taylor, however, was not the only male deponent on whom Hannah depended. Samuel Mann, an acquaintance of William Coombs's, provided a particularly graphic testimony that left no room for speculation about either William's crimes or Mann's opinions about them. Mann charged that William often used "lewd and lecherous language" in his presence, while William bragged about keeping the company of women of "loose character" with whom "he could do what he pleased." William scoffed at Mann's apparent disgust, jeering, "Now, you would not do such a thing if you could?" Mann's attempts to give William an opportunity to deny the insinuation of adultery fell on deaf ears; William instead declared, "I'll be damned if I ever let a good opportunity pass." Mann even remembered an instance in which he and Coombs passed the house of a woman named Mrs. Lewis, at which point William announced his intentions: "I want to get a stroke." Lewis, William added, "gives the best stroke that ever I got of any woman," from which Mann interpreted that William had committed adultery with this woman in the past. Mann testified that he refused to let William stop at Lewis's home, absolving himself of any complicity in William's affairs. Mann's betrayal of William's trust provided the exact fodder Hannah needed to gain a divorce from her husband, freeing her from the confines of her marriage with a philandering cad.[70]

Women often relied on men who acted as character witnesses to provide legitimate evidence of their virtuous, dutiful wifely behavior to the court, even in the face of their husbands' iniquities. This very much mirrored the techniques of women's petitions themselves, with the added, legitimating support of male voices to attest to women's appropriate behavior within the confines of patriarchal authority. Celeste Kemp's uncle, Augustin Guigue, characterized his niece as "always" behaving "as a virtuous & good Woman." He further emphasized that he had a "constant opportunity" to witness and observe her behavior, thus legitimating his (and her) claims. Once women could prove that they had behaved as upstanding wives, this ostensible crutch became a mechanism that they could employ to their advantage. Women like Celeste Kemp used legitimating male voices to manipulate seemingly impossible standards of behavior imposed on them and instead turned these constraints into tools that would work to their advantage.

Having a man testify also allowed a woman to indirectly attack her husband's character without giving the appearance that she was transgressing her spouse's authority. Jacob Screiner provided testimony against George Griscom in order to bolster his wife, Catharine Griscom's, case for divorce. In Screiner's opinion, Catharine was "a woman of reputable connections and irreproachable character" who was, with the help of her family and friends, able to support herself and her children without George's assistance. George, on the other hand, never contributed to the support of his family, lived "almost constantly in a state of intoxication," and often cursed his wife and threatened her life.[71] Likewise, David Christie chastised Samuel Tallman for "frolicking with lewd women" and contracting venereal disease as a result of his misdeeds. In defense of Mary Tallman's character, Christie berated Samuel, insisting that "no man need have a better woman for a wife than he had."[72] James Tiffin's treatment of his wife aroused such disapprobation from the community that his business suffered significantly, and he acquired tens of thousands of dollars of debt as a result.[73] These patriarchs-by-proxy used the privileges inherent in assumptions about masculine authority to lend credence to women's claims.

Women even employed a team of male witnesses to testify on their behalf and thus magnify the legitimacy of their claims. In Mary Howley's case, the defense questioned ten witnesses, and seven of the ten explicitly vouched for her and bolstered the claims in her petition.[74] Lawrence O'Neil argued that far from any abusive language or behavior, Mary Howley always treated her husband, Patrick, well, often "endeavouring to coax him into good-temper" and going to great lengths to provide Patrick with a separate meal from the other boarders when he "got sulky."[75] William Whitby swore that Mary always behaved with the "utmost kindness" toward her husband.[76] Witnesses also testified to Patrick's awful behavior. Edward Talbot averred that Mary often felt compelled to give Patrick money "in order to escape from his ill-usage." The defendant allegedly "kept the neighbourhood in a constant uproar."[77] A number of the deponents in this case claimed that Patrick stabbed himself and threatened to kill his wife, which confirmed the accusations in Mary's petition.[78]

Ultimately, then, these depositions were a necessarily utility for women, and in certain cases determined their very survival. While Elizabeth Black's own assertions of her husband's cruelty leave the reader devoid of the particulars of her situation, a number of witnesses filled in the gaps of her petition. Jacob Graff testified on behalf of his sister-in-law, contending that her husband, James, twice threatened to set fire to the couple's house (with Elizabeth locked inside) and on another occasion "threatened to blow her up." Graff also declared that he and his brother-in-law, Frederick Shingle, both went to Chester County (where the Blacks lived for a time prior to their residence in Philadelphia) to rescue Elizabeth from James's abuses.[79] Likewise, Henry Graff, another male relative, woke one night between midnight and one o'clock in the morning to Elizabeth's screams, and confirmed with her the next morning that James had threatened to set fire to the bed while she lay sleeping in it.[80] Elizabeth's male family members lent credence to her accusations of her husband's cruelty. They were also witness to a number of threats made on her life, and thus also witness to the abject failures of the patriarchal system meant to protect Elizabeth.

That women relied on men's testimonies to legitimate their claims in divorce petitions seems to undermine, at least to some degree, the fact that they were ultimately attempting to free themselves from one particular form of dependence on men. Yet women's rhetorical strategies, in these cases, were circumscribed by standards set by the patriarchal state. They were effectively required to do so by the confines of the law and social custom; women were thus limited in terms of which strategies they could employ. Even in especially egregious cases, like the Obers' divorce case, a male advocate helped to strengthen a woman's claims. John Barber Frost testified against a fellow mariner, John Ober, claiming that Ober "led a very dissolute life," living with several different women while in Alexandria and Norfolk, Virginia, while his wife was back in Boston. Frost presented graphic details in his deposition, having observed Ober undressing three specific women whom Frost was able to name, knowing full well that Ober had spent the night with these women. Frost's deposition demonstrated his great concern for Ober's wife, Catherine, who worked as a seamstress in Boston and to his knowledge was ignorant of her husband's illicit activities, along with his concern about John's having contracted venereal disease.[81] That Frost's statements passed judgment on Ober's actions lent credence to Catherine's claims, thereby reinforcing her dependence on the larger system of patriarchal authority.

* * *

Women adapted their rhetorical strategies for exploiting the terms of their marital obligations in accordance with the legal strictures of the colony or state in which they resided. In Boston and Philadelphia, women engaged the mutual if uneven spousal obligations of husband and wife to validate their claims for divorce. Boston women were able to employ this strategy from the late seventeenth century, while Philadelphia women did so more readily after 1785. Although Boston and Philadelphia women's ability to exploit these tactics began at different points and the laws and customs of Massachusetts and Pennsylvania varied, the linguistic techniques these women employed in their pleas remained consistent. Their petitions stressed their own compliance with the wifely duties of submission to and dependence on male authority in the form of their husbands, juxtaposed with these men's failures to perform their husbandly duties. Wives upbraided their husbands for emotional and physical abuse, for infidelity, for desertion, and for failing to provide financial support, all of which violated the terms of the early American marriage contract.

At the same time, however, women's individual challenges to the patriarchal system—namely, within their homes and marriages—required that they ultimately consent to its larger structure and inequities. Women painted portraits of themselves as helpless victims, as defenseless innocents, as precisely the figures the patriarchal state expected them to be. Their petitions depicted wives who fulfilled their spousal duties, who bought into conceptions of female dependence and subordination. Women likewise relied on male witnesses to bolster their claims, to legitimate their critiques of their husbands, and in some cases, to be the very vehicle for these critiques. Often, women's silence in their own petitions was superseded by male witnesses' testimonies, as women refrained from voicing their own concerns in the specifics of the case and had men speak on their behalf. Such a tactic ultimately helped to free individual women from the clutches of abusive, adulterous, and absconding husbands. Yet, on a larger scale, this strategy demonstrates that the law compelled women to tacitly consent to the very foundation of the patriarchal state's power, perhaps enhancing its strength in the process.

3 /   Sole and Separate

Elizabeth Pinckney Bellinger married Dr. John Townsend, just after the two signed a marriage settlement on November 26, 1793.[1] The widow of William Bellinger Jr., Pinckney was born into a wealthy and well-established South Carolina family whose patriarch first arrived in the colony in 1692.[2] In their marriage settlement—a prenuptial agreement regarding the division and ownership of property between spouses—the couple agreed that as Pinckney's "marriage price," Dr. Townsend would receive five hundred pounds. In turn, Townsend would be compelled to relinquish control of a portion of the property Pinckney would bring to their marriage. Townsend was obliged to acknowledge that the remainder of her estate, along with its rents, "issues," and profits, be assigned for her "sole and separate use," and that she would have the right to manage, direct, and have "enjoyment" of her property "without the controul or interference of her said Husband."[3]

The Pinckney-Townsend marriage settlement was meant to protect Pinckney's property that she had acquired prior to their nuptials through her marriage to her first (late) husband, William Bellinger.[4] Though few early American women availed themselves of this legal opportunity, those families with extraordinary wealth had this door open to them. It provided several benefits: with a marriage settlement, a young bride would be protected from the potential hazards of marrying a profligate spouse; a woman could retain a separate estate or property in the event that her husband should go into great debt (and thereby protect this property from his creditors); or, the landed elite used these settlements to ensure that wealth remained within their own families for generations, despite men's possible financial failures.[5]

The Pinckney-Townsend case gives the observer a chance to study what occurred when one party breached the terms of one of these marriage settlements—an important, often (but not always) premarital contract. In extant records, it is evident that Dr. Townsend undermined the terms of the contract he signed with his wife. With the help of her "next friend," Pinckney petitioned the South Carolina Court of Equity in March of 1797. Citing the "Treaty between" herself and her husband, Pinckney's plea demonstrated her dismay when she learned that Dr. Townsend had entered into a contract with an Edmund Bellinger and other "persons unknown" to her, which had the effect of "[depriving] and defeat[ing] your Oratrix of the benefit of the said Deed of settlement."[6]

On his part, Townsend first (inexplicably) insisted that the marriage settlement did not exist. When clear evidence arose to the contrary, he shifted tactics, arguing that the settlement was "invalid and irregular, and being in restriction of the marital rights, and ought not to be carried into Execution."[7] Townsend's rationale for insisting upon the illegality of the contract likely spoke to the well-understood and accepted notions of coverture. But, unluckily for the good doctor, South Carolina law recognized the legitimacy and enforced the legality of such settlements. The entire case hinged on one piece of parchment—the marriage settlement—a document to which both parties in this marriage consented. While the extant records do not provide a clear conclusion to the Pinckney-Townsend case, Pinckney recognized the powerful role she could play in advocating for herself by working with the strict legal code set for women in early South Carolina. And, she advocated for herself within a patriarchal system, utilizing that very patriarchal system, despite her husband's continued insistence that he owed her no property or money.

Women and South Carolina Law

Protracted legal battles over marriage settlements like the Pinckney-Townsend case, while not a frequent occurrence in early America, were also not unique. Women in early America negotiated a variety of marital settlements, ranging from divorce to separate maintenances to financial independence, even within marriage. In a number of ways, South Carolina law as it pertained to women, marriage, and property was unique. Women in revolutionary-era South Carolina could not obtain divorces from their husbands, as the practice was prohibited in the state through the late nineteenth century (and even then, was only briefly permitted before being restricted again).[8] Significantly, Janet Hudson posits that "South Carolina's insistence on denying divorce during the antebellum period seems to have been a rigid means of upholding the patriarchal structure which had served as the essential underpinning for both the family and slaver."[9] South Carolina's slave society inherently influenced other relationships and legal institutions in this patriarchal system, like marriage. White male property holders and enslavers in early South Carolina intended to bolster their own patriarchal authority by enshrining power, control, and, in the case of enslaved people, ownership of human beings in the law. At the same time, elite and middling white women claimed a unique position of power, existing on the spectrum below that of white men (i.e., their husbands) but above the people they enslaved.

While this legal system imposed restrictions on women's freedoms and rights, it simultaneously created opportunities for white women in particular to negotiate a variety of marital settlements using the terms of their dependence. The maintenance of the stranglehold of patriarchal power demanded that concessions be made in the form of protections and benefits to dependents.[10] Married white women in South Carolina were endowed with different rights in regards to property than their counterparts in places like Massachusetts and Pennsylvania. The unique nature of South Carolina's legal system created distinct circumstances for women living within that jurisdiction. In particular, South Carolina women employed several legal measures to compensate for their inability to seek legal divorces.

South Carolina women managed their marital difficulties and gained a degree of independence by challenging their husbands in the Court of Equity, as Elizabeth Pinckney Bellinger Townsend did. South Carolina women turned to equity courts, which mediated suits and petitions relative to trusts and real property, to enforce marriage settlements for two main reasons. First, women attempted to protect the property they brought to the union through marriage settlements from husbands' abuses of these agreements, highlighting that these men were poor providers and had the capacity to squander these women's estates and bring the family to ruin. Second, women attempted to protect themselves and their children through seeking legal intervention via the courts in order to keep the property they earned while their husbands purposefully deserted them. Women used the equity courts to protect from the more nefarious aspects of coverture the assets they had earned independent of their husbands' contributions.

South Carolina women who brought their cases to the Court of Equity did not construct their own interpretations of femininity. Rather, they regurgitated and performed these standards with targeted precision. South Carolina women employed the contractual terms of marriage and mimicked the language used in divorce petitions by women in other jurisdictions to negotiate various financial arrangements within the framework of colonial and state law. In the absence of the ability to seek divorces, South Carolina women performed the role of good wife and dutiful mother, consistently referred to the contractual nature of marriage, and expected enforcement of the mutual and reciprocal duties of spouses in their quests for ownership of property and financial agency. These women exploited the patriarchal protections inherent in the law to suit their own purposes, much in the same way women who sought divorces in other regions presented their cases.

Charleston women had another particular legal advantage at their disposal that most other women in revolutionary America did not. South Carolina was the first state—and one of only three states from the colonial period through the early republic—to allow married women to achieve *feme sole* trader status. From 1712, women in South Carolina could obtain—albeit, with their husbands' consent—the ability to conduct business in their own names, while still remaining married to their husbands, and legally still being defined as *feme covert* in certain matters.[11] This law provided women with what one scholar has called a "strong commitment" to protecting the rights of married women to own their own property.[12] While Charleston women were endowed with this specific right, they manipulated the law much in the same way their peers in Philadelphia and Boston did in divorce petitions. They invoked their husbands' failure to uphold his marital duties—namely, to provide for their families—in order to achieve the legal distinction of *feme sole* trader and thus gain a measure of independence over their financial lives.

South Carolina law allowed for women to be granted *feme sole* trader status in one of two ways: usually by her husband's overt or tacit consent, often in the form of deeds, but occasionally by the state's acknowledgment of a woman's operation of a business without her husband's conspicuous objection.[13] Many women were also able to claim *feme sole* trader status because of their husband's inability to provide for them for a variety of reasons. Women whose husbands had abandoned them, for example, were able to make the argument that these men could no longer provide for them, and that therefore these women should be able to conduct business in their own name.[14] In this way, Charleston women used their position of dependence as wives to argue for and achieve a measure of financial independence from their husbands, while still remaining married to these men.

The mechanisms of *feme sole* trader status are a bit more complex relative to those used by women seeking to enforce separate maintenances and marriage settlements. These *feme sole* traders, for instance, often explicitly undermined the masculinity of their husbands, highlighting the ways in which these men were poor providers, and insisted that they—that is, these wives—could do better. In ways perhaps more overt than those of women seeking divorce, then, wives seeking *feme sole* trader status undermined norms of the patriarchal household, turning the assumption about which sex ought to protect and provide for the other on its head. But, at the same time, this process still conformed to the larger structures of the patriarchal hierarchy, especially at the state level. First, husbands had to at least tacitly consent to their wives' new status. Likewise, much of the motivation behind the patriarchal state's assent to this upending of the gendered power balance in the home and in the economy involved absolving the state of the responsibility to care for its most vulnerable, dependent citizens: wives and children of failed family patriarchs. And most obviously, women still remained in otherwise legally, socially, and culturally subordinate positions within marriage, the household patriarchal system. Ultimately, then, women who sought *feme sole* trader status and women who enforced marriage settlements through the Court of Equity undermined the patriarchal system on a local and individual level, but contributed to sustaining it on a broader scale.

Property, Privilege, and Patriarchy

While the state of South Carolina imposed explicit restrictions on women's ability to divorce their husbands, Charleston women faced several unique legal conditions that, in turn, opened up opportunities for different kinds of marital settlements.[15] Women who sued their husbands in South Carolina's Court of Equity, for example, demonstrated how their husbands violated both their marriage settlements and their husbandly duty to provide for and protect their dependent wives.[16] The language Charleston women employed in their petitions to equity courts reflects that used by women in both Boston and Philadelphia when seeking divorces. These women all engaged with the contractual nature of and obligations within marriage; they cited their ever-important roles as mothers to future citizens of the United States; and, they reinforced that their behavior had been in line with that prescribed of their gender both by law and by contemporary literature while their husbands had failed at this ever-important task.

Charleston women made use of a specific kind of marital contract—the marriage settlement—to enforce the mutual obligations of husband and wife. These women sued their husbands in South Carolina's Court of Equity to protect their property under the terms of these original settlements. Elizabeth Peronneau Lightwood, for example, challenged her husband in South Carolina's Court of Equity in May of 1797. The couple signed a marriage settlement on December 28, 1769, prior to their wedding on January 1, 1770, in order to protect Elizabeth's property.[17] This included a plantation on James Island and the "several Negro slaves" who labored there.[18] Here, significantly, Elizabeth's claim to protection for herself and her property included her assertion of selfhood and privilege in relation to the enslavement of others.

The marriage settlement provided Elizabeth with a certain amount of property with which she could do what she wished. Under the terms of the settlement (for which Elizabeth's uncle, William Webb,[19] was trustee), Edward was to provide Elizabeth with four hundred pounds annually "for her sole and separate use benefit and behalf free and clear of all deductions whatsoever and without . . . being subject or liable in any wise to or for the payment of any of [Edward's] private debt"; likewise, Elizabeth was to "have the use work labour and hire of the said Negroe [Bellah] with all her future issue and increase for ever and ever," again without the interference of her husband. Here again, Elizabeth asserted her own right to ownership of another human being by claiming Bellah as property while simultaneously operating from a position of subordination as a *feme covert*.

This marriage settlement should have operated smoothly, like the dozens of others signed during this period, yet Edward, in deliberate breach of contract, attempted to sell the plantation and mortgage Elizabeth's property in enslaved people, all while failing to provide Elizabeth her annuity for twenty-seven years. This meant that Edward, according to the terms of the Lightwoods' marriage settlement, owed Elizabeth 10,800 pounds, plus interest.[20] Evidently, Elizabeth—and her trustee, William Webb—frequently prodded Edward to provide her with the sum to which she was entitled over the twenty-seven-odd years of their marriage. Edward, however, eluded making these payments by either leaving town when he sensed that Webb or Elizabeth would insist he provide his wife with her annuity or citing that his actions were done for the benefit of the Lightwood family. He insisted that "it would be more for the interest of their family to let the same remain in his hands," contending that providing Elizabeth with her regular annuity would "alarm" his creditors (presumably, signaling his incompetence at his sudden loss of capital) and thus have "ruinous consequences" for their family.[21] Webb lived in "the northern states," which logistically inhibited him from bringing a suit against Edward.[22] It was up to Elizabeth, then, to challenge her husband in court in order to uphold the terms of the settlement. Notably, she had to be careful not to challenge her husband's actions *too* forcefully.

Elizabeth conformed to the court's expectations of genteel, white femininity by demonstrating that her reluctance to bring the suit over these many years was part of her performance of wifely duty. One might assume that the frustrations Elizabeth experienced over twenty-seven years of being denied funds allocated to her per her marriage settlement would justify an impassioned harangue against her husband's misdeeds. Instead, Elizabeth expressed *remorse*, indeed her "repugnance" at having to bring her marital issues to court, "which might tend to interrupt the tenderness and harmony which subsisted between her and her said husband." Elizabeth demonstrated her willingness to endure decades of financial maltreatment and, frankly, *unlawful* actions, in an attempt to maintain the "harmony" in her marriage. Recall that contemporary prescriptive literature cautioned women against chastising their husbands, and insisted that it was part of a wife's duty to attempt to reform her husband's transgressive behavior. Like Boston and Philadelphia women who brought divorce suits against their husbands in court, Elizabeth Lightwood demonstrated in her petition that she prioritized the execution of her wifely duties over her own happiness. Indeed, she had long been willing to overlook the illegality of her husband's actions.[23]

This rhetorical foundation was a requisite step before Elizabeth could legitimately accuse her husband of shirking his husbandly duties. Only after laying this critical foundation could Elizabeth formally rebuke Edward's character, his ethics, and his inability to perform the duty of a husband. Before she could criticize her husband's behavior, she had to provide a foundation of social justifications for stepping into the masculine realm of the court. She detailed nearly thirty years of mistreatment, all the while confirming that during that period, she had remained a dutiful, affectionate wife, never pushing her requests for her rightful share of the annuity beyond a gentle prodding. This rhetorical performance proved a necessary and ultimately successful strategy for enforcing the settlement between Elizabeth and her husband, Edward.

What eventually brought Elizabeth to court, as she explained, was the family's unfortunate financial situation. Edward, who had become "very much embarrassed" by all the debts he had accumulated, was facing suits from his creditors demanding payment on these debts. Likewise, Edward "expressed his total inability" to pay his wife the debt he now owed to her. Most significantly, Edward insisted that Elizabeth was "not entitled to demand" any interest on the money he owed her, despite their marriage settlement providing clear evidence to the contrary. In order to remedy her own situation, Elizabeth requested that the court compel Edward to pay the debts he owed his wife, per the contract the two had signed nearly thirty years prior. If he could not, she suggested, he should be forced to sell the enslaved people of whom *he* claimed ownership to make up the difference. If he *still* fell short of the sum due to his wife, Elizabeth insisted, Edward should be obliged to sell *his* land as well.

In his response, Edward countered none of the charges that Elizabeth lodged against him. He agreed that he was bound to pay his wife four hundred pounds each year; that he owed her twenty-seven years of back payments; that he never believed Elizabeth intended to abdicate her property rights; and that Webb and Elizabeth were both prevented by Edward himself from procuring these payments. He even admitted to the "reasonableness and justice of paying and satisfying" the arrears due to Elizabeth. Edward, however, insisted that all he did, he did out of the interest of his business and his family, fearing that selling his bonds too soon would provide less profit than they were worth, or that providing Elizabeth with her annuities would alarm his creditors. On top of all of this, Edward insisted that he was unable to meet his wife's demands and that Elizabeth's claims to interest were unjust. Yet, Edward ultimately acquiesced to his wife's dictates: he conceded that he was "ready to submit to any decree this Honorable Court may think proper to make."[24]

Like the Pinckney-Townsend case cited at the start of this chapter, the exact conclusion of the Lightwoods' legal battles is unknown. But, with extant probate files and wills, census records, and Charleston city directories, we can piece together what happened in the aftermath of their legal battle. Elizabeth was eventually free of her husband, and retained a significant portion of property that she owned in her own name. By 1800, Elizabeth was listed as head of household on the census records, with eight other "free white" persons under the age of twenty-five and twenty-six enslaved people also listed among that group.[25] Later, Elizabeth lived with her son, the attorney Edward Lightwood, at 220 Meeting Street, while her husband continued to live in the home they shared prior to this separation, at 226 Meeting Street.[26] By 1806, Elizabeth was listed as a "widow" in the directory, and after her son's passing in 1808, she lived alone at 119 Meeting Street.[27] In 1809, she was the lone Lightwood in Charleston's city directory, which designated her occupation as "planter," thereby indicating that she retained her possession of a number of enslaved people while living free of male control.[28]

Charleston women also used equity courts to protect themselves and their children against the financial strains caused by adulterous and absconding husbands, much like their counterparts who sued for divorce in other jurisdictions. While infidelity and desertion provided clear justifications for divorce in other colonies and states, South Carolina women could not utilize this legal mechanism. Yet, the rhetoric some employed in their interactions with the equity courts provided an outlet for South Carolina women to compel their husbands to abide by similar arrangements of physical separation and financial freedom. Even those women who had no marriage settlement to enforce their claims sought financial protection from the courts. Maria Beaury, for example, filed a complaint against her husband, Jean, in the wake of his desertion. Having threatened to leave his wife and two children for some time, Jean made good on his warning in June of 1809. Three years later, Maria finally presented her case to the Court of Equity. What propelled her to speak out against her absconding husband in court after this long stretch was her increasingly untenable situation. Maria found "her means of support exhausting, her Children burthensome." She noted that her husband "had left her regardless of their welfare." Jean, Maria held, shirked his husbandly duties without any just cause or reason.[29]

Like those women in other states who petitioned for divorces, Maria Beaury also demonstrated her own performance of wifely duty, presented in stark contrast with Jean's abandonment. She labored for years in an attempt to provide for her family in her husband's absence, because "she felt herself obliged to make every exertion for the maintenance of herself & Infants." Though this duty was not prescribed to her, Maria took on the role of provider in an attempt to ensure her family's survival. She belabored the point, making sure to emphasize how she had been backed into a corner by her husband's actions, before she detailed her own independent business venture. It was under these strained circumstances, and not by her own volition, that she ventured into this traditionally male-centered realm.[30] She entered into a partnership with a man named John Collins, and the two ran a grocery store together.[31] Because of her efforts, Maria was able to support her children during the entirety of Jean's absence, and likewise acquired "three negroes & some Groceries & other articles without the least assistance" from her husband. All that she earned for herself and her children, she earned by her own labor (and, though it went unmentioned, by the labor of the people she enslaved).[32] Like Elizabeth Lightwood, Maria Beaury positioned herself simultaneously as helpless before the law in regards to her status as a *feme covert*, yet empowered and emboldened by her control over enslaved people who existed in this system for her benefit and the benefit of her children.

It seemed that Maria had created a life for herself and her children, but it was her husband's *return* that interrupted this stability. Here, of course, Maria would have to tread across a very delicate line; her husband's return would prompt the reunification of her family, and his ostensible supplanting of his wife as the financial provider. But, Maria naturally worried that Jean would return briefly, take possession of the wealth and property she had acquired in his absence, and leave his wife and children as destitute as they had been three years prior. Maria thus took the drastic legal measure of preempting the threat of Jean's presence by submitting a complaint to the Court of Equity. Jean, of course, presented his own side to the story. He claimed that "as her husband" and per the doctrine of coverture, all of Maria's property that she had earned "during the time he absolutely abandoned her & her Children" was, in fact, "his own." Technically, of course, Jean was right. Under coverture, anything Maria earned—even during the period Jean deserted his family—was under his control.

Maria relied on the extenuating circumstances of her case, which included Jean intentionally and maliciously failing to provide for his family the protections and benefits of a husband and father. Maria begged the court to consider the details of her situation: if Jean had his way, she argued, he would take control of her property and abscond again, leaving his wife and children "absolutely destitute" and in the same position as she had been three years prior. Maria pleaded not just for herself but for her children, "who rely on her alone for support." She requested that the court order that Jean be served with an injunction preventing him from interfering with her property.[33] Judge DeSaussure granted Maria's request; he ordered that Jean Beaury be prohibited from "intermeddling with the property acquired by his wife, during his desertion of her & her children."[34]

Like women in similar circumstances who sought divorce, Maria needed to demonstrate that her children would suffer if their father returned, and that she herself constituted a better parental figure and financial provider than he could be. In inserting herself into this firmly masculine role, Maria had to construct her rhetoric carefully, and always nod to the fact that this behavior was truly an extension of her role as mother to young children.[35] Like women who petitioned for divorce from absconding husbands, Maria accounted for her financial independence by invoking her children, and underscoring her role as the consummate mother.

Maria's situation seems particularly frustrating to a contemporary reader. Because Maria's husband abandoned her, necessity compelled her to support herself and her family in a world that not only did not expect that of her but often admonished women who performed the traditionally masculine role of family head and provider. Nevertheless, she persisted, and succeeded, creating the means by which she could support herself and her children. When her hard work was in jeopardy, she sought the legal advocacy and protection provided by the patriarchal state. Social and legal standards compelled Maria to present her breach of gendered norms to the court ruled by wealthy, white South Carolina gentlemen. So, she presented the performance they expected of a middling, white woman. To cover for her challenge to her husband's authority, she focused her narrative on her exemplary performance of motherhood—an exceptionally critical role for women in the early American republic. She couched her petitions for protection from her husband by emphasizing the ways in which she did conform to the comportment expected of proper femininity.

Notably, enslaved people played an important role in a number of these heated marital battles between elite and middling white South Carolinians. They were humans treated as items to be mortgaged to pay for debts, as property to be protected from the possession of profligate spouses, as tokens to be used as currency in a courtroom struggle in which a white woman argued that human beings were commodity goods entitled to her to ensure her financial security. In this way, the Lightwoods and the Beaurys asserted their position of white privilege. Likewise, the Lightwoods' and Beaurys' ability to mark enslaved Black Americans as property in their court battles demonstrates a clear division between white and Black marital privilege.

While Elizabeth Lightwood's and Maria Beaury's actions can be construed as a form of resistance against patriarchal authority, they achieved their goals on the backs of men and women of color. They defined their positions of power by designating themselves as the helpless dependents of men but also as the enslavers of Black Americans. Elizabeth Lightwood and Maria Beaury, both disadvantaged under the law in many ways, could still claim a level of privilege because of their race and the degree of protection they were owed as white wives. This was a crucial component of the patriarchal state's continued oppressive power, and these women actively assented to its terms, despite the ways in which their behavior subtly undermined certain components of it.

This racial and economic privilege was essential to the success of both Beaury's and Lightwood's cases. Unlike women in jurisdictions that allowed for divorce, Charleston women found their best legal opportunities for marital separation within the realm of the Court of Equity. Women's ability to file petitions with this body, however, was contingent upon access to their own property, distinct from their husbands'. Without that propertied privilege, South Carolina provided few mechanisms through which women could live financially and maritally free from their spouses. The case of Jane Hedderley demonstrates the limited prospects afforded to women in these scenarios. She presented a petition to the South Carolina Court of Equity that mimicked Beaury's complaints while also detailing the extensive emotional abuse she suffered through years of her husband's deceptions. Jane married William Hedderley in Nottingham, England, in 1783. Soon after, the couple came to the United States and eventually settled in New York. After two months in the city, William received an offer to work as a carpenter in Hartford, Connecticut, bringing his wife with him. There, she gave birth to a son, named after his father. William then left for Boston, where he continued his carpenter trade, while Jane remained in Hartford for a time before joining him further north. In Boston, Jane gave birth to a daughter, Elizabeth. William then settled his family in a home in that city, but later returned to New York again to be a carpenter in a theater. From that point, Jane's life fell into a downward spiral. William's absence caused his wife and children a great deal of financial trouble. Soon after he arrived in New York, William demanded that his wife move to "cheaper lodgings" in Boston because he no longer had adequate work. This, Jane insisted, was the last time she ever heard from her husband; eight years stood between the letter to which Jane referred and the bill of complaint that she submitted to the court.

Like other women who transgressed their husbands' authority by filing complaints in court, Jane Hedderley insisted that William's indefinite departure and failure to communicate with his wife came with no explanation, despite her consistent attention to her wifely duty. She never found their marriage to be an unhappy one, insisting that the two had "no disunion or quarrel" between them (despite his absence). They "lived on terms of affection," and up until that point, had not met with any significant challenges threatening their marriage. Despite William's continued silence, Jane wrote to her husband "frequently . . . without any satisfactory answer." She attempted to contact him through his brother, George, asking for any news of her husband's whereabouts. Jane made every effort to fulfill her wifely duty, while caring and providing for her children, throughout her husband's prolonged—and unexplained—absence. Then, Jane heard an unfortunate report of her husband's death.[36]

Faced with the frightening reality of William's passing and the definitive knowledge that he would never again provide them with any support, Jane and her children struggled in destitution. They remained in Boston for several years "in great poverty and distress." Jane found some work as a maid, yet not on a consistent basis; she and her children also had to resort to the city's almshouse for "aid and sustenance." Most unfortunately, Jane's "miseries . . . were most cruelly aggravated by the impossibility to save from prostitution her unfortunate daughter." Jane had attempted to place Elizabeth in service, but instead the sixteen-year-old was "secured to an house of ill-fame." Jane claimed to have "rescued" her young daughter from a life of prostitution, and sent her to serve in the house of a "reputable family" in Boston before Jane and her son left the city. Jane later learned of "her unhappy daughter's return to her former disgraceful . . . State." Following William's departure from his family and his death, Jane and her children fell into a life of want, misery, and sexual impropriety.[37]

As it turned out, however, William had *not* died. Instead, he had ignored his husbandly duty, and—quite literally—his wife and children, and taken up with one Mary Edwards, who worked in the theater where William first found work in New York.[38] The two had then left for Charleston. Learning of her husband's deception, Jane sent several letters to him there, all with no reply. Jane continued to attempt to find work by any means necessary, selling goods in the public market, working in service, and "more than once in the low and painful duties of a Cook or Housemaid, or whatever service could protect her from starving," as her husband was clearly unwilling to do the same. Later hearing that

William had gone to Philadelphia, she traveled there to inquire of him from his brother, who insisted (again) that William had died. Shortly after this second blow, Jane learned that she had been deceived another time; William was *still* alive and "doing well in business in Charleston."[39]

In an attempt to fight for her own survival, Jane traveled to Charleston to confront her husband. Along with her friend, Mrs. Brown, "to whose benevolence humanity and hospitality she is indebted for food & shelter," Jane laid several charges at her husband's feet. She reproached him for his "barbarity in having thus cruelly, and without cause deserted and abandoned her, his lawful Wife, & her Wretched Children, to misery and disgrace." She accused him of "squandering on the unworthy Woman with whom he cohabits." She blamed him for deliberately hiding from her when she came to his home, where Jane instead faced Mary Edwards—her husband's paramour—who offered nothing but "intemperate and indecent language" before slamming the door in Jane's face. Echoing language of abused, maltreated wives who petitioned the courts for a divorce, Jane lashed out against her husband for failing to live up to his husbandly duties, and indeed for purposefully and blatantly sentencing his family to a life of destitution, with no regard, compassion, or respect for their lives.[40] She could not have used such disparaging language, however, without first demonstrating her steadfast, and at times seemingly naïve dedication to her husband and their marriage.

Determined to hold her husband to task for his years of cruelty and injustices, Jane approached a lawyer in order to gain "a competent and suitable maintenance for herself & children."[41] In an attempt to defend himself against the onslaught of his wife's accusations, William denied that they had ever been married, along with invoking his own colorful narrative replete with "scandalous and unfounded insinuations" against Jane's "fame and reputation." But Jane fired back with her depiction of William's odious lack of feeling toward his children. She confessed to the court her assumption that upon the "sight of [his] infant Son," William would have "felt the pangs of remorse for his past cruelty and misconduct." She hoped that he would play the honorable man, leave his mistress, and return to his position in Jane's family as father and husband. Instead, William persisted in his barbarity, conspiring to keep Jane from receiving her "just matrimonial rights," namely, an adequate support from her husband. If the court were to believe William's counternarrative, Jane and her children would find themselves "utterly destitute of relief in the premises." She submitted to the court her plea for a separate maintenance, requesting that her husband not be permitted to leave the state lest he fail to provide "a proper suitable maintenance for herself and children."[42]

The Hedderleys' case proves a strange contrast to the cases presented in this chapter thus far. Puzzlingly, the Hedderleys' marital clashes took place on the battlefield of South Carolina's Courts of Equity, *not* in the Suffolk County Court where a number of Boston women successfully won suits for divorce. She and her husband lived in a number of different states, and Jane could have legally sought to divorce William in Massachusetts. She would have presented a solid case with evidence to prove desertion, neglect, and her husband's failure to provide for his family, along with his having committed bigamy as well. In fact, the narrative within her bill of complaint read exactly as hundreds of other petitions for divorce from this era do. Jane, however, made a choice to file a complaint with the Court of Equity in South Carolina, where divorce was not permitted. There, she could seek a separate maintenance, a regular and legally mandated payment that William would provide his wife for her care and for the care of their children. We cannot know why Jane made this specific legal choice, and the records do not provide evidence as to whether the court made a decree in Jane's favor. Perhaps she was advised to do so by counsel; perhaps she thought it was easier to obtain a separate maintenance through the South Carolina court system; or perhaps she preferred this particular form of redress. Divorce in Massachusetts would have freed her from the confines of her marriage, but would not necessarily have provided the legal requirement of continued financial support from William as her former spouse. The Hedderleys were not a family of means, even prior to William's absconding, and Jane may have gambled that the form of legal redress that could best offer her children protection for the future came from suing her husband in South Carolina's equity court.

Jane's *lack* of economic privilege here limited her options and her opportunity for success. Even if the court found in her favor, there was no guarantee that William would comply with legally mandated support payments. In fact, we can reasonably surmise that he would not have done so, given his track record of behavior towards his wife and children. But Jane was desperate, and like many other women struggling through financial destitution, she sought the best solution to her problems, even if there was no guarantee of success or survival. Unlike Pinckney, Beaury, and Lightwood, Jane Hedderley had no economic privilege on which to depend, and no amount of performative white femininity would save her from poverty. In the case of women in South Carolina, racial and economic privilege along with the proper performance of the expectations for wives and mothers were all critical components in negotiating the terms of their marital settlements and separations.

Married and *Feme Sole*

Obtaining separate maintenances and enforcing marriage settlements, however, was not the only way for Charleston women to obtain a relative degree of financial independence from their husbands. In addition, they could achieve *feme sole* trader status, securing them the right to buy and sell property and to do business in their own name, all while remaining married, and legally *femes covert*. Between 1750 and 1820, a significant number of Charleston women achieved *feme sole* trader status under South Carolina law.[43] They, along with their husbands, applied for this status for a number of reasons, including alleviating their family's economic need, helping diminish their family's debt, and, most frequently, attempting to assuage their husband's financial inadequacies.[44] Charleston women, therefore, used the terms of their dependent status as wives—through language and through the literal consent of their husbands—to gain a relative degree of financial freedom from these men and the confines established by the patriarchal state. While Charleston women were not legally capable of divorcing their husbands, achieving *feme sole* trader status served as a remedy to their marital problems in much the same way that a divorce may have.

Importantly, this legal privilege was contingent on at least the tacit consent of their husbands when men could not support their families. Dr. John Mackie, for instance, declared that it had "long been intended" by him "for various good and Solid reasons to authorize and empower" his wife, Anne, to act as a *feme sole* trader in any business in which she "might find herself competent" or "to which her interest might lead her."[45] Therefore, rather than wives declaring their dependence on failing husbands, most sources reveal husbands coming to terms with the fact that they themselves were poor providers and pathetic patriarchs. In these cases, husbands acknowledged that it was foolhardy to force their wives to be financially submissive dependents while these men themselves could not provide adequately for them and their children. Significantly, then, *feme sole* trader deeds demonstrate the ways in which husbands also undermined the absolutist notion of women's dependence and financial ineptitude. In these cases, husbands themselves subverted their own patriarchal authority in the home and requested that the state intervene.

Like their counterparts in Boston and Philadelphia, Charleston women underscored their husbands' failures as providers for their dependents in order to procure *feme sole* trader status for themselves. In 1761, for example, Mary and Thomas Langley signed an indenture granting her official *feme sole* status. Her husband, Thomas, an "Indian trader," had thirty years prior absconded from her as well as from her children, leaving them "Destitute of any Support; Cloathing or Maintenance." Because of Thomas's desertion and failure to fulfill his husbandly duty, Mary went from financially dependent wife to *feme sole* trader. She, "by her own Labour, and Industry . . . Supported and provided for herself and Children by the said Thomas Langley." She also had the written support of several of her acquaintances: Elijah Postell, William Saunders, and Richard and Mary Saltus. At the urging of these acquaintances, Mary submitted an indenture to the state in order to protect the real and personal property that she had earned as a *feme sole* trader, which included forty-five enslaved people (a number of whom were mortgaged to pay Mary's debts). As in the aforementioned cases in the equity courts, Mary Langley's racial identity provided her with a measure of privilege in this patriarchal system.

Significantly, Mary also agreed to provide *Thomas* with some financial support, if he acquiesced to allow her, in the future, to have all the rights of a *feme sole* trader, thus providing her with the ability to make contracts and sue in her own name.[46] In this case, the Langleys turned the patriarchal system on its head: Mary would provide a regular maintenance for Thomas. In the state's view, an emasculated head of household was preferable to an entire family brought into destitution and reliant on the state for assistance. Mary successfully gained a measure of independence from her deserting, irresponsible, and financially inept husband by highlighting his inability to fulfill the role of independent, bread-winning head of household.

Some husbands granted their wives *feme sole* trader status in order to prepare for the future in the event that they might become insolvent or otherwise unable to care for their families, thus acquiescing to their wives' financial independence. In 1763, Christopher Sheets suggested that his wife, Susannah, earn *feme sole* trader status for that very reason. Susannah had already been running a shop in Charleston (evidently with her husband's tacit consent), but Christopher filed with the state so that "in case the said Christopher through any misfortune or accident should become insolvent," Susannah would be able to continue to conduct business on her own account, and not be liable for any "Contracts Debts or

Encumbrances" that fell to Christopher. The couple took this precaution "for the better providing, maintenance and Support" of Susannah and their children, preparing for the instance in which Christopher might not have been capable of fulfilling his masculine duty as husband and provider.[47]

Because these deeds required a husband's consent, circumstances essentially compelled men to emasculate themselves by highlighting their failures as providers for their dependents. Peter Horn, for example, admitted to have "greatly Lessened and Reduced the fortune" of Elizabeth Horn, his wife. He also recognized that even if the family were to earn a sufficient living in the future or perhaps receive financial support from friends and family, "Elizabeth might by leaving it in the power of her said Husband be totaly strip[p]ed of the same and of the means of producing a future support and subsistence." Peter thus recognized his past as well as his potential failures, and therefore decided to ask the state to grant Elizabeth *feme sole* status in order to better improve the lives of his ostensibly dependent family members.[48] Similarly, James Farrell conceded that since he had married his wife, "the fortune which the said Mary then Brought to the said James hath been from various Losses and unaccountable Misfortunes happening to the said James Farrell totally wasted and imbezled." Like Peter Horn, James Farrell recognized that if the family's future finances were left to him, "in all Probability" they would "be wasted and imbezled," as he had done with his wife's former fortune. James recognized his wife's financial acumen in addition to his failures to provide security to his family, and therefore granted Mary *feme sole* trader status.[49] Men's open admission of their failure to live up to patriarchal standards undermined the social and legal prescriptions of gendered behavior in revolutionary America, but alternatively relieved the state of having a number of new dependents on the public dole.

By consenting to their wives as *feme sole* traders, husbands likewise vacated the role of independent providers, and instead passed this baton to their wives. James Clark, "by reason of Misfortunes and disorders in Mind," declared himself "unable to carry on any Business for the support of [him]self and family." He similarly asserted that his wife, Rachel, on the other hand, was "by her Labor and Honest Industry . . . capable of gaining a comfortable lively hood for herself & family—without my Interfering there with." Here, because James professed himself unable to perform his husbandly duties, he designated that Rachel, who should have been cared for in her role as dependent wife, would usurp the role of financial head of household due to his inadequacies.[50] Edward Johnston deemed himself "at present incapable" of providing support and maintenance for his wife and children. He therefore agreed that his wife, Sarah, should, "not withstanding her coverture," become a *feme sole* trader to conduct business "at her own free will and pleasure without the controul or Intermeddling" of her husband. Edward attempted to redeem his character by stating that he signed the indenture out of "the Natural Love forever and affection, which he hath for, and beareth towards his said Wife and Children."[51] Certain language men presented in these deeds indicates their own performative attempts to salvage their husbandly reputations and provide a semblance of a justification for their abdication of patriarchal household duty.

While it is unclear whether most of these husbands independently made the decision to designate their wives as *feme sole* traders, some records show that wives exerted a significant degree of power in coercing their husbands' actions in this way. Robert Howard, for instance, who "thro misfortunes" was "rendered unable" to pay his Creditors and "support . . . [his] Wife and family," chose to grant his wife *feme sole* status so that she "may be at Liberty to provide for her own Childrens maintenance." This choice, however, was not his own; he made it "at the Special request of my said Wife Mary."[52] George Thomson also named his wife, Jane, as a *feme sole* trader because of her "advice, & Consent."[53] Though women's agency is rarely made explicit in these deeds, it is likely that many women pressed or cajoled their husbands to consent to their freer economic status.

Feme sole traders often turned to this role in conjunction with their husbands in order to earn extra income to support their families and to help raise their families out of debt. In the cases of Charleston women, this independence was always achieved with their husbands' at least tacit consent but often with their explicit consent, as seen in the deeds granting women *feme sole* status. Women in South Carolina who achieved *feme sole* trader status could use this designation as a pseudo-divorce, or substitute for divorce, when the law would not permit such a separation, so that they might better provide for their families. The language of *feme sole* trader deeds challenged traditional expectations about marriage, undermining husbands' authority while accommodating wives' desires for more freedom within their marriage, but by treating these cases as individual aberrations from the patriarchal norm, the state bolstered its power as it continued to exercise patriarchal authority on a broader scale.

* * *

Charleston women, subject to a different set of laws from their counterparts in Philadelphia and Boston, were not afforded the same ability to petition the court for a divorce. They could, however, employ other legal statutes to gain a similar measure of independence from negligent husbands. They also engaged strikingly similar tactics in these parallel marital arrangements that remained relatively consistent over time. Some wives sued their husbands in equity courts for violating the concrete terms of their marriage settlements. Others saw their own husbands openly admit to their failure to provide for their families and in turn designate their wives as *feme sole* traders. In these ways, Charleston women acquired a degree of financial independence from their husbands while still existing as dependent *femes covert*. In all of these cases, women employed the legal, social, and economic frameworks of feminine dependence to their advantage, much in the same ways their counterparts in other jurisdictions did when they sued for divorce.

Notably, in a colony and, later, state in which divorce was not an option, Charleston women's ability to take advantage of the protections afforded to women in this patriarchal system hinged on their access to property and the privilege of their whiteness. Property, in the cases examined here, was often the ultimate determinant in these women's fates. This is, perhaps, unsurprising in South Carolina, a place steeped in the idea that human beings could be designated as property, as capital, and as wealth that bestowed power on white Americans. Women claimed their place in this chain of privilege by virtue of their whiteness, which allowed them and encouraged them to set themselves apart, as special figures in need of protection granted by the patriarchal state. Ultimately, though, to take advantage of these protections, women would be required to acquiesce, at least tacitly, to their disempowerment, their subordination. In order to invoke this power and privilege, they were made to be—wittingly or unwittingly—complicit in continuing the systemic oppression of others, including other women.

4 /   Matriarchal Allies and Advocates

On December 11, 1799, Mary Hopps filed for divorce from her husband, Samuel. In her petition, she noted that the two had been married for seven years, but for "a considerable time past," Samuel had "totally alienated his affections from" Mary, had "given himself up to habits of intoxication," and had completely neglected "the means of providing a maintenance for his family." Worse still, Samuel had "assaulted beaten and otherwise maltreated" his wife "in the most cruel and barbarous manner." In just over three hundred words, Mary Hopps summarized years of abuse and sought a separation from her spouse.[1] Distressing though Mary's complaint is, it pales in comparison to the details provided by her neighbor, a mantua maker named Ann Dennis.

Ann's deposition described the extraordinary lengths to which she went to protect Mary from her husband, the man who was tasked by law and social custom to protect his wife. On at least two occasions, Ann intervened to stop Samuel Hopps from attacking his wife with various weapons. She held back the axe in Samuel's hand as he rushed toward Mary, threatening to call their neighbors if he would not yield. In another instance, Samuel ran at Mary with a butcher's knife he found lying on the counter that he had concealed by his side; fortunately, Ann spotted this and quickly grabbed the knife from Samuel's hand before any additional harm could befall Mary. Ann had observed other occasions in which Samuel had been violent towards his wife both in word and in deed, striking her in the face with a brush and otherwise threatening to kill Mary a number of times. Believing that Samuel's behavior was so unpredictable and violent, Ann felt warranted in her decision to take the knives and a hatchet from the Hopps' home and hide them, "fearing that [Samuel] would do mischief with them."[2] Ann not only saved Mary's life on at least two occasions but also took measures into her own hands by stealing weapons from Samuel's possession, which he could have used in future attacks against his wife. Importantly, she testified to these observations under oath, and helped Mary earn a legal separation from her husband.[3]

Ann Dennis's deposition—though brief—reveals a powerful, long-lasting force in revolutionary-era women's experiences. An array of legal sources, including legislative petitions and court records, illuminates an otherwise invisible world of well-established women's networks that served to support each other, especially when patriarchal authorities failed to protect and provide for them. Early American women, in certain cases, disregarded some boundaries imposed by their legal, social, and economic subordination, bypassing their dependence on men in favor of their *inter*dependence on and with other women. Early American women's shared gendered experience fostered empathy and elicited allyship and advocacy among other women. In the absence of patriarchal protections, these women filled the roles traditionally held by men. In many ways, then, matriarchal allies and advocates were critical to women's survival in the revolutionary era.

Matriarchal allies and advocates were female family members, friends, and women in local communities who supplanted patriarchal authority.[4] The term "matriarch" generally denotes women who have "the status corresponding to that of a patriarch."[5] In the context of the American revolutionary era, however, matriarchal allies and advocates did not have the legal or social status of patriarchs. Yet in many ways, they acted as the protectors and defenders of women in the stead of patriarchal authorities—namely, husbands and the state—who failed to fulfill their duties.[6] They built and fostered female networks of interdependence, replacing the hierarchical, unbalanced relationship between patriarchal authority and female dependents with communal support among women. While the Revolution altered gendered conceptions of dependence and independence, it did not alter women's tendency to rely on each other in the years following the war, although the circumstances of the conflict may have enhanced this interdependence among women.[7]

Importantly, matriarchal allies and advocates did not desire to have or exert power over their fellow women. In advocating for one another, women instead upset the balance of gendered power by usurping, at least performatively if not literally, the masculine roles of household and state authority. The instability of wartime and the uncertain future of the state created a space for women to take advantage of blurred gender boundaries, defending each other in the process, and in many ways being more dependable than the men who were tasked by society to protect and care for them. When husbands proved themselves to be failed patriarchs, particularly through spousal abuse, neglect, or financial incompetence, women interceded to protect—physically, emotionally, and financially— their female friends and family members. Likewise, women deponents stepped into the masculine space of the courtroom, thus replacing patriarchal figures in certain ways. These advocates bore witness to men's transgressive behavior, and in so doing empowered themselves and female victims in the process. Ultimately, these witnesses demanded that the state fulfill the role of surrogate patriarch in the absence of legitimate husbandly authority, granting divorces and providing legally mandated financial support for wives in these situations. Matriarchal allies and advocates stepped in to defend women when patriarchal authorities failed to do so.

Matriarchal Allies

Women's shared gendered experience gave them an empathetic understanding of each other's plight. In particular, female family members— especially mothers and daughters—advocated for each other in their daily lives and, if necessary, through legislative petitions and in the courtroom. When Mary Pedley's husband's abuse became too much to bear, for example, she took up residence with her mother, who gave her refuge from William Pedley's violent temper.[8] Likewise, Mary Cooper's daughter solicited her assistance after her husband died. Cooper, out of the "obligation and Parental affection from a tender Mother to an only child now in the utmost distress," begged Pennsylvania's Executive Council to grant her a pass to travel to and support her widowed daughter and fatherless grandchildren.[9] In these cases, the love and bond between a mother and daughter manifested in physical protection and legal advocacy.

Matriarchal allies demonstrated selfless love and an astute understanding of effective petitioning strategies, particularly in mothers' support for their daughters. Mary Cumming petitioned the South Carolina General Assembly for permission to sell portions of her late father's property upon her husband's desertion. It had, of course, belonged to her absconding husband upon their marriage according to the customs of coverture, so she enlisted the assistance of female family members to make her case to the legislative body. Mary contended that because of her particularly distressed situation, her two sisters and her mother agreed to apportion her a piece of her father's estate. In a show of motherly devotion, Mary's mother even agreed to renounce her own claim of dower—a widow's right to one-third of her deceased husband's property—thus strengthening Mary's claim to her deceased father's property.[10] Mary was dependent on both her sisters' support of her claims and her mother's continued dedication to her prescribed parental duties.

Matriarchal alliances extended beyond familial ties, too. Occasionally, entire groups of women came together to support one of their own. One such case is that of Mary Fraser. In her petition, Fraser recognized the "unfortunate" decision of her husband to side with the British government during the Revolutionary War. Because of his "becoming obnoxious to the American Government," Dr. James Fraser's name appeared on the list of offenders of the Confiscation Act of 1782. The narrative Mary presented diminished her husband's true influence and activities. In her view, James followed the law, left the country, and had been in exile at the time of her petition for thirteen years. Further demonstrating her performance of wifely duty, Mary, "being bound in duty as well as by Affection to follow the fortunes of her Husband, was obliged to quit her Native Country, to abandon her Aged Mother and all her relations and friends, and to take refuge in a foreign land, where she has been made to taste, in Common with her young and unoffending Offspring, of the bitter cup of Sorrow and Affliction."[11] Mary was deeply torn between, on the one hand, her love of country, family, and friends, and on the other, her dedication to her husband and her marital responsibilities.

On the occasion of her mother falling ill, Mary begged the assembly "to be re-admitted to the bosom of her Country" with her children and husband in tow in order to care for her ailing parent. Mary and her children had already returned to South Carolina; her petition attempted to gain legal sanction for their (and for her husband's) return to the state. Mary was convinced that her husband had already "been severely punished" by the confiscation of his property, "to which he submits without reluctance," as well as by the family's thirteen-year exile from their home. In her petition, Mary emphasized that she and her children were merely "the Innocent victims of his political errors" and begged for the legislative body to have mercy on her family's situation. The only way, in Mary's view, for these "innocent victims" to receive justice would be for the legislature to forgive her husband's "political errors"; as "the Law . . . banishes her said Husband," it also "virtually banishes your petitioner and her nine helpless Children." Mary clearly demonstrated her dedication to her husband despite his poor political choices, and begged the legislature to express their mercy as well.[12]

Mary's strategic deployment of the language of devotion to her husband and dedication to her motherly (and daughterly) duties was typical of these sources. What made her plea extraordinary, however, was that she submitted her petition along with another signed by 191 other women, presumably those "relations and friends" whom she expressed great regret at having to leave upon her husband's exile. These nearly two hundred signatures all came from other women, who felt compelled to submit a separate plea to the South Carolina General Assembly. Convinced of the injustice of the 1782 law, these numerous women explained to the body that "the punishments Imposed . . . reach in their operation far beyond, the person offending." The women were similarly assured that "all who seek should be allowed to enjoy the protection of our mild and excellent Government which above all others knows how to forgive." Here, the 191 petitioners highlighted the patriarchal state's responsibility to provide "protection" to its citizens, particularly dependents and innocents. The female cosigners both emphasized Fraser's dependence on her husband and implicitly recognized her dependence on their support as they petitioned for her husband's offenses to be forgiven so that Mary might spend time with her ailing mother and return to her home, "which she desires above all earthly blessings."[13] Unfortunately, even though she did everything right—providing a sympathetic narrative asserting her own affection for America and gaining the support of the community—the extant evidence suggests that her claim was denied.

Matriarchal allies highlighted the suffering of their sex more broadly. Evidence of a sense of shared empathy among women was particularly strong when they pointed to the deleterious consequences of men's actions. In her petition, Margarett Brisbane acted as the champion of dependent women and children. This was likely a step too far, however, penetrating the boundaries of gender roles through the opportunities presented in wartime to a degree the South Carolina General Assembly found unpalatable. Brisbane's husband, James, left the country during the war after being accused of harboring loyalist sentiments. Like Fraser's, though, Brisbane's petition undervalued the true scale of her husband's actions, and the assembly well knew this. James later absconded from his wife and family, leaving them without any support. Margarett made no attempts to repudiate the case against her husband; instead, she made sure to distance herself from his politics, claiming that "her Sentiments with regard to the present Contest never coincided with, but were always contrary to her Husbands."[14]

Here, Margarett stressed her independence of thought, while simultaneously reiterating the unfortunate situation of her dependence on her absent husband. This was an implicit critique of women's larger social and marital roles, beyond her own individual situation, and proved problematic. In her case, James left behind an eighteen-month-old infant and a pregnant wife, as well as several children from a previous marriage in Margarett's care. What he did not leave, however, was a proper method of "support, and Maintenance, or some portion of her Husband's late property."[15] Margarett's petition, then, was similar to others made for the same reasons, but hers included a brave declaration calling on the assembly to recognize her critique of the patriarchal structure that brought her to such an unfortunate position.

Margarett asked that an exception be made not only in her case but in the case of *other* women and children unfortunate enough to find themselves in the same situation. Margarett boldly made her case to the assembly: "Called on by Humanity toward her Offspring, she finds herself impell'd to make this Request, & flatters herself with Hopes, that when the House reflects on the weak and Defenseless Situation of women & children, who are not the promoters of the War, nor, from their Sphere in Life, can possibly be disadvantageous to the Contest; and whose Opinions seldom avail, and do not frequently operate on the Judgment of Men," that the body would grant her petition.[16] Brisbane's petition highlights the devastating problem of women's dependence, especially set against the upheavals of war. Her husband, James, was able to leave the country, while she was forced to remain at home not only with her infant son and soon-to-be-born child but also with his children from a previous marriage. The stipulations of the law meant to punish James had the adverse effect of imposing the bulk of the consequences heavily on Margarett and her children. The war, and the state's actions, put her family in this precarious situation, and the patriarchal system had failed her and other women. Margarett, however, refused to remain silent and acquiesce to it.

Margarett's petition drew attention to the injustice of the South Carolina Confiscation Act—that dependents, whose political choices were considered either irrelevant or nonexistent, were made to pay for a husband's, father's, or brother's political affiliations and wartime activity. She went beyond the mere advocacy of her own situation or that of a friend or female family member. Margarett instead called upon members of the assembly to think of the broader consequences of their actions, namely, the ways in which the law had a disproportionate effect on the state's most vulnerable citizens. "Impell'd" as she was, Margarett became the epitome of a matriarchal ally, critiquing the very structures undergirding the patriarchal household and state in the process. Margarett's language, her accusations, and her overt challenge to the gendered status quo, compounded by her husband's behavior, however, ultimately served to undermine her case; the body rejected her petition.[17] When women did not perform *with precision* the expectations of helpless femininity, the patriarchal state felt no obligations to those dependents purported to be in their care. Matriarchal allies had to be very careful as they pushed against the boundaries of gender during wartime.

Matriarchal allies shared strategies for successful petitions with each other to bolster their own claims for aid, relief, or assistance from the state. Women depended on informal networks of communication to advise each other on shared experiences and particular outlets at their disposal in order to obtain relief, demonstrating the ways in which matriarchal alliances extended outward within female communities. A group of Boston women, all wives of sailors who were taken prisoner, petitioned the Massachusetts General Court for financial compensation, employing identical or nearly identical language. Mary Booth, Hannah Horner, Ann Saunders, Isabella Whaland, Mary Casey, Rachel Richards, and Ann and Elizabeth Johnson all submitted petitions requesting remuneration for the loss of their husbands between January and April 1761.

Booth was the first to submit her petition. Her husband, John, served on board the ship *Prince of Wales* when the French overtook the vessel and impressed him aboard their man-of-war. He had yet to return at the time of Mary's petition. Mary mentioned having "been inform'd" that the government would provide a sum of money to prisoners of war from the *Prince of Wales*. Although John Booth himself could not submit his own petition for the money the state owed him as a result of his capture, his wife, Mary, took it upon herself to request that "she may be impower'd to receive said allowance," which the General Court granted.[18]

As a result of their shared experiences, Booth's female friends all submitted requests for compensation in language either identical to or echoing the same sentiments as Booth. Four days after the body approved Booth's request for remuneration, granting her ten pounds, Horner's identical request was granted as well, garnering her the same compensation.[19] That same day, the legislature also passed a resolve to grant Ann Saunders ten pounds, her husband having been captured while serving on the *Prince of Wales* as well. Saunders's petition matched Horner's down to the punctuation and spelling, indicating that Saunders likely copied Horner's plea word for word.[20] Isabella Whaland used similar language to Booth's, Horner's, and Saunders's petitions, but she went further in her description of her husband's trials during his capture, perhaps angling for greater sympathy from the legislature.[21] Regardless, given the similarities of the languages of their petitions, it is likely that Booth, Horner, Saunders, and Whaland worked together in some way in the crafting and submission of their petitions.

Other wives of those captured aboard the *Prince of Wales* made direct references to their collaboration in their petitions. Casey, for instance, asked the legislature to "allow her" a sum of money "as you have others in the same Circumstances."[22] Using language comparable to the petitions of these other women, Casey demonstrated that these women *did* collaborate, and she brought their network to the body's attention. Not only did she depend on these matriarchal allies—their words and their assistance—in drafting her petition, but she used her dependence on them as a justification of her worthiness for aid. Casey pointed to the fact that other women in the same situation had received compensation—which they likely told her—to argue that she, too, was deserving of money that the state owed her husband in his captivity. Deploying a slightly different strategy, the remaining women chose to submit their petition together, signing their names to one joint request to the legislature. In doing so, they demonstrated both their common goal and their interdependence on one another for practical and emotional support. Ann and Elizabeth Johnson, who submitted their plea along with several other women whose husbands were captured while on board the *Prince of Wales*, signed their names to a copetition for compensation as the executors of the estate of William Pike.[23]

A few years prior, other women had employed a similar tactic. Widows Heziah Holman and Sarah Simpson submitted a petition for the wages of their late husbands *and* to dispute a claim against their husbands' estates. The French took Hugh Holman and Jeremiah Simpson prisoner when their forces captured Fort William Henry during the Seven Years' War. Jeremiah died in captivity and the French brought Hugh back to France, where he later died. In the wake of this news, the two widows submitted a petition together requesting wages in their late husbands' names during the time of their captivity. Heziah and Sarah jointly emphasized the "great Hardship & Discouragement" during their widowhood, and used their suffering to justify their claim. Likewise, they disputed the state's charge against their late husbands' accounts for guns lost as a result of their capture. In solidarity, they complained about the injustice of making widows accountable for guns lost during a skirmish *and* of considering stopping soldiers' pay while they remained in captivity, "when they undergo so much more Toil & Difficulty and Distress." Not only did Heziah and Sarah receive compensation "in full consideration for their . . . Sufferings mentioned," but they also joined together in an accusation of injustice perpetrated by the patriarchal state, which successfully negated the charges against their husbands held in captivity.[24]

Wives seeking divorces often depended on the advice and counsel of other women who had gone through the same process. Some of these women had verbal confirmation from their friends or acquaintances who had similar experiences, and advised them either to take a certain course of action (e.g., file a divorce petition) or to mention their names specifically. Sarah Rust first unsuccessfully petitioned for a divorce from her husband, Francis, in January of 1784.[25] The court granted her request for a separation, but because of Francis's intervention, did not ultimately find Rust deserving of either alimony or a full divorce from her husband.[26] Just six months after the court refused to grant her request for alimony, though, she filed another petition, this time providing significantly more detail about her husband's failures. Sarah accused her husband of being cruel and an adulterer, and she wished to divorce him for those reasons in addition to her desire to protect herself and her earning potential, as "the fruit of her daily Industry is now liable from day to day to be taken for the same purposes."[27] Sarah Rust, like other women, thus described one of the cruel ironies of coverture: that women were not seen as capable of caring for themselves, so when their husbands failed to provide for them financially and wives had to pick up the slack, their work, and their earnings, did not belong to them. Several months later, she would try again.

The most striking portion of Sarah's second petition, however, was not how her language became more pointed, aggressive, and confident in its tone than in her first (though this language did mark a change from her first plea). Instead, her invocation of another woman's successful divorce petition proved a particularly convincing element of her second plea. "She has been informed," Sarah divulged, "that since your Excellency and honors were pleased to dismiss her libel one Mrs. Bayard has in Circumstances not so desperate as hers obtained a divorce."[28] Helena Bayard, an acquaintance of Sarah Rust, effectively manipulated the conditions of her marriage and her coverture to accuse her husband of cruelty and was granted a divorce.[29] These legal actions all happened within several months of each other, indicating that Helena Bayard and Sarah Rust were in close and regular contact with each other throughout the process. Clearly, Rust had spoken with Bayard, and the two worked together in some way to craft a second, more effective petition for Rust's divorce. Because of the coalition the two formed in drafting Sarah Rust's second petition, she was finally granted a divorce from her husband.[30] Although the court initially failed Sarah Rust, her friend, Helena Bayard, did not.

Matriarchal allies' coordination extended to the use of identical language in petitions submitted to state legislators. Ellinor and Judith Gaillard, married to Theodore and John, respectively, were sisters-in-law who pled for the return of their husbands after the Whig government banished these men from the state of South Carolina during the Revolutionary War. Both women explained that their husbands accepted commissions from the British in an attempt to "please [their] Parishioners, and protect a numerous and helpless Family from the insults of a conquering Enemy." The two explained that their husbands' actions were in defense of their neighbors and largely a result of their "tenderness and affection for [their] Famil[ies]."[31] Smartly, the Gaillard women engaged with tropes of both femininity and masculinity according to the expectations of the General Assembly. Echoing other petitions to the body, Ellinor and Judith Gaillard defended their husbands' deeds in terms of protecting their community and kin.

Although containing differences in spelling, capitalization, and punctuation, the language of Ellinor's and Judith's petitions is identical, save for their husbands' first names. This suggests that neither Ellinor nor Judith mindlessly copied the other's words, but instead that the two sat down and drafted the petitions together, while electing to submit them separately. Ellinor's and Judith's petitions demonstrate the multilayered nature of women's dependence in this period: the two were dependent upon absentee husbands; they were dependent on the state to return their husbands and thus their source of financial support; and finally, they were dependent on each other to navigate the performative expectations and rhetorical strategies necessary for their petitions to be successful. In the end, the assembly granted both of their requests.[32]

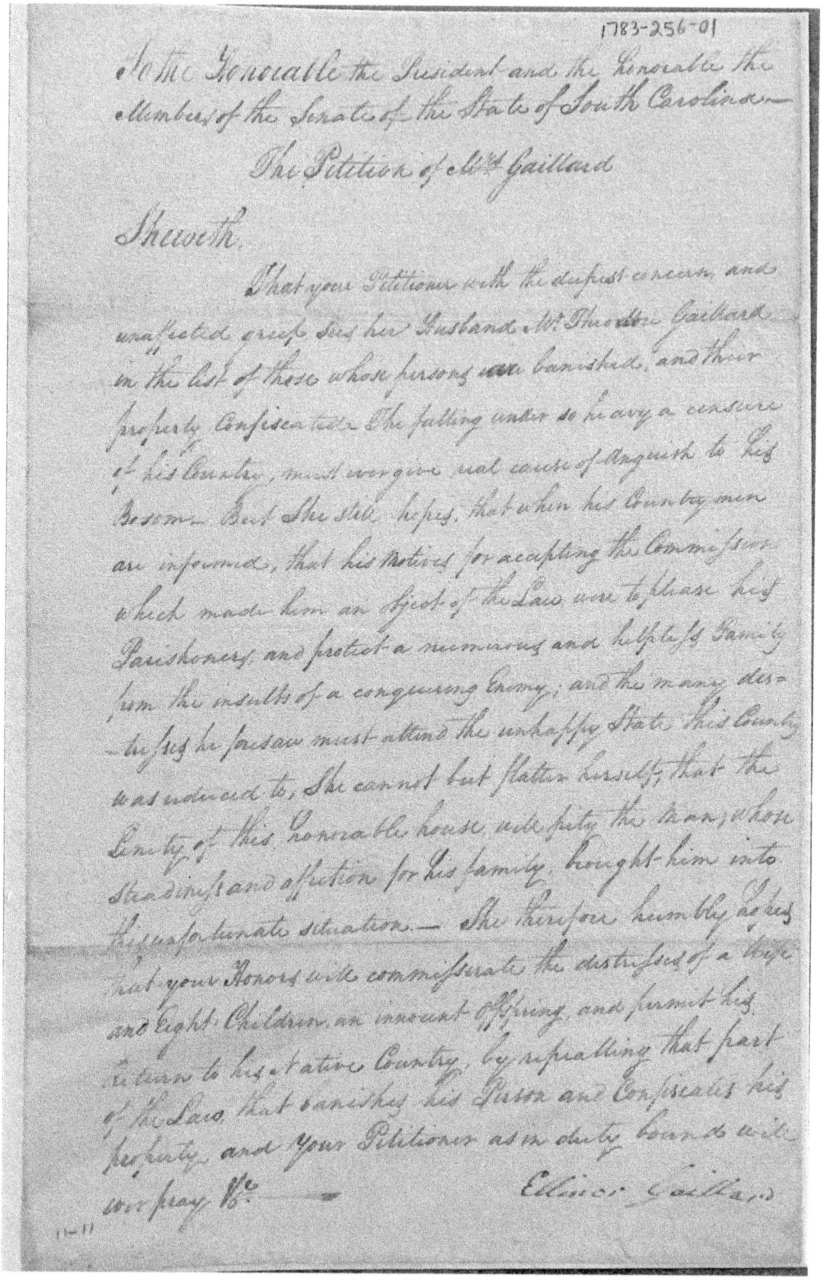

1783-256-01

To the Honorable the President and the Honorable the Members of the Senate of the State of South Carolina—

The Petition of Mrs. Gaillard

Sheweth.

That your Petitioner with the deepest concern, and unaffected grief, sees her Husband Mr. Theodore Gaillard in the list of those whose persons are banished, and their property confiscated. The falling under so heavy a censure of his Country, must ever give real cause of Anguish to his Bosom.— But She still hopes, that when his Country men are informed, that his motives for accepting the Commission which made him an object of the Law, were to please his Parishoners, and protect a numerous and helpless Family from the insults of a conquering Enemy; and the many dis- tresses he foresaw must attend the unhappy State, his Country was induced to, She cannot but flatter herself, that the Lenity of this Honorable house, will pity the man, whose steadiness and affection for his family, brought him into his unfortunate situation.— She therefore humbly begs that your Honors will commisserate the distresses of a wife and eight Children, an innocent Offspring, and permit his return to his native Country, by repealing that part of the Law, that banishes his Person and Confiscates his property, and your Petitioner as in duty bound will ever pray &c.——

Ellinor Gaillard

FIGURES 4.1. AND 4.2. Ellinor and Judith Gaillard, sisters-in-law, submitted two separate petitions using identical language on the same date. The punctuation, spelling, and capitalization of these petitions, however, differed slightly, indicating that the two worked together in crafting the petition but did not copy each other's writing exactly.

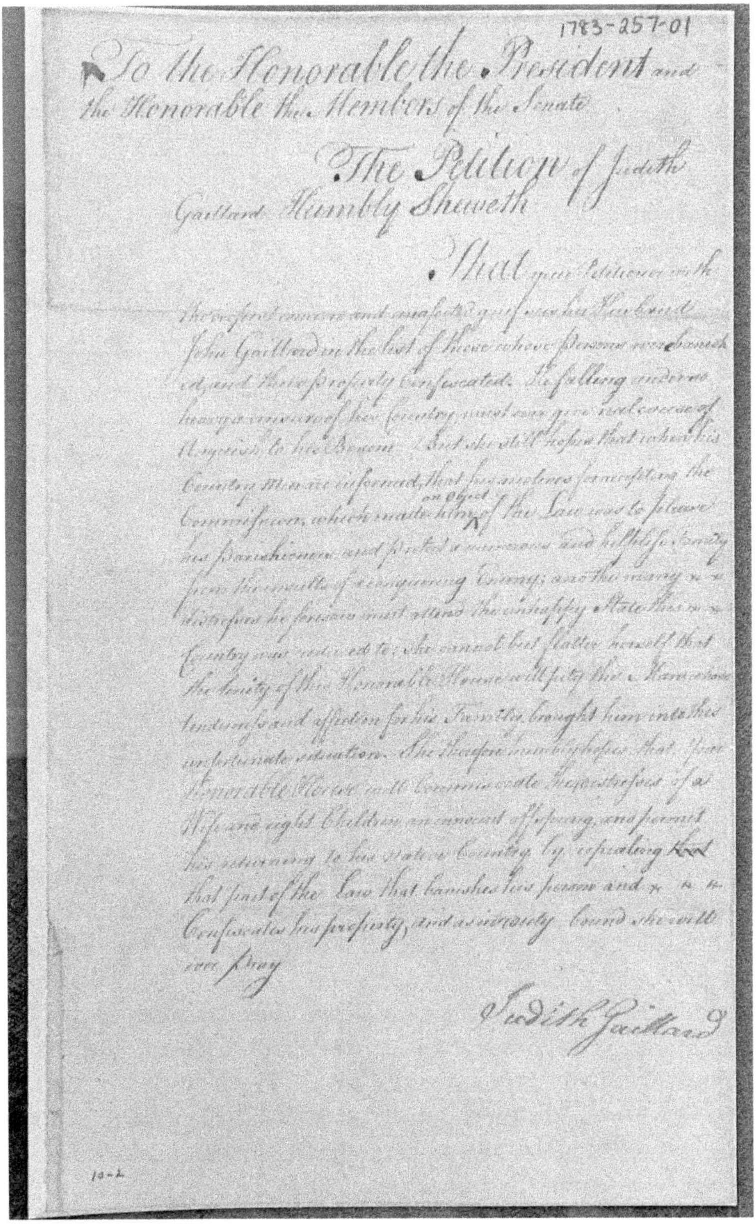

FIGURES 4.1. AND 4.2. (*continued*). Sources: Petition of Ellinor Gaillard, 15 February 1783, no. 256, and Petition of Judith Gaillard, 15 February 1783, no. 257, *Petitions to the General Assembly*, South Carolina Department of Archives and History, Columbia, SC.

Matriarchal alliances were especially effective when deployed in legal procedures, particularly in exploiting tropes of female helplessness and ignorance, thus magnifying the power of joint petitions. When suffering under the same circumstances, women submitted a jointly signed petition to amplify their case to their state legislatures. Mary Coughran and Mary Rone presented a single plea together to the Pennsylvania Council of Safety to relieve their mutual distresses. Both women's husbands were engaged in the war; finding these men's wages "so Low that It is emposable for us to Live," they jointly complained of the insufficient rations and their inability to support their families in their husbands' absence.[33] Because Coughran and Rone submitted a petition in which they highlighted their shared sufferings, this plea does not read as a complaint about the hardships of war or a critique on the council's inability to properly provide for women in certain situations. Instead, their petition has the appearance of a simple request for sympathy from the body and a suggestion that the council be obligated to recognize and alleviate the particular distresses suffered by a number of women as a result of the war. Coughran and Rone's copetition demonstrates the ways in which matriarchal alliances could critique the policies of the state without undermining patriarchal principles underlying its foundation.

Establishing a pattern of female suffering had the effect of softening petitions that might otherwise read as accusatory towards legislative bodies or transgressive of feminine comportment. In their joint petition, Mary Sneff and Catherine Winckeler lamented the state's inability to provide for their families. Their husbands, Martin Sneff and Henry Winckeler, helped to take a prize of significant value from the British during the war, and Mary and Catherine complained of never having been compensated during their husbands' lives. As war widows, Mary and Catherine insisted that they were "entitled" to a portion of the prize as compensation for their husbands' efforts. Contending that they were "greatly distressed" by their husbands' deaths, "which happened in the service," Mary and Catherine implied that the government was responsible for providing them with appropriate relief, especially as these women had "nothing to depend on now for their Support and maintainance."[34] By positioning themselves as distressed and impoverished as a result of their husbands' deaths and linking themselves to their late husbands' service, Mary Sneff and Catherine Winckeler collaborated to emphasize their entitlement to assistance from the patriarchal state based on their dependence as widows but also their own vicarious sacrifices to the American cause. They did not go so far, however, as to critique the

policies that led to their husbands' deaths. As with all women petitioners during the revolutionary era, successful pleas required a carefully
executed performance of femininity.

The upheavals of the Revolutionary War created circumstances that
disadvantaged legal dependents, including women. With husbands at
war or banished from their homes for their problematic politics, women
(and often their dependent children) were left to fend for themselves in
an uncertain world. Neither their household patriarchs nor the patriarchal state seemed up to the task of mitigating their suffering, and in these
instances, women turned to their female friends and family members to
provide a safe haven from the dangers and uncertainties of war. During
the Revolution, the British occupied several American cities for a number of years, causing disruption to the stability and safety of early American women's lives.[35] While some women implored legislative bodies to
join their husbands abroad after Whig governments banished these men
from the state, other women found sanctuary with their matriarchal
allies. Especially when their husbands had deserted them, gone off to
fight in the war, or been banished for their political ideologies, women
turned to their mothers, sisters, daughters, and female friends.

The sentiments imbued in these petitions were not unilateral, with
desperate dependents petitioning the patriarchal state to join their female
family members elsewhere, often in more favorable political conditions.[36]
Some women devotedly entreated their female family members to join
them in places like New York, Halifax, or England when the upheavals
of war proved too much for them to bear. Sisters, mothers, and daughters
actively wrote to their female family members, imploring them to take
advantage of their relationships and depend on women in their family
to rescue them from poverty and destitution. Mary Graves, for instance,
contended that her sister "in Affluent Circumstances" requested that
Mary go to Halifax to "live with her & be supported by her." Mary, who
presented her own "Circumstances" as "hard & difficult," could depend
on her sister, who actively offered to provide her with the support she
needed.[37] Rachel Lehr also noted "Repeated & earnest solicitations from
her sister in [New] York to pay her an immediate Visit" due to Rachel's
declining health, and her being "entirely Destitute of any Relations or
near Connections in that City." Because Rachel had no other forms of
support in Boston—especially a man on whom she could depend—she
requested to be allowed to leave the city and reside with her sister. There,
she could receive the assistance "which is now become necessary for
her Recovery."[38] Women's gendered empathy facilitated and sustained

matriarchal alliances throughout the Atlantic world, and supplanted patriarchal protections when they proved deficient.

Mothers and daughters in particular relied upon one another under these circumstances. Women who petitioned to join their mothers, who were often characterized as "elderly" or "infirm," demonstrated the mutual benefits of these relationships in the revolutionary era. Ann Calvert, who found herself in "the unexpected necessity of hard suffering," asked the Pennsylvania Supreme Executive Council to give her a pass to join her mother in New York. Having no man on whom she could depend, Ann believed that her "tenderly fond mother, in easy Circumstances," would be able to provide her with support. Ann also offered that with her sister's recent death, her "infirm" mother had no one to look after her (or her property). Ann's petition reveals that if the Executive Council were to grant her a pass to travel to her mother, the state would grant them *both* relief: Ann would receive financial support from her mother while fulfilling her filial duty to care for her mother in her old age. Fortunately, Ann Calvert's request was granted, and she was able to travel to New York to care for and receive support from her aging mother, revealing the mutually beneficial nature of mother-daughter relationships in this period.[39]

Matriarchal alliances existed on a more equal plane than the deeply hierarchical and unequal relationships between men and women. Relationships between sisters, for example, demonstrate this equitable interdependence within these kinship networks. Sarah Johonnot's (unnamed) sister, for example, offered an invitation to Sarah in her husband's absence. Gabriel Johonnot had left his wife to travel to France, and Sarah held that in all likelihood, he would not return for "a very considerable time." She also claimed to have no friends or relations in Boston "with whom she can pass so solitary an interval as she must experience during the absence of her husband." Sarah's sister, however, had offered "repeated sollicitations . . . to tarry with her" in Halifax, Nova Scotia, during her husband's absence. Staying with her sister in Halifax, Sarah argued, would make her situation "less tedious" because she could enjoy the company of a female family member, but also had the added benefit of "saving her considerable expence."[40] Johonnot's petition reveals that not only would Sarah benefit financially from the assistance of her sister, but the enjoyment of her sister's company would prove a welcome respite in the absence of affection that should have been offered by her husband. Women openly offered assistance to their female family members, expecting nothing in return. When the world of men—the household patriarchy and the patriarchal state—created insurmountable obstacles for women, they turned to their female familial networks to save them.

Matriarchal Advocates

In addition to fostering these supportive alliances, women also actively advocated for each other in the revolutionary era, often through direct engagement with the patriarchal state. This advocacy is most readily visible in divorce papers, particularly in those depositions in which women swore under oath to the verity of their claims. Female witnesses provided colorful commentary on the ways in which husbands broke their marriage contracts. Their testimonies were often more accusatory and aggressive than those provided by male witnesses. Female deponents could empathize with the situation of women petitioning the court for divorce, having a real understanding of the challenges of their particular gendered experience. Women's testimonies proved especially detrimental to adulterous and abusive husbands. These women empowered those suing for divorce by providing vividly detailed accounts of these men's violent and lascivious behavior. Women thus depended on each other to provide witness testimony that often led to women gaining a divorce and even alimony from their husbands. Ultimately, gender played a pivotal role in the construction and effectiveness of such depositions, though scholars have paid little attention to or have been dismissive of the powerful impact of women's testimonies.[41]

As was the case with legislative petitions, divorce depositions reveal the extent to which the mother-daughter relationship proved critical in women's daily lives. Additionally, women within these kinship networks actively advocated for the patriarchal state to alleviate the suffering of dependent women. Ann Hawke petitioned for a divorce from her husband, James, in the spring of 1805. Her mother, Lydia Shaw, was clearly not an admirer of her son-in-law, and used the opportunity in her testimony to defend her daughter's honor and attempt to help Ann Hawke receive a divorce from her husband. Ann and James Hawke had been secretly married just over six years prior to Shaw's deposition, when Ann was not yet fourteen years old; given that she had included this information, it is apparent that Shaw did not approve of her daughter's clandestine marriage at such a young age, and sought to have the court consider her daughter's vulnerable position, which she implied James had exploited.

Shaw's opinion of James was validated just two years after the couple wed. She witnessed him in the act of adultery with a hired servant in their home. The situation was made all the more deplorable as Ann was recovering from childbirth and being taken care of by her mother at that time. Shaw quickly told her daughter what she had witnessed, and refused to let her daughter sleep out of Shaw's own room in the future. Three months later, Shaw's fears of her son-in-law's potential for physical abuse were realized, as she learned of James having broken his wife's collarbone. Just a few days later, Shaw came home to find her son-in-law intoxicated and further abusing his wife. Shaw heard James, in his drunkenness, threaten Ann's life and the life of their child, and warned him to change his behavior "or," she threatened, "I would find a way to make him, for I would not suffer my daughter to be treated so." He quieted and sat down, but when Shaw left the room, Ann came toward her mother, crying, begging her mother to take her and their child away from their home. So, Shaw sent Ann and her grandchild to Ann's uncle's home, where she remained through the time of the suit.

Shaw did not shy away from denigrations against James's character, either, and used the opportunity to challenge the legitimacy of his patriarchal authority. In addition to his myriad abuses, which she outlined in great detail, Shaw characterized James's behavior as "rugged, surly, and ill tempered." He did not support his family, which forced Ann and her young child to subsist on what little she was able to acquire from her friends and family. Shaw claimed that if Ann were to make a living by her own industry, James "would drink it" away. Shaw testified to having to drag a drunken James down the stairs after he attempted to take Ann's bed during her lying-in.[42] While Ann herself could not transgress her feminine comportment by criticizing her husband in this way, her mother did, and Shaw's testimony supplied the character assault as a loving and devoted mother whom Ann desperately needed to secure her divorce, along with the physical and material protection that James could not provide. Ann's mother, therefore, usurped the role of protector-patriarch when her husband failed to fulfill his duties in every way. Yet at the same time, Shaw validated gendered assumptions inherent in the patriarchal system by holding her son-in-law to those standards in her testimony to the state.

Financial support was a key component of patriarchal authority, and a justification for the power these men held over their wives. Yet husbands often fell short of these obligations, leaving their wives financially destitute, forcing them to turn elsewhere for this support. In certain cases, it was women who fulfilled the provider role when men failed to do so. Women's depositions in divorce cases reveal the extensive networks of financial support that matriarchal advocates and family members provided one another. Mary Knider gave evidence of her own fiscal and emotional support of her sister, Catharine, when the latter's husband, George Griscom, deserted her. Shortly after the Griscoms married, they moved first to Burlington, New Jersey, and later to New Bern, North Carolina; during their absence from Philadelphia, Knider reported that she "heard that the Defendant [George] treated the plaintiff [Catharine] very ill"; evidently, Catharine complained to her sister of her husband's maltreatment from afar, likely through their correspondence. When the Griscoms returned to Philadelphia, they lived with the Kniders, but shortly after their homecoming, George departed the city and never returned. Catharine and her children remained with her sister until two months prior to her testimony, when her father began paying her rent and she supplemented his assistance by working as a seamstress to support her family in George's absence.[43] Mary's deposition helped Catharine receive a divorce from her absconding husband, while also presenting evidence of the financial and emotional support she provided to her sister in the wake of George's desertion.

Matriarchal advocates could disrupt traditional familial structures, as women chose to defend each other by challenging the power of their own brothers, fathers, and male acquaintances. Elizabeth Martin, the sister of Mibsom Martin, whose wife shared her name, defended her sister-in-law in her petition for divorce, and in the process, disparaged her brother's behavior and character. Mibsom's sister blamed him for not having supported his wife almost from the time of their union. Instead, Elizabeth (Mibsom's wife) had supported *her husband* for the majority of their marriage. Mibsom had taken to drinking constantly. His sister testified that if he came home sober one night, he would certainly be drunk four or five nights after that; she described her brother as "a man deranged." Elizabeth was wholly on the side of her sister-in-law, with whom she ran a school for both of their support. On at least one occasion, Elizabeth stopped her brother from hitting his wife. Both Martin women had clearly reached the end of their ropes with Mibsom.[44] Despite the fact that she was Mibsom's sister, Elizabeth was disturbed enough by her brother's intoxication and profligacy, and perhaps so moved by a sense of shared empathy, that she testified on behalf of her sister-in-law against her own blood relative.

Having the ability to empathize with other women because of their mutual experience of female dependence gave some matriarchal advocates the impetus to go to great lengths to protect their friends and neighbors from their profligate husbands. Jemma Brown testified on Maria Moore's behalf to support Maria's claims of her husband John's adultery. Jemma declared that she knew John had been to a brothel, because she had seen him there with her own husband! Jemma's husband had evidently been missing for "several nights" and in her hunt for her absent spouse, she checked the local "house of ill fame," finding him there with John Moore. On another occasion, Jemma found John in the company of a young woman who inquired to her about renting a room. Jemma found out later that John had been intimate with this woman for a time when she found them in bed together.[45] Based on her own experience with an adulterous husband, Jemma could empathize with Maria's situation and provided evidence in her neighbor's defense in order to help her gain a divorce from her husband.

Women's own individual moral compasses and distaste for adulterous men often motivated them to challenge these cads in the court and even in these men's own homes. Mary Angel and Abigail Galloway testified in the divorce suit of Martha and Adam Air. The two were neighbors of the Airs and swore that although Martha's "general Character has been good," they often heard the woman scream on account of her husband's beating her (the "thin Partition" dividing Angel from her neighbors allowed her to hear the couple's altercations through the wall). On another occasion, the two women heard strange noises coming from their neighbors' home; armed with the knowledge of Adam's prior violent offenses, the two decided to investigate the commotion. With the window open, Angel and Galloway observed Adam "in the Act of Copulation with one Priscilla Brichford." They took it upon themselves to enter the Air home, "& stood behind [Adam and Priscilla] as they lay on the Floor." After apparently standing there for quite some time, Galloway prodded Adam, asking "if he was not ashamed of the act . . . when he has a Wife at home." In response, Adam declared "one Woman was as good to him as another." Appalled by Adam's brazen misogyny, Galloway and Angel were further disturbed when the man "exposed his nakedness" to them. Abigail Galloway's testimony revealed that in addition to this scene, Adam's character had overall "been very bad, neither taking care of his Wife, nor confining himself to her but . . . keeping the Company of other women."[46] Angel and Galloway's clear disgust for Adam Air's behavior was evident in their colorful testimony, and helped secure Martha the separation from her husband that the two witnesses clearly believed she deserved.

Some women even testified against the men with whom they committed adultery, siding with the women they had wronged, wittingly or unwittingly. Although most of these women were likely compelled by the court to testify and likewise incriminate themselves, they still chose *not* to lie on the stand or to fail to appear as some of their male counterparts had done under similar circumstances. When accused of adultery, many husbands conveniently failed to come to court to respond to the petitions their wives filed. When men shirked their responsibilities, however, women supplanted that role. Mary Brown revealed her own guilt in a deposition filed in the Coombses' divorce case. "So you know that the said William Coombs at any time and what time was in bed with any woman who was not his wife?" the lawyer inquired. Brown replied bluntly: "Yes—He was in bed with me in the year 1812 and I was not his wife." In case this rather stark admission was not clear enough for the court, she further stipulated that "the said William Coombs did lay with me in Boston in the year 1812 and pass the night with me in bed and then had Carnal knowledge of me."[47] Women who admitted to committing adultery with married men conceded their own iniquities to benefit female plaintiffs in divorce cases. Female adulterers' depositions in favor of their lovers' wives demonstrated the power of female empathy over allegiance with their male paramours.

Women who defended their female friends and family members in depositions acted as matriarchal advocates, undercutting men's authority over their families by diminishing and delegitimizing these men's power. In her deposition in the Scaleses' divorce case, Mary Learned described her distaste for men who were openly unfaithful to their wives. Learned lived in the poorhouse in Watertown, Massachusetts, where she saw Dr. Abraham Scales pay an improper visit to a woman named Sall Saunders, despite his already being married to a woman named Elizabeth. Upon his arrival at the poor house, he went straight upstairs with Sall. Learned was so disturbed by what she saw ("I did not like their carrying's on") that she ran upstairs after them, wielding a club with the intention of "driv[ing] him down" from Saunders's room. By the time she arrived at the woman's bed chamber, she witnessed Scales "in a very suspicious & unchaste situation with Sall." Upon realizing his misdeeds had been discovered, Scales quickly ran out of the house.

In court, Learned passed judgment on him and exposed his lascivious intentions and exploits. When questioned, she identified Saunders as "a woman of evil fame" who was known to have "the foul disease."[48] Learned's identification of Saunders as a sex worker who was infected with venereal disease helped to substantiate another deposition given by a man named Dr. Jeffries in which he claimed that Abraham and

Elizabeth's newborn died just two days after its birth as a result of a sexually transmitted disease "which it must have derived from its parents."[49] Learned's depiction and castigation of Abraham Scales as a lecherous adulterer and, implicitly, a murderer helped convince the court that Elizabeth Scales deserved to be divorced from her husband.[50]

Women who testified in divorce cases often came to the defense of wives suing for divorce more readily than did male witnesses, both demonstrating the widespread sense of female empathy among women and reinforcing patriarchal assumptions that men would not challenge each other's authority. Daniel and Love Woodman both provided witness testimony in Margaret Cross's suit for divorce from her husband, John. John boarded with Love and her husband, Daniel, in Newburyport, Massachusetts, during the time he had absconded from his wife and children. Love noticed that John paid "attentions inconsistent with the character of any man" towards Mrs. Thompson, a woman hired by the Woodmans. John told Love that his wife had a child during his absence, but regardless of his marriage to Margaret and the birth of his baby, he intended to marry Mrs. Thompson. Love's husband, Daniel, even told his wife that he saw John and Mrs. Thompson in bed together. Love, clearly sympathizing with Margaret, testified that she "spoke to [John] repeatedly on the subject" of his behavior and infidelity. She also judged John Cross to be "an immoral man."[51]

While Love's account provides a clear opinion on John Cross's moral transgressions, her husband Daniel's account was not nearly as accusatory or reproachful as that of his wife. The details of his testimony matched Love's, but Daniel's tone was much less disparaging. He confirmed that he knew John had a wife, and that John "did not intend ever to live with her again nor to maintain her." Daniel knew of John's plans to marry Mrs. Thompson, despite already being married to Margaret. Daniel even fulfilled John's request to enter his intention to marry Mrs. Thompson with the Newburyport town clerk! Despite John's abandonment of Margaret, his failure to provide for her, and his clearly having committed adultery (John himself admitted to having "carnal knowledge" of Mrs. Thompson "many times"), Daniel seemed to find no issue with the situation. In fact, Daniel admitted, "I did not at the time find so much fault with them [John and Mrs. Thompson] as they both assured me it was their intention to be speedily married."[52]

Juxtaposing these two testimonies demonstrates women's willingness to bear witness to the plight of their female peers, to have their opinions weigh in on the moral elements of divorce cases, and to come to each other's aid. Daniel's testimony did provide clear evidence of John's inability to uphold the vows of his marriage covenant. Yet Daniel found no fault with the man's behavior—or at least, he refused to express the disgust his wife conveyed in her deposition. Instead, he seemed to defend John's behavior, explaining away the affair and intended bigamy by insisting that his desire to "speedily" marry another woman nullified his crimes. Love's testimony, however, was dripping with disdain. Her testimony, however brief, recalled John's actions, and forced the court to recognize the immorality and illegality of those actions. Her tone compelled the judges to sympathize with the victim of John's depravity—his faithful, dutiful wife, who remained in Boston, devoid of any "maintenance and support."[53] Along with the evidence of the case, Love Woodman's testimony helped to persuade the court to grant Margaret Cross a divorce, thereby freeing her from an adulterous, unsupportive husband.[54]

When called to testify in divorce cases, male witnesses were less likely to cast judgment upon male defendants than were female deponents. Two depositions in the Kinsey divorce case, for example, give contradictory accounts regarding Philip Kinsey's actions towards his wife, Jane. While Robert Correy described Philip as "much distressed" over his inability to support his family (compelling Correy to lend the man money for that purpose), Sibilla Bickham's testimony reveals that she had little sympathy for Jane's husband.[55] Instead, Bickham complained that Philip "left the whole burthen of supporting the said family to his said wife." Bickham also provided details of the physical abuse Philip inflicted on his wife (which Robert Correy either ignored or did not know of), causing him to be taken to jail to answer his wife's charges.[56]

Gendered empathy, then, worked both ways. Some male deponents in other cases seemed bothered by the offenses made by husbands against their wives, but were unwilling to truly intervene on women's behalf and ultimately undermine their peers' patriarchal authority within the household. William Snyder, who boarded with the McKanackers one winter, testified that he once heard Rosanna McKanacker cry "murder," and saw her come into the shop where he worked with a gash on her head and her "Legs and Thighs . . . bruised and much discolored." Snyder could not, however, testify that these severe wounds and her cries of "murder" were a result of her husband Daniel's abuses.[57] Apparently, Snyder could envision a wide range of events that would cause Rosanna to be screaming for her life and arriving soon after with wounds all over her person, *other* than her husband's physical abuses. Another male witness in the same case speculated that he had seen a mob recently near the

McKanackers' house, so he could not be certain as to who exactly gave Rosanna her bruises.[58]

While men seemed hesitant to speculate in their testimonies regarding spousal abuse, women who did not directly witness husbands abusing their wives often took their friends' word at face value and testified in their favor. Elizabeth Hughes, for example, claimed that although "she never actually heard or saw" Robert Murray abuse his wife, she heard various details of his misdeeds from his wife, Mary. When Mary came to Elizabeth, she was "in a very bruised condition, her arms shoulders and breasts bearing marks of violence, her mouth bleeding, and one of her teeth loosened by a blow." Mary asked her how she had received her injuries; Elizabeth replied that her husband gave them to her.[59] Elizabeth Hughes wholeheartedly trusted and advocated for her friend, despite not having witnessed the incident in question.

Men could even prove unwilling to defend women in physical altercations with their husbands while their female friends deliberately put themselves in danger to protect these victims of domestic abuse. In the Henderson divorce case, for instance, William Barry testified that while "several" other people were in the room, a drunken Alexander Henderson slammed his fist upon the stove and then struck his wife in the chest, causing her to lose her breath. Later, Barry, along with Robert Nelson, witnessed Alexander come down the stairs naked; upon astutely perceiving that Alexander was likely intoxicated and that "some disturbance" was about to take place, Barry conceived himself "determined to watch" rather than to stop any potential abuse from happening. Later that night, Barry heard screaming coming from the Hendersons' bedroom. Instead of intervening on Mary's behalf, both Barry and Nelson entered the room and instead decided to coax Alexander to "go peaceably to bed," leaving Mary in a "hysteric fit," a notably gendered criticism of her reaction to abuse.[60]

When Barry and Nelson failed to stop any physical abuse beyond their attempts at wheedling Alexander to sleep, the female deponents in the Henderson case demonstrated how they intervened to defend Mary against her husband's attacks and against the male witnesses' apathy and inaction. When Lucy Brown heard screams coming from the Hendersons' house, a few doors from her own home, she rushed to check on Mary, just in time to witness Alexander threaten his wife; he called out to Mary, "You damned bitch and whore, you have a Bastard in your damned guts—I will run my hand into you, and tear it out." Fearing the verity of Alexander's threat and for Mary's life, Brown bolted to the scene, and stood between the victim and her would-be attacker, giving Mary time to escape Alexander's brutality.[61]

It is notable, too, that Lucy Brown rushed from her home down the street to defend Mary, while the several men witnessing Alexander's violent behavior *in the same room* were unwilling to do the same. Other of the Hendersons' female neighbors took similar action. Hester Fisher testified to stepping between Alexander and Mary when the former pulled out a pen knife and threatened to stab his wife.[62] Sarah Nelson once saw Alexander draw two knives on his wife; at that instant, Sarah called out to the people in the street for assistance in restraining the would-be assailant.[63] The women deposed in Mary Henderson's defense saved her life on at least three occasions, and ventured to defend her in court by being witness to the abuses she suffered at the hands of her husband. When the household and community patriarchs had abdicated their responsibility to protect Mary, her matriarchal advocates demanded that the state intervene to supplant that role.

These depositions reveal the extent to which women relied on and advocated for each other within two potent and interlocking patriarchal systems: the household and the law. Both Henry Armbruster, the local tavern keeper, and his wife, Mary, testified on Catherine France's behalf in her suit for divorce. While Henry's deposition provides clear evidence of John France's abuses, he failed to go to the same lengths as his wife in physically defending Catherine and in her verbal defense in court. Henry knew of and often heard John getting drunk, beating his wife, keeping her out of their home, and failing to provide for his family. Henry, however, mentions only one occasion—and does so quite briefly and disinterestedly—in which he and his neighbor, William Cummins, stepped in to stop John's abuses, despite his testimony that these violent acts occurred regularly.[64] Mary Armbruster, however, did not tolerate John's abuses as her husband so often did.

Mary's testimony underscores the scale of John's abuses, as well as her own willingness to intervene in the Frances' marital problems time and time again in defense of Catherine's life and well-being. Hearing her neighbor cry through the thin wall that separated their houses, Mary, "thinking it a pity that no person should go in to help her," stormed into the Frances' home and berated John for his cruelty, especially as Catherine was pregnant at the time. Mary's husband, Henry, lived in the same home and could hear John's abuses through the same thin walls, yet his testimony remains devoid of the pity, empathy, and concern necessary to intervene on Catherine's behalf. Instead, it was his wife who "often had to come between [Catherine and John] to keep them off from one another," even when Mary's own life was in danger (on at least one occasion John ran after her with fireplace tongs).

It is clear, too, that Mary was Catherine's confidant; Mary knew details of Catherine's life—John's regular intoxication, his spendthrift ways, his failure to provide necessaries for his family—that she would not have otherwise known if Catherine had not shared her distresses with her neighbor. Mary even claimed to feed the France children in her own home when the Frances did not have enough money to do so.[65] Mary Armbruster defended her female friend not just in court but in her daily life, providing Catherine with support and protection that none of her male neighbors seemed willing or able to give. Mary acted as the supplemental patriarch in Catherine's life, as John was clearly not up to the task.

The power of gendered empathy, for both men and women, ultimately reinforced patriarchal norms in the household and under the law. In their interactions with the state in cases in which women sought separations and divorces, male witnesses rarely criticized the behavior of husbands. Conversely, women deponents regularly professed their negative opinions of transgressive husbands, highlighting the ways in which these men had failed to uphold their duties as household patriarchs—husbands and fathers who would protect the dependents in their care. These women acted as matriarchal advocates, supplanting men's household authority by providing financial, physical, and emotional protection for embattled wives. In other ways, however, their insistence upon pointing to individual men's failures served to reinforce patriarchal standards of gendered comportment. Rather than critiquing the system that put women in these unfortunate situations, matriarchal advocates instead lambasted individual men who fell short of patriarchal expectations.

* * *

Matriarchal allies and advocates disrupted the gendered status quo during the revolutionary era. Women relied on each other in difficult circumstances—in many cases brought on by the war and its aftermath—because patriarchal authorities and institutions failed to properly protect them. Female friends and family members cared for each other in their daily lives, shared their knowledge of successful strategies for legal intervention, and provided material support when husbands were neglectful, absent, or dead. Matriarchal advocates stepped in—sometimes quite literally—to protect women who had been abused by their husbands;

their bearing witness in the masculine space of the courtroom disrupted the traditional balance of gendered power, and highlighted the ways in which individual men failed to live up to the standards of their own gender.

While these matriarchal allies and advocates made a great difference in the lives of individual women, these events elicited no form of collective action among the carefully constructed network of women's communities. Ultimately, women petitioners and their allies employed the framework of feminine helplessness familiar (and preferable) to legislators and jurists. Whether these women believed in these tropes of their own subordination is immaterial in this case; use of the constructions of women's dependence served to provide at least tacit consent for these ideas. So, while patriarchal authority may have been challenged on an individual level—importantly, by women advocating for each other— these women also reinforced a collective acceptance of patriarchal norms that necessitated their subordination to male authority in the household and of the state. Thus, despite the individualized empowerment women experienced from their interdependent alliances and the ways in which they exploited the fluidity of gender norms during wartime, they ultimately remained firmly dependent within this dual patriarchal system.

5 /   The Problem of Dependence

Elizabeth Browne made clear in her petition that she was struggling. The distraught widow penned her brief plea, framing it with the tropes that the Massachusetts General Assembly had already come to expect of its supplicants; she presented her missive as a "humble petition and prayer," imploring the elite authorities who, in that moment, had the power either to safeguard or endanger Browne's future. Her note was as brief—its contents amounting to sixty-six words—as it was vague in its lack of detail about the precise nature of Browne's situation. She called upon the "known goodness and compassion" of the legislative body, and expressed her hope that under their "wise and compassionate consideration," they might "take her melancholy and Distress'd Case" and provide her with relief they would deem to be "just" under the circumstances.[1]

The General Assembly approved her request, but with a certain and rather patronizing precondition. While they ordered that Browne receive ten pounds "for the support of the Petr," the committee required that "the said sum be paid into the hands of the Honl John Erving Esqr to be dealt out to the Petitioner as he shall think may be most for her Comfort."[2] The assembly agreed that Browne was deserving of aid but did not allow her to control the money herself. Instead, another man had control over how this relief would be distributed to her; this man had the authority to decide how best to support her; and, furthermore, this man had the authority to withhold such support from her if he so desired. The General Assembly's decision thus facilitated an additional, perilous level of dependence in Browne's life.

Women's positions of dependence portended significant precarity over the course of their lives. Yet, as we have seen, there were a number of instances in which women were able to exploit the legal, sociocultural, and economic terms of their dependence to regain some semblance of control and agency over their lives. Even so, while this dependence provided spaces and opportunities for some women, it was utterly incapacitating for others. Poor women, women with no familial or communal networks, and those who refused to conform to traditional standards of feminine deportment were unable to successfully deploy the terms of their feminine subordination to work to their advantage. Women who, for various reasons, chose to lambast the actions of the patriarchal state in their petitions, sometimes even subtly, would often see these patriarchal authorities reject—formally or through inaction—their pleas.

Poor women faced a double bind imposed by their class and gender.[3] These women were simultaneously expected to present themselves to the state as women who conformed to the strictures of white femininity—which they were unable to do in practice—while also demonstrating that they were worthy of the state's aid. They could not meet the expectations of white womanhood, because these gendered standards implied a level of financial privilege to which these women did not have access. They likewise found extraordinary difficulty proving that they deserved financial and material assistance from the patriarchal state and their local community. Particularly as the new nation grew, ideas about poverty and who exactly was "worthy" of aid changed. The bar for assistance included work requirements and confinement, which undermined genteel white femininity. For all of these women, dependence was not an avenue through which they might gain some semblance of power over their individual lives. Instead, for certain women, gendered dependence was a burden that they could not successfully exploit to their advantage.

Performing Unfemininity

The success of women's petitions to the patriarchal state for aid or relief was often contingent upon their careful rhetorical performance of white femininity. Women who saw their petitions rejected were often those who employed harsh, accusatory language towards male authorities. Refusing to humble themselves completely before their legislators, these women offended male officials by transgressing the boundaries of traditional feminine comportment and challenging white male authority. Women who, rather than conforming to traditional expectations of feminine behavior, performed *un*femininity, saw their petitions ignored or denied by their legislators.

In their considerations of petitions and applications for relief, patriarchal authorities used their unilateral authority in the decision-making process, frequently failing to provide any explanation or justification for rejecting women's applications for aid. After a petitioner submitted her plea to state legislatures, these officials formed committees to discuss and review the plea and recommend a decision to the larger body. These decisions generally followed the recommendations made by the committees appointed to each case. Those petitions that were not recommended to have their requests granted could be referred to further committees for debate, tabled for further discussion by the larger body at an often unknown future date, provided with leave to withdraw their petitions, or flat-out rejected by the committee. Those petitions that were tabled or given leave to withdraw were effectively—through inertia and neglect—rejected. Committees recommended these modes for a variety of unknown, unspecified, but sometimes political reasons.[4]

While women who employed submissive, deferential language that reinforced tropes of femininity in their petitions often found success, those who rebuked state officials, choosing instead to strike a more belligerent tone, saw their petitions rejected. The language of Ann Swift's

FIGURE 5.1. Rate of successful versus unsuccessful petitions submitted by women in Boston, 1750–1820. See "A Note on Sources" for an explanation of the sources of and deficiencies in the data.

petition, for example, did not adequately cushion the blow of her transgressive behavior. At first, she followed the pattern of many other effective pleas by her contemporaries, demonstrating evidence of helplessness, motherly devotion, and an inability to recover without the intervention of the patriarchal state. Had Swift ended her request there, it might have succeeded. Instead, she complained of the cruel treatment she endured by the Continental soldiers who occupied her home during the war, and likewise, the disrespect they showed to her property. "For there own pleasure," these men "tore my house allmost to peices—burn[ed] all my fence and as many of the trees as served there turn." The soldiers also destroyed the fruit and grain she had planted on her property. Because of these actions, Swift found herself "Allmost Incapable to support my Fatherless Children (some of which are Babes)." Emphasizing her widowed status, she continued by condemning the Continental soldiers, and by extension, the legislature itself, for propelling her children into starvation: "Now Gentellman by the Law of God, and man I . . . have a consideration for takeing my Childrens bread from out of there Mouths." Her distaste for the government's handling of soldiers' discipline reverberated in her deprecatory petition, yet likely hurt her chances of receiving compensation from the state.[5]

Women's hostile language undermined their declarations of dependence and seemed to pose a threat to male authority, especially when these women invoked any anti-American political sentiments. Mary Freeman claimed that at the start of the Revolutionary War, "an inveterate and cruel Enemy" seized her husband's property. In case the Massachusetts assembly was confused as to whom Freeman was describing as an "Enemy," she explicitly defined her terms: "These Epithets she does not bestow on the British Army, but on those Americans who made that Army their Protection while they plundered those who resolved in Defense of their Country." Freeman's petition highlighted the base behavior of American soldiers who hid behind the mantle of the army during the war, and the dire consequences such behavior had on society's most vulnerable.

While not explicitly opposed to the American cause of independence from Great Britain, Freeman railed against those "who have by their cruel Machinations involved the Country in Bloodshed and ruin." State authorities and military officials, she said, compelled her husband to flee to the country, leaving his family and his personal property unattended and unsafe. She also assigned blame to government officials for creating "the Distresses of his Family," which "sunk his Spirits and has[te]n[e]d him to his Grave." Freeman thus blamed the state for her husband's untimely death. While she closed her petition declaring that she was "obliged to raise her supplicatory Hands to your Honours," her humility seemed too little too late and, frankly, rather disingenuous considering the tone of the bulk of her petition. Freeman's numerous accusations detracted from her brief attempt at submitting a humble entreaty; the state referred her petition to a committee and never addressed the matter further.[6]

When women declared their dependence on husbands who espoused loyalist sentiments yet failed to explicitly rebuke these policies, their connections to these men often hindered their ability to convince legislatures that they played no part in the politics of the war. In her petition, Ann Dunkin never once steered away from her spouse's loyalism, refusing to denounce it or provide any justifications for his misdeeds, as a number of other women had done. Robert Dunkin served "his Britannic Majesty" during the Revolution, and as a result, she "as his Widow . . . is entitled to receive a Pension from the board of Admiralty of Great Britain." Ann had already submitted an application and arranged for a friend to receive and transmit these funds on her behalf, but the papers had been lost in transit. She petitioned Pennsylvania's Executive Council for a pass to travel to New York, where she would leave for England in order to prove that she was, indeed, still Robert's widow. Ann attached a letter signed by two men verifying that she was "of a respectable Character" and "well attached to the Liberties and Independence of the United States"; she never once, however, stated these sentiments personally, nor did she attempt to explain the reasons behind her husband's politics. Her petition was referred to the next session, but was not discussed again.[7]

It is telling, too, that Ann was not requesting any direct relief from the council, and instead sought to leave the state entirely, ensuring that her care would not be under the purview of Pennsylvania's patriarchs. Yet it seemed her husband's politics, and her inability to distance herself from them, proved an obstacle too great to overcome. Ann Williams, on the other hand, openly rebuked those who harmed her husband's reputation and livelihood. Citing the "weakness and inefficacy upon liberal minds"—taking a direct jab at the masculinity, or lack thereof, of Pennsylvania's patriarchal authorities—Ann reprimanded those who, due to "private prejudice and resentment . . . operated considerably to the disadvantage of" her husband, Robert. Ann claimed to be "uninfluenced by motives of resentment," but the scathing tone of her petition suggests otherwise.[8]

Ann made futile attempts to reign in her aggressive language toward the end of her petition. Her plea sought to recover her husband's property, which he had transferred to her name in early 1782, just ahead of the passage of the Confiscation Act, when her husband "incurred" this "legal disability." The act, however, nullified maneuvers meant to skirt the statute, explicitly rejecting "colusion or fraud, or . . . an intent of eluding a forfeiture."[9] Ann, having been made aware of this stipulation, moved forward with her petition anyway, suggesting that Robert decided to transfer the property to Ann's name *before* the start of the war, but had simply not acted on these wishes. Ann begged that the assembly not follow through with their decree to confiscate the Williamses' property, as it was "all she depends on for support, herself and numerous family, consisting of eight helpless Children" who would be "reduced to experience calamities" in such an instance.[10]

While Ann's petition did, eventually and in part, follow the traditional rhetoric of supplication and deference, the assembly rejected her plea. It is likely that her defiant, caustic language cost her the relief she sought. While a number of women transgressed the boundaries of their gender comportment in the language of their petitions, those who saw success despite these offenses were more careful in their performance of unfemininity, couching their challenges to male authority in conceptions of traditional feminine comportment. Ann, however, failed to balance these delicate tensions in her petition. Backed into a corner as a result of the legislature's unforgiving position, she and her children were forced to join her husband in England, where they lived the remainder of their lives.[11]

Ann's failure to conform to submissive feminine standards of comportment by challenging male legislative and political authority influenced the committee's decision to reject her plea. Successful female petitioners whose political ideologies diverged from those of their husbands stressed their dependence on foolish men, their husbands' defense of family over loyalty to the budding nation, and their conformity to male legislators' authority. In order to have their petitions granted, women who transgressed the boundaries of traditional feminine comportment by challenging their husbands' authority simultaneously needed to submit themselves to the authority of the state. Likewise, those who criticized state authorities needed to demonstrate their capitulation to their husbands' authority, a hallmark of traditional feminine comportment, which excused their defiance of state officials. If critiquing one patriarchal authority, women were required to acquiesce to the other, at least rhetorically.

Women's failed petitions thus provide evidence that male officials were uncomfortable with women posing a threat to these men's power and authority. Unless the female petitioners simultaneously asserted their acquiescence to male authority in other ways, the state routinely rejected or ignored their pleas. Some women insisted on holding male officials accountable for the wrongs perpetrated against them, while others failed to adequately demonstrate their proper submission to male authority. Their aggressive, censorious language likely offended the committees to which they applied for aid. Rather than viewing these women as sympathetic, vulnerable victims, these committees responded to the belligerent tone of these petitions with disdain for these supplicants. Women's petitions that employed hostile, accusatory, or combative language rarely succeeded, reinforcing the notion of the importance of a petitioner's deference to authority, and of the requirement for a woman petitioner to employ traditional tropes of feminine behavior in order for her petition to succeed. Male officials, in other words, often reacted negatively to challenges to their authority, especially when these threats came from women.

Gender and Poor Relief in the Revolutionary Era

Much scholarly work has drawn attention to the plight of the urban poor in the revolutionary era.[12] Social historians have reconstructed the lived experiences of the "lower sort," largely in eastern port cities, while also drawing attention to the particularities of the lives of poor women and the ways in which gender influenced one's experience of poverty in the period.[13] The complicated intersections of poverty and womanhood, however, deserve more careful attention, particularly the ways in which poor women navigated their doubled dependencies in their interactions with the patriarchal state. Ultimately, they were unable to employ the same rhetorical strategies that their middling, elite, and more well-connected counterparts did. Bound both by a gendered poverty and an impoverished femininity and thus unable to fully claim the protections enjoyed by middling and elite white women, poor urban white women continued to exist on the margins in the revolutionary era, incapacitated by a multifaceted dependency imposed on them by the forces of the patriarchal state.

Poor white women faced even greater limitations in their ability to overcome the obstacles imposed by their gendered subordination than did their more financially stable counterparts.[14] Because of their socioeconomic status, poor women were precluded from deploying the rhetorical strategies of helpless, vulnerable femininity to relative success. Unlike white women of means, poor women often did not have the resources necessary to petition their state legislatures, or the community and familial networks on whom they could rely in dire times. Instead, in early American cities, impoverished women appealed to other public, patriarchal institutions through their applications for outdoor relief and admission into the city's almshouses or workhouses. They sought various forms of assistance directly with these institutions when their survival depended on it. Notably, the language that poor women used in order to apply for relief in Boston, Philadelphia, and Charleston was filtered through the perspective of patriarchal state officials; many of these women were illiterate, and the extant source material detailing their lived experience—such as minute books and application logs—exists within institutional files. Both in reality and in much of the surviving archive, poor women's lives were more circumscribed by the powers of the patriarchal state than those of their middling or elite counterparts.

Local overseers, managers, and commissioners directed these institutions, and dictated the policies, rules, and regulations governing the mechanisms of public relief. Boston's overseers, for example, were elected officials and, most often, members of Boston's merchant elite who worked closely with the city's town selectmen.[15] Charleston's commissioners were likewise locally elected officials.[16] Philadelphia's overseers (later called "guardians," further evidence of the paternalistic nature of these institutions) were appointed by members of the Corporation of Philadelphia, which included the mayor, the recorder, the alderman, and city councilmen.[17] In Philadelphia, too, there was a special organization specifically dedicated to reforming impoverished sex workers. Led by a group of reform-minded Episcopalian men, the Magdalen Society of Philadelphia eventually built an institution to house, employ, and ultimately regulate the behavior of poor sex workers.[18]

Male officials distributing relief to the poor in urban areas provided aid in three ways. First, authorities distributed "outdoor relief" in the form of necessities: food, clothing, firewood, or modest pension payments. But this relief was only available to a relatively small group of paupers who were able to earn approval from their assigned overseer or commissioner. These outdoor pensioners were those who, "because of age, infirmity, or 'some other immediate causal circumstances,'" could not otherwise provide for themselves.[19] Second, if these authorities deemed a pauper unworthy or unfit for this type of assistance, officials sent applicants to live and labor in the city's workhouse. Workhouse authorities tasked these people with performing mundane and tedious work to prove their worth. A number of poor women, for example, were employed in making oakum and coffins, spinning cotton, or breaking rocks to earn their keep.[20] Third, those deemed either unworthy of outdoor relief or incapable of working could seek admission to the almshouse, where they resided until their situation changed, if ever. Significantly, the population of these urban institutions was overwhelmingly female.[21] In a number of cases, officials also authorized indemnities for children of single mothers. The aid they received was not necessarily regular and could be cut off at any moment, for any reason. Ultimately, the overseers and commissioners of the poor—men who were wealthy and had a relative degree of power in their communities—exercised nearly unilateral authority in deciding who was worthy of receiving aid, the majority of whom were women.[22]

The decades following the American Revolution saw an increased hesitancy among the nation's wealthy elite and middling citizens to provide aid to their impoverished contemporaries, a diminished willingness to bend the law to accommodate applicants for aid, stricter regulation for almshouse "inmates," and fewer acceptances overall. An editorial that appeared in Charleston's *Southern Patriot* in 1818 demonstrates this shift in attitude: "Any fixed provision made by law for the relief of the poor is always likely to be more productive of evil than of good, as it leads many to depend rather on what they consider to be their authorized claim to relief than on their own economy and industry."[23] The requirements both for admission to the almshouse as a resident and for the receipt of outdoor rations thus became stricter over time.

In colonial American society, however, local communities often felt a collective responsibility for the poor, and few public institutions existed.[24] Throughout most of the eighteenth century, people often welcomed the poor into their homes, and communities dispensed relief without long investigations into the recipients' character or circumstances.[25] Between 1790 and 1830, however, a steady population increase led early Americans to reinvestigate the origins of both crime and poverty.[26] Some determined that the root causes of these social ills were the failure of parents to properly raise their children and the lack of legal justice served to criminals. In response, some communities created a special institution to house "deviants."[27] Thus, due to moral and budgetary concerns, almshouse admissions in the early American republic decreased dramatically from previous decades.[28] Poor women, then, faced the additional hurdles of community apathy and even hostility on top of the myriad challenges they faced due to their poverty and their gender.

Increasingly, society viewed the poor as a drain on public resources as well as a danger to social morality and stability.[29] So, too, did the public deem the poor culpable for their condition, rather than assuming that their poverty existed because of larger social problems or structural, systemic inequality.[30] Almshouses, which often required work of their residents, were established in increasing numbers across the nascent nation.[31] Almshouse inmates were thus subjected to increased regulations, harsher treatment, stricter application standards, and the decreased likelihood of overseers bending the rules in sympathy for poor Americans' plight. Poor women's declarations of dependence, then, became a significantly less effective strategy for survival as the years of the early republic wore on.

Importantly, public relief was often a last resort for the revolutionary era's urban poor. Even though many women were able to receive assistance from local overseers or commissioners of the poor, they experienced these services as an indignity; those who entered these institutions were desperate, "naked, helpless and emaciated."[32] The conditions of almshouses and workhouses were abysmal, residents and inmates received little in the way of sustenance, the housing was inadequate, and men and women often fled these institutions. Inmates and residents preferred to be bound out as apprentices because anything seemed more desirable than a life in the local almshouse. Some even preferred the uncertainty and dangers of homelessness to life in the almshouses or workhouses.[33] Others "declared in a Solemn manner that they would rather perish through want" than reside in these local institutions.[34] Life inside the almshouse was strictly regimented; residents could not leave without permission, for example.[35] As the revolutionary era wore on, then, there was an increased hesitancy among the general public to provide relief to the urban poor, and a consistent disinterest in being a recipient of such aid unless it was absolutely necessary for one's survival.

Almshouse officials held power over both poor women and poor men. These patriarchal authorities often attempted to make poor men conform to middle-class standards of male deportment, emphasizing individual character and encouraging industriousness among this particular group of paupers. In many circumstances, poor men faced much the same treatment as poor women. Poverty and dependence in the revolutionary era made an individual subject to the judgments of various officials. But poor women struggled on a different, and often harsher scale, due to their magnified dependencies based on the intersecting forces of their class and gender.[36]

We must see poor white women, then, as subject to two different yet powerful forms of dependence. This analytical framework thus illuminates the simultaneous limitations imposed on them by their gender as well as their class status. Existing at a nexus between the challenges confronting impoverished early Americans in general and early American women in particular, poor women faced obstacles additional and unique to those of their wealthier female and poor male counterparts. They were simultaneously subject to the challenges of poor men and those faced by wealthier, yet still dependent white women. At the same time, then, they were forced to comply with certain standards of male comportment and with other standards of female comportment. This rendered them neither fully feminine nor fully members of the "worthy poor" and thus never adequately protected by either station of dependence or able to fulfill the complicated gender roles to which they were subjected by patriarchal authorities in society at large.

The Problem of Female Poverty

Poverty hit women especially hard. Pregnancy, single motherhood, widowhood, and marital desertion compounded poor women's suffering.[37] Women thus made up a significant portion of the urban almshouse population, "overrepresented at all levels of poor relief."[38] One historian has shown that the population of women at the Boston almshouse, for example, was so large as to make it a "female space organized around the lives of poor women." This "female space," however, existed "within a male-centered society."[39] The almshouse had a patriarchal structure, too. Women were expected to be the subordinates of men even within the almshouse, cooking and serving meals, cleaning clothes, tending to their ailments, and providing other domestic services.[40] Assumptions about gender roles were likewise instrumental in constructing the rules, procedures, and daily life of outdoor relief, almshouse admissions, and workhouses in these revolutionary-era cities.[41] With wealthy, elite men holding positions of power on the boards of urban institutions of relief, poor women often fared worse than their male counterparts on the basis of their gender.

There was a clear trade-off in the gender dynamics of the almshouse. Women could more easily procure relief from this source of last resort, yet they had significantly more difficulty obtaining their freedom from their detention than did men, according to those same gendered assumptions. While women had to demonstrate their virtue and worth for admission to the almshouse, they were more likely than men to be admitted if they demonstrated need (and their poor health). This is perhaps due to the expectation that men could and should have been able to work and earn money, while it was presumed that women would depend on an industrious, bread-winning, male head of household (in the ethos of middling Americans). The belief that women were dependent beings and thus less likely to be able to support themselves often led to overseers' willingness to grant them relief or admission to the almshouses at higher rates than men.[42]

By contrast, it was more difficult for women to make the case that they should be allowed to *leave* the almshouse once admitted. The warden passed judgment as to whether almshouse residents were "fit" to be released. This fitness corresponded to expectations of male comportment, and generally required residents to be able to demonstrate their ability to subsist without any further assistance from the state or community. A woman named Elizabeth Boon was judged "fit to do something for her own Maintenance," for example, yet the authorities decided she should remain in the almshouse. By contrast, most men in similar circumstances were granted permission to leave.[43]

Likewise, the rising focus on alleviating the needs of the "industrious" poor adversely affected women. Because women were supposed to be dependent on men—their fathers, husbands, and sons—for financial support, these men became the central focus of the overseers' reforming efforts. Local authorities began prioritizing the amplification of masculine independence, rather than attenuating the negative effects of feminine dependence.[44] If local efforts to mollify the struggles of the urban poor were focused on reforming men, patriarchal authorities assumed that the successful effects would eventually trickle down into the lives of their family members. This, of course, presumed that the trickle-down effect would be successful, and that enough poor women had men in their lives who, once rehabilitated, could provide for them in ways preferable to women relying on local, institutionalized relief. When neither was the case, women suffered significantly.[45] It is evident that the patriarchal structures built into these institutions disadvantaged poor women.

Because overseers' policies prioritized the assistance of male paupers in order to propel these men into their roles as women's financial providers, much of the relief offered to women was intended to be a temporary measure until these women could find themselves a male support system. This was a mechanism that utilized the forces of the patriarchal state to bolster the power of the patriarchal household. For women in almshouses or receiving outdoor relief, then, these forms of assistance rarely provided any significant, long-term relief or any reasonable solution to their financial situation. This point is made clear by the significant number of women who sought aid in these cities who submitted repeated or even regular applications for relief or admission to their local almshouses after they had been discharged.

As soon as women found viable alternatives to their almshouse or workhouse residency, they left their confinement. Many, however, were compelled by their circumstances to return to their dependence on state aid, as their alternative means of support was either temporary or inadequate to attain self-sufficiency. Women's frequent and repeated applications for relief demonstrate both that they intended these stints to be temporary, stop-gap measures and that the assistance they received from the patriarchal state was largely inadequate to transition them to a position in which they could support themselves. Poor women's implied dependence on often nonexistent male support meant that they returned time and time again to these paltry and utterly insufficient forms of public relief.

The rhetorical strategies employed by relatively well-situated or well-connected white women were not consistently effective for poor women seeking relief from the patriarchal state. Even when poor women employed tropes of middle- and upper-class white femininity, they often found that the problems of their poverty outweighed the problems of their gender. When poor women could not justify their plight to the satisfaction of these male authorities, they became subject to the often capricious judgments of local overseers. Ann Varnov, for example, applied to the Charleston commissioners for outdoor relief, believing herself worthy for their consideration. Yet because these officials faced budgetary constraints and a changing tide of social policy toward impoverished Americans, they were more prone to offer outdoor relief to men who were responsible for their dependent wives and children than to these women themselves, who were viewed as less productive or industrious members of society. In Varnov's case, they decided that she was capable of working to earn her relief, and thus they sent her to live and labor in their institution instead of granting her outdoor relief.[46] In order to receive relief, Varnov thus was forced to acquiesce to the oversight and control of patriarchal authorities in the almshouse.

Women seeking assistance were often seen less as humans worthy of aid and more as social problems threatening to place undue burdens on their communities. Especially when men failed to provide for their dependents, poor women suffered significantly. Thomas Rote Potter's wife came to Philadelphia's overseers, pregnant and unable to procure a subsistence. One of the overseers demanded that Thomas pay the required security for his wife's care, but he claimed to be unable to do so. Potter had but "nine half Johanneses,"[47] which the overseers retained until Potter was able to obtain more funds so that, notably, "the public shall not suffer by his neglect of duty to his family."[48] Mrs. Potter's suffering went unrecognized. Instead, she was kept in the custody of the overseers, while her husband lived free from the authority or punishment of these officials, despite it being his legal and social obligation to care for his wife and unborn child.

Those deemed able to work saw their applications for admission into the almshouse or for outdoor rations denied.[49] Sarah Shults's request was rejected because the committee determined that she was "capable of earning a livelihood," and thus, they were of the opinion that she did not truly need their assistance.[50] The commissioners also rejected Frances Jacobs's application for residency in the almshouse, as they found her "not being a sufficient object for this institution."[51] In order to demonstrate their worthiness for admission into the almshouse, these women had to prove both their inability to work (which would convince male authorities to provide relief to poor men) and their helpless dependence (which often convinced legislators to provide white women with relief).

Unlike women who received relief from their state legislatures, women who sought assistance from almshouse officials were often compelled to work to earn this aid. Early Americans, especially in the early republic, believed that it was better—both for society and for paupers—to work to earn money, rather than to be given relief with no stipulations: "To enable a poor Woman to earn six or seven Shillings a week by Labour would be much better than to grant her a Pension of five Shillings for the same Time."[52] Of course, requiring applicants to labor to "earn" their assistance had the added benefit, in the eyes of the overseers, of taking the burden of relief off the taxpayers and themselves. From late February 1774 onward, for example, the overseers of the poor in Philadelphia insisted that "any Poor distressed Objects" who requested relief from the body would be ordered into the House of Employment.[53]

Applying to the overseers of the poor for admission into the city almshouse or being compelled to "earn" one's support through confinement in the local workhouse reinforced early Americans' powerlessness and dependence. In the early to mid-eighteenth century, the overseers and

the general public had at least some understanding that people's capacity to work to care for themselves could be inhibited by circumstances
that designated them as impotent poor, or those who by no fault of their
own were incapable of earning a subsistence. Mary Gaskall, for example,
was a poor Philadelphia woman who was so ill that the managers of the
House of Employment found that she was "not . . . in a Condition to
be removed" from her home or to be required to work for aid; instead,
these men gave her fifteen pounds of assistance without demanding that
she work to earn this assistance.[54]

Cases like Gaskall's, however, were few and far between. On most occasions, poor women who had no one else on whom they could depend were
forced to labor for some form of relief. Elizabeth Lee, after being cleared
of perjury charges because she was found to be "not Right in her Sences,"
was sent to the House of Employment.[55] Despite her being deemed men-
tally incapable of committing a crime, the managers of the Philadelphia
workhouse did not designate Lee as incapable of earning her keep. Poor
women could easily be deemed "idle" and therefore be required to work
for their relief through a life in the workhouse, whereas wealthier women
were not subject to these kinds of stringent expectations.

Likewise, many rules and regulations governing admissions and
inmates applied both to men and women, regardless of their gendered
experience in poverty. Between 1800 and 1820, for example, the commissioners of the almshouse in Charleston placed an increasing number of
restrictions on applicants for residency and outdoor rations. They did not
take into account, however, that women made up a significantly larger
portion of those paupers receiving outdoor relief and occupying the
almshouse than did men.[56] Each increased restriction, then, hit women
harder and in bigger numbers. Holding men and women to the same
behavioral standards necessary for relief when they suffered through
different gendered realities had the adverse effect of disproportionately
penalizing impoverished women for their poverty and their gender.

As time wore on, more women than men faced enhanced restrictions
on the amount of rations and support they would receive from Charleston's commissioners. The board had found that "impositions have been
practised by sundry out-door pensioners or their connections in receiving rations of Bread and Beef," despite the fact that these pensioners
either left Charleston or died. Because they felt it "necessary and proper"
to stop such behavior, the commissioners passed a number of new bylaws
regarding the distribution of outdoor rations. The master of the poor
house was required to give only one ration to each pensioner daily; he

was also required to distribute these rations *only* to the intended recipient.[57] These kinds of restrictions limited not only women's access to relief but also their ability to claim their rations if they had been approved after the vigorous vetting process. Mothers of young children, for example, already had limited mobility and access to relief, and these changes proved a further undue burden on their suffering.

The lives of women receiving outdoor relief faced further scrutiny in later years, as local officials surveilled their behavior in closer detail. Beginning in 1819, the regular lists of outdoor pensioners became more detailed, including recipients' addresses, ages, places of birth, and number of children.[58] By June of 1820, the commissioners began listing diseases and other miscellaneous "observations" made regarding those receiving outdoor relief.[59] By early 1820, the commissioners required that any pensioner receiving outdoor rations and having children between the ages of six and fifteen send these children to Sunday school in order to continue receiving rations.[60] Even by 1820, the commissioners of the almshouse set out to further restrict the behavior of those to whom they provided rations or housing. Because women made up a disproportionately large number of outdoor pensioners, these policies affected poor women on a larger scale than they did poor men.

Additionally, mothers and children in Charleston received rations in smaller quantities as the years passed. Earlier in the almshouse's history, the commissioners doled out one ration to each member of the family. As the years of the early republic wore on, however, the commissioners seldom provided the number of rations they had doled out in earlier years. A mother of three, for instance, might receive only three outdoor rations per day. Mary Fernando applied for rations for herself and her two children, but was only granted two rations, without explanation.[61] In this case, Fernando would have to split an insufficient amount of food between herself and her children, or perhaps choose to go without so that her children would not suffer because of the commissioners' increasingly restrictive policies that disadvantaged vulnerable dependents.

As with wealthier women, poor women's applications for relief were most successful when they obtained recommendations from "respectable" men with standing in their community.[62] Although it was not originally required, letters from family members, acquaintances, or neighbors often made an applicant's request for assistance stronger.[63] It was more difficult for these poor, less connected women to obtain such recommendations. Over time, male authorities in these cities began *requiring* recommendations for almshouse inmates and outdoor relief recipients in an attempt to curtail the amount of relief doled out to those deemed unworthy. While some women were able to procure such recommendations, it was more challenging for others who were impoverished in part because of their clear inability to rely on anyone else for any form of support. Women without these networks suffered from their inability to have their hardships legitimated or confirmed by patriarchal voices.

Some institutions eventually began to require applicants to supply recommendations not just in support of their worthiness for aid but also on their character. Elizabeth Goper was temporarily given rations until the next meeting of the Board of Commissioners, "at which time she is to produce a good recommendation otherwise her support from this Institution will be stopped."[64] Similarly, Sarah Rhodes was required to supply a "recommendation from some respectable citizens" within two weeks' time.[65] Before her petition for outdoor relief could be granted, the commissioners determined that Mr. Curtis, a board member, would "visit her habitation & if found deserving . . . give her two rations."[66] In the case of Sarah Rhodes, she was subject to both increasingly harsh regulations and the imposition of a male authority in her home, casting judgment upon her and deciding whether she was a person who deserved the institution's support.

Like those who could not provide recommendations to garner public relief, women who were labeled transients or "strangers"—i.e., not established or known members of the community—also faced increasingly stringent regulations over time. Like other restrictions confronting impoverished revolutionary-era Americans, Boston's progressively harsh warning-out policies adversely affected women on a larger scale.[67] Warning out was a process by which community leaders, no longer able or willing to provide public relief and assistance to a particular person, used the law to forcibly remove a person then residing in their jurisdiction and compel them to return to their previous place of residence. Although the overseers were only supposed to dole out aid to those women who could prove their residency in the city, prior to the Revolution, there is significant evidence to demonstrate that even if women were deemed "strangers" or could not prove their residency status, the overseers still provided these women with relief. In the years of the early republic, however, the institution was stricter about regulating or warning out these women. Transient women with no place to turn were often forcibly removed from Boston's city limits in postrevolutionary years. As women had fewer economic opportunities than did men, this newly

enforced warning-out policy adversely affected women who found themselves without any networks of support.

Women with no connections—familial, neighborly, or otherwise—
were crippled by their social and legal dependencies in ways that women
who had networks on whom they could rely were not. The detriments of
detachment from familial or neighborly networks were evident in the
preponderance of settlement laws in dictating relief for impoverished
early Americans. Those who had no connections, no sponsors, and no
one to provide security on their account were "warned out" of cities in
which they had not established or could not establish residency. Overseers who warned out the local poor were largely motivated by budgetary
concerns, as these men feared their cities would be overcome with "idle
strangers."[68] Poor women who faced the threat of being warned out of
these cities had insult added to injury: not only did they not enjoy formal
belonging in the community, but their lack of connection to a place or to
a support system jeopardized their very survival, as they faced the probability of forcible removal.[69]

Overseers of the poor worked in conjunction with local officials to
warn out poor women to their last known place of residency, forcing
them into greater hardship than that which they faced in their current
state. The Philadelphia overseers requested that Nicholas Wall, a local
attorney, draw up a warrant to have Elizabeth Morgan removed from
the city to Lancaster, and gave him fifteen shillings to do so. The overseers, however, made no note of any assistance that might be provided to
Morgan to travel over seventy miles.[70] For fear of Bridget McCall becoming "Chargeable to this City," the overseers requested that local officials
"take her away" and remove her by warrant, if necessary.[71] Women
whom patriarchal officials identified as "strangers" could also be labeled
"vagrants" due to their lack of connections. Elizabeth Riley, one such
stranger-turned-vagrant, was forced to be committed to the workhouse,
and was only set free when she promised to return to her previous place
of residency in Colchester, Virginia.[72] Poor women often lacked the networks that their wealthier counterparts used to combat the ill effects of
their feminine dependence.

The Problem of Impoverished Womanhood

The overseers and commissioners of the poor dictated how poor women
were expected to behave and evaluated their applications, in part,
on the basis of society's vision of middle-class white femininity and

womanhood. A number of female applicants for public relief proved their worthiness to receive such aid by manipulating tropes of comportment in ways similar to those of women who applied to state legislatures for assistance. Grace Ingraham, "being in a very low state of health," received rations for herself and her children.[73] Fanny O'Brien's husband was "absent," and as she was in "low Circumstances" with an ill child to care for, the Philadelphia overseers provided her with a paltry sum.[74] The overseers paid Ann Harkin one dollar per week while her child was sick. Stipulations came with Harkin's aid, though; she only seemed deserving because she had an ill child whom she was nursing back to health.[75] The language of these applications mirrors that of those petitions submitted by women who, because of their husbands' death, political affiliation, or financial deficiencies, requested financial aid from their state legislatures.

Overseers often considered poor women worthy objects of assistance if they could clearly and unequivocally demonstrate both that their husbands or other patriarchal figures could not provide for them and that these women were truly unable to support themselves. These women were frequently admitted to the almshouse or provided with rations in these circumstances. James Carter's wife and child (both unnamed in the historical record) were permitted to continue to reside in the almshouse in Charleston until Carter recovered from his "ill health."[76] Jane Walker requested rations for herself and her child; the commissioners granted her request because her husband was unable to work.[77] Charlotte Smith similarly requested rations for herself and her children until her husband was well. She claimed he was "very much indisposed with a Splinter in his hand." Because the commissioners knew her husband to be "an Industrious man," they granted Smith three rations for herself and her children.[78] In Smith's case, she had to demonstrate her own need, her husband's inability to provide for her, *and* the fact that he was otherwise a hard worker, all of which made her a "deserving object" of the overseers' pity. In all of these cases, too, it is notable that these women's needs were temporary, not indefinite.

Certainly, there are a number of instances in which poor women could demonstrate their helplessness and need for relief in much the same way that white women applied to state legislatures for aid. Yet, even if poor women received this aid, they were subject to the watchful eye of male authorities even after they were deemed worthy to receive such assistance. Women who succeeded in their applications to state legislatures for relief would not have had to deal with the regular oversight of these male officials after their request was granted. But, this was not the case for women who turned to local overseers or reform societies for relief. Instead, women who resided in these cities' almshouses and workhouses were subject to patriarchal authorities' continued exercise of capricious and often uncompromising mechanisms of control long after their applications were accepted.

Women who earned public relief were thus subject to extensive and regularized patriarchal surveillance over their lives. In submitting to the discipline of the almshouse regime, poor women substituted one kind of dependence for another—even harsher—system. Once residents were admitted, their activities, property, and rights were carefully controlled by the commissioners and overseers. Just as women's applications were subject to the whims of officials, so too were those who resided in the almshouse or were confined in the workhouse under the surveillance of the overseers and their employees. Overseers in Philadelphia appointed managers to regularly "examine such poor and Indigent persons" admitted to the almshouse to determine "who do not appear suitable Objects" and thus "may be Removed."[79] These managers, who made weekly strolls through their assigned wards, also had the authority to remove young children from their parents' care if these men did not find the child's upbringing proper or adequate.[80] They likewise were permitted to "administer suitable Correction to such Idle, dissolute Vagrants, that refuse to work, and who are other ways disorderly when in the House of Employment." Both the overseers and the managers had "discretionary power" to administer the oversight and the day-to-day activities of the almshouse and workhouse.[81]

Patriarchal authorities in revolutionary-era cities thus used the institutions of poor relief as much for "social control" as for assistance for the needy.[82] City overseers and commissioners regularly seized property belonging to residents of the almshouses and inmates of workhouses, including women. Maria Chevalier was admitted to the Charleston almshouse in 1806, and when the committee learned of her owning "a certain valuable property," they determined to "keep [it] from her." Two men were appointed to "search into the particulars so as to Obtain if possible the same," with no further directions given.[83] Mrs. Salts, a deceased resident of the almshouse, was found to possess several silver spoons and other valuable items, which her daughter Susan petitioned to recover after her mother passed away (Susan was the ward of a man named Mr. Gillison). Before making a decision, the committee first required "proper enquiries" into Susan's claims.[84] The investigation revealed only twelve silver spoons and one ladle to be the property "of value" left by

Mrs. Salts, which the committee decided to place in the hands of the chairman of the board until Susan reach the age of eighteen.[85] Isabella Edwards, who was confined in the Philadelphia House of Employment, was forced to convey her estate to the overseers in order to cover the costs of her support. Rather than allowing her to take back her property when she was prepared to support herself, the overseers decided to assemble a committee to discuss and make decisions about Edwards's readiness to leave the almshouse.[86] Once women applied to the overseers for assistance, their property was subjected to men's probing and harsh oversight.

Women who turned to the overseers of the poor rather than state legislatures for assistance in dealing with negligent husbands found that their rights to certain property were restricted for the ostensible purpose of their protection. The Philadelphia overseers sent a committee to visit Mrs. Morgan's home, and upon finding her "much distress'd and not able to support herself & four children," took it upon themselves to intervene in the Morgan family's affairs. Thomas Morgan, who had allegedly been cruel and neglectful toward his family, owned significant property.[87] The committee found that Thomas "persisted in refusing any kind of support to his Wife and four Children," so they seized his effects, which included a number of pieces of mahogany furniture, silverware, china, linens, "and a Negro Boy named Robert," the combined value of which amounted to 127 pounds, two shillings, and nine pence. Because Mrs. Morgan and her children had evidently run up a bit of debt by living in the almshouse when Thomas refused to care for them, the overseers decided it was appropriate to hold the Morgans' property as bond until the debt was repaid.[88] Whereas women who sought divorces or separate maintenances through the court system could retain control over their estranged husbands' property, women who, as a last resort, had to turn to local overseers of the poor to intervene in these matters accumulated debts that restricted their access to their husbands' property.

Poor women who desired to separate from their husbands did not, in most cases, have the capabilities or resources to seek redress through the court system like their more well-off or well-connected counterparts. Even if these poor women could demonstrate that their husbands had deserted them or failed to provide for them adequately, their applications for aid were not necessarily met with success. When Catharine Carney's husband deserted her, she requested assistance from the Board of the Almshouse in Philadelphia in her attempt to sell her husband's property. After meeting, the committee appointed to Carney's case decided that "they do not consider her entitled to relief."[89] A simple mention or verification of a husband's desertion and failure to provide an adequate maintenance for his wife and family could secure middling and upper-class women divorces. Yet Carney, who did not have the resources to seek a divorce through the court and instead turned to local overseers, failed to find a solution to her problems.

As with their property, the behavior of residents and outdoor pensioners was highly regulated and controlled from the application process through discharge.[90] Although the boards in these institutions approved the residency and outdoor pensions of a significant number of its applicants, the behavior of residents and those receiving rations was strictly monitored by the commissioners and overseers of the almshouse. In Charleston, the commissioners conducted regular inspections of rooms and work areas, requiring certain standards of order and cleanliness.[91] They also inquired into the "Characters and Circumstances" of the residents of the almshouse.[92] Beginning in August of 1802, the commissioners determined that regular oversight of the outdoor pensioners was required to ensure that those receiving rations were not unlawfully taking advantage of their assistance. They appointed a committee to "enquire into the circumstances of the out Door Pensioners and to report from time to time to the Board" on their findings.[93] Applicants who received rations were later required to appear before the committee every three months "to undergo an examination to judge" whether they should continue to be "on the Bounty" or instead struck "off the list, as [they] are no longer an object of charity."[94]

Because the almshouse was a last resort for women, they did not experience empowerment by declaring their dependence on local overseers, as those who sought relief from state legislatures sometimes did. On the contrary, this reliance on men who dictated how they were to behave reinforced their dependence and powerlessness. Some women received outdoor relief, but that was not enough to pull them out of poverty or even to allow them to subsist beyond squalor. At least with successful legislative petitions, women had the possibility, the distinct hope, of supporting themselves, of freeing themselves from certain confines of their dependence. Women who resorted to almshouses, however, had no choice, were completely desperate, and did not *desire* to be confined and controlled by the overseers. They did so merely because, by the double dependence of their sex and class, they had no other option for relief.

Policing Poor White Women's Bodies

Poor women were also subject to control over their bodies and sexuality by patriarchal authorities. Neither poor white men nor wealthier women who submitted petitions to the court faced this kind or level of scrutiny and control over their behavior. Women whose sexuality did not align with traditional expectations of female comportment could see themselves confined and often punished for their behavior. Facing the double binds of expectations of sexual purity and the strains of poverty, poor women who transgressed society's sexual expectations for women found themselves under close scrutiny, control, and discipline by the forces of the patriarchal state.

Pregnancy, of course, was a unique, gendered burden that fell especially hard on poor women. The pages of the minute books of the Philadelphia overseers of the poor are filled with notations of pregnant women seeking assistance and accusations of local men fathering "bastard" children. Pregnant women who would not find consistent support for themselves or their children were deemed unwanted and viewed as potential burdens to the community. Rather than attempting to protect poor pregnant women in their dependent state, the city sought to escape culpability for supporting them by holding the fathers of illegitimate children accountable for supporting these infants. These fathers, however, were often unable or unwilling to provide the financial support required by local authorities, so they denied fathering these children, or they left the city entirely. Even married women whose husbands could not support them were often sent to their local almshouse with a small security to guarantee their support. Local overseers, then, often acted out of self-interest when they intervened to demand that fathers of illegitimate children pay security for them. The overseers did not enforce the collection of securities out of concern for the pregnant woman and her inability to care for herself and child, however. Instead, overseers sought bonds for illegitimate children so that women and their infants would not become a financial burden on the city.

Women whose husbands and paramours refused to pay a security to local officials were effectively punished for these men's failures. Women pregnant with illegitimate children who could not secure a bond were literally kept in confinement. In their minute books, the overseers stated, "We are of Opinion, that all such Women, who are delivered of Bastard Children in the House of Employment, and who will not discover the Father of such illegitimate Child (of which they are delivered,) may be obliged to serve a reasonable Term, to defray the Expence, which the City may be at for their Maintenance."[95] Again, this punishment reveals local patriarchal authorities' true intentions in regards to poor women's welfare: because of their ostensibly illicit sexual behavior, they ought to *earn* the relief that they received from the public dole, rather than be given it. Men who fathered illegitimate children in these situations could more easily escape punishment by leaving the city, abandoning the women whom they impregnated.[96] Their children, once they were of age, were often forced into apprenticeships.[97] The overseers were clearly interested in punishing women who became pregnant while unmarried. In their desperation, then, pregnant women often accepted the unfortunate tradeoff, residing in the almshouse until their child was born, and then laboring in the workhouse afterward to compensate for the relief they received.

Overseers' treatment of pregnant women also became harsher over time. By 1810, the Philadelphia overseers apparently found that women carrying illegitimate children had become enough of a problem to warrant clarification on the regulation of admissions. The overseers saw an increased expenditure for servants who by their "imprudent conduct" got pregnant while unmarried. In the future, they agreed, the overseers were not to admit any pregnant servant unless her master or mistress agreed to pay all of her expenses up front, and she was required to leave with the child once mother and child were both well enough to do so. This was all done with the purpose of "checking the evil" that they believed flourished among female servants in early republican Philadelphia.[98] By 1811, the overseers had deemed it necessary to form a "Committee on Bastardy," whose sole purpose it was to deal with these cases.[99] The committee amounted to patriarchal oversight of poor women's bodies. These women were more line items on overseers' budgets than objects of empathy for local overseers.

Local patriarchal authorities also sought to police, control, and reform poor sex workers. In Philadelphia, a group of white male Episcopalians founded the Magdalen Society, which sought to reform women who, for various reasons, turned to sex work.[100] Like the overseers who attempted to reform "indolent" paupers through institutionalization, the Magdalen Society decided to keep these fallen women in an asylum, "untill their virtuous resolutions are formed into habit."[101] Of course, members of the Magdalen Society—elite white men—were those who ultimately determined when these women had acquired sufficiently virtuous habits to warrant their release from captivity.[102] The efforts of the Magdalen

Society reflected elite anxiety over the behavior of members of the lower classes, and targeted their efforts in an attempt to control women's bodies and sexual activity.[103]

The white male members of the Magdalen Society in Philadelphia took advantage of poor women's dependence and helplessness in an attempt to control their behavior under the guise of protection and reformation. The group took in the city's sex workers in an attempt to reform their sexual mores through a strict regimen of work and religious indoctrination. Magdalen Society members promised these women food and housing in exchange for their work and their desire to reject their current life, which may have seemed an appealing offer to some. But the society simultaneously imposed a system of control over its residents. In the cases of women admitted to the Magdalen Society's asylum, little to no freedom came from their dependence on white male authority. Their poverty, and especially their sexual history, prevented them from using the language of their dependence as a strategy for survival in the same way that women who had not turned to sex work could do.

The Magdalen Society, like patriarchal officials who operated revolutionary-era almshouses, only focused its efforts on women whom they considered to be worthy objects of reform.[104] Women's "situation and temper" were both subject to the judgment of the society's members. The Magdalen Society's biases—against poor women and especially against those whose sexuality did not conform to its members' moral code—were evident in the way that they wrote about women who did not mindlessly subject themselves to these men's authority. They lamented the "insensibility that generally prevails among these deluded females and their backwardness to accept the charitable assistance gratuitously offer'd to them."[105] The expressions of the Magdalen Society make evident that these men were largely devoid of empathy for sex workers, and neglected to understand the circumstances that might compel them to make the choice to engage in this labor.

After admission, these poor women faced severe restrictions on their behavior. And, depending on the conduct of the asylum's residents, society members might alter their opinion of these women and change the terms of their relief. When these women resisted the controlling reform efforts to which they were subjected by running away, for example, patriarchal officials denigrated them as ungrateful, immoral, and "deluded." Yet if they demonstrated an openness or willingness to remain in confinement and change their behavior according to members' wishes, these women were seen as "unhappy victims of seduction."[106] Often, members of the Magdalen Society seemed more interested in social control and in enforcing poor women's acquiescence to patriarchal authority than they were in ridding the streets of Philadelphia of sex work.

The Magdalen Society's attempts to control poor women were carried out under the guise of paternalistic protection. Suggesting that "fallen women" were powerless to control their own behavior, society members insisted that "however affected with remorse or desirous of returning to a life of rectitude" these women were, they could not "in such a place be protected from the assaults & temptations of insidious men until their virtuous resolution are confirmed by habit."[107] Members worried that these "magdalens" would be brought back to their lives of vice by men who called to them from the street, thus undoing all the hard work of reforming in which society members had invested their time.[108] So too did the society's membership regularly keep these "magdalens" confined for longer than they originally anticipated, "in order the more effectually to wean them from the vicious habits."[109] Using the pretense of protection from sin and the influences of vicious men, the Magdalen Society confined and controlled poor sex workers for periods longer than those to which these women had originally acquiesced.

Rather than making their first concern the protection of poor women, though, the Magdalen Society of Philadelphia, like city overseers, prioritized their own sense of morality and focused their energies on fixing what they perceived to be dangers to society. The building of a physical asylum had always been a priority of the Magdalen Society, which firmly believed that "seclusion from the world for a certain period" was "absolutely necessary for the objects of this institution." Likewise, these men feared that, "in moments of weakness," residents might act as a "force of temptation" to inhabitants of the surrounding neighborhood.[110] These anxieties justified, in their view, the decision to build a tall fence around the property, demonstrating the society's interest in preserving the morality of the neighborhood perhaps more so than their desire to reform residents of the asylum; walls keep people in as much as out.[111] Women who declared their dependence on the Magdalen Society were literally secluded from their former lives, segregated from the institution's neighbors, and kept under close surveillance by these male authorities.

Like inmates in city workhouses, residents of the asylum of Philadelphia's Magdalen Society were expected to work to earn their keep. Because of their fall from virtue, these women were not considered deserving of the same aid or relief without labor that a more pious or chaste woman may have received from other sources. The society focused on labor and industry not only as a way to reform these sex workers but also as a way for them to repent for their sins. Women who declared their dependence to local overseers or reform societies were not deemed worthy of this assistance by virtue of their situation but had to earn their worthiness for aid. Because of their poverty and their sexual history, male authorities required these poor sex workers to work while diligently reforming their behavior.

Magdalen Society members kept tight control over their residents, whose lives and daily routines were regimented and highly surveilled. These women needed express permission to leave the asylum, to which society members were unwilling to consent unless they deemed that residents had fully reformed their formerly vicious ways.[112] These men also made sure to emphasize that they were providing social benefits to these women, who ought to be grateful for these acts of benevolence. The minute books reflect members' attitudes that fallen women who were admitted to the asylum were to be "recipient[s] of the moral as well as . . . pecuniary privileges" of the home. They therefore insisted that residents "be willing to subject themselves to the salutary rules and regulations of the Institution."[113] Poor sex workers, then, were subject to extensive, continued control and judgment even after they had already been deemed worthy of relief by these male authorities.

The Magdalen Society's rules and regulations became more stringent as the first decades of the nineteenth century wore on. In the society's early years, members placed aid recipients in the homes of local families whom they believed could have a positive, reformative influence on fallen women. Later, the society only placed women in these homes once they deemed them ready for a transitional period—if they were capable of leaving the asylum but not quite ready, or habitually virtuous enough, to return to life outside the purview of the society's dictates. These families served as transitional surrogates for the social control members exercised over women once they acquired the funds to build an asylum to house, and confine, fallen women. So, even when these poor sex workers deemed themselves worthy in the eyes of male society members to leave the asylum, they were still subject to this surrogate control because of their sexual history.

* * *

Ultimately, then, early American women's capacity to strategically deploy their dependence to work to their advantage was limited, particularly for those who did not or could not properly conform to standards of white femininity. Those women who petitioned their state legislatures using aggressive or accusatory language that was not properly couched in terms of feminine submission to male authority threatened to upset the delicate gendered hierarchy. Poor women faced the complications of an intersectional gender identity, confronting the dual burdens of their class and gender. Impoverished women, who were overrepresented in all forms of poor relief, had to cope with the uniqueness of female poverty. Increased rules and regulations implemented by the patriarchal state over time paid no attention to gender difference. Poor women, then, were held to male standards of comportment in poverty, while combating the unique obstacles of their gender. Other women whose sexuality transgressed traditional norms of feminine comportment faced further oversight and were subject to the nearly constant control of male authorities. Throughout the revolutionary era, poor urban women consistently struggled to combat these increased regulations and the limitations imposed upon them by their dependence.

6 /   To Have and to Hold Herself

On January 19, 1779, Carolina Lamboll, a free Black man from Charleston, attested to his purchase and subsequent manumission of an enslaved woman named Jane.[1] Lamboll testified that the amount Jane paid him for her freedom was a mere twenty shillings. Such a sum seems puzzling when juxtaposed with hundreds of deeds in which enslaved people were often sold for hundreds or even thousands of pounds. Lamboll, however, was not concerned with Jane's monetary value as human property. Instead, he offered as his motivation for manumission "the Love and affection" he possessed for Jane, as her husband. Lamboll purchased his wife from an enslaver named Rachel Caw, and used his power as a free man to liberate his wife from the institution of slavery.[2] In the midst of a violent, bloody civil war that ravaged South Carolina, and fewer than three years after Jefferson penned his famous Declaration, Jane was free. She earned that freedom, her legal independence, and the freedom of all future generations of her family by working in tandem with her husband.

Out of more than three hundred deeds of manumission of formerly enslaved women in the Charleston area during the revolutionary era, one phrase appears just once in these records.[3] With the stroke of a pen as he made his mark on this binding legal document, Lamboll declared that his wife, Jane, should henceforth be legally entitled "to Have and to hold herself."[4] Lamboll's diction, especially amid a set of sources that often follow a specific and repetitive pattern, is significant. Rather than present the South Carolina secretary of state with the same rote language employed by the white men and women whose business it was to trade in human beings, whose power and socioeconomic status was grounded in robbing enslaved people of autonomy, of dignity, of freedom, rather than use the words of the patriarchs who instituted and strengthened a system of bondage across the state, Lamboll and Jane chose their own words. As a result of their union, of their love, Jane would have ownership over herself. Jane and Carolina Lamboll's future children, their grandchildren, their great-grandchildren, and all generations that followed would enjoy the same, all descending from a free, female line.

At the same time, however, the patriarchal state dictated the process by which Lamboll and Jane worked together to seize her freedom and that of their future children. Seeking to legitimate Jane's freedom under the law, Lamboll purchased his wife, and therefore (albeit briefly) owned her. In those moments, Jane was—legally—enslaved property belonging to her own husband. It was the intermediary point between slavery and freedom that the two facilitated together; it was temporary, a means to an end, a technicality of sorts; it was a necessary step to ensure Jane's freedom in the eyes of the patriarchal state.

Black women's relationship to freedom and to the patriarchal state was fraught with contradictions.[5] Following the example of scholars who have recently pushed us to rethink the structural inequalities inherent in and the violence perpetrated by the traditional archive, this chapter seeks to uncover components of that fraught relationship and purposefully recover the voices of Black women through and in their

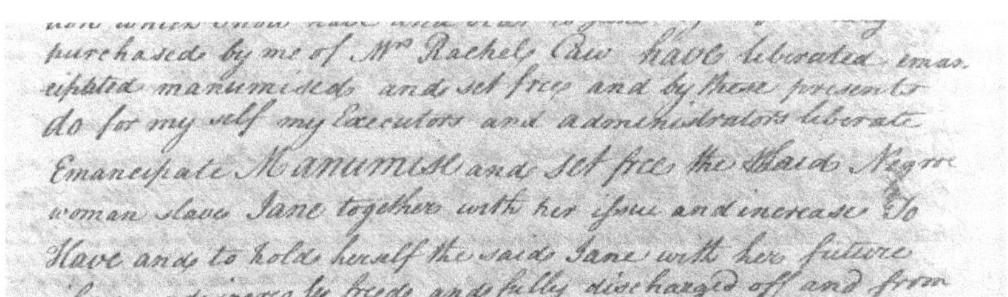
purchased by me of Mrs Rachel Caw have liberated eman-
cipated manumised and set free and by these presents
do for my self my Executors and administrators liberate
Emancipate Manumise and set free the said Negro
woman slave Jane together with her issue and increase To
Have and to hold herself the said Jane with her future
issue and increase freed and fully discharged off and from
the Bonds of Slavery and Servitude to me the said Carolina

FIGURE 6.1. The choice of language in the manumission deed that freed Jane Lamboll from enslavement is notable; likely working together, Jane and her husband Carolina wrote that she was to be entitled "to Have and to hold herself." Source: Manumission Deed of Jane, purchased and freed by Carolina Lamboll from Rachel Caw, 19 January 1779, vol. RR, 586, *Miscellaneous Records*, South Carolina Department of Archives and History, Columbia, South Carolina.

interactions with the patriarchal state.⁶ In order to truly analyze how Black women navigated the confining sociolegal systems created by the patriarchal state, we must expand our conceptions both of "petitioning" and of "the patriarchal state"; we must likewise look beyond the traditional legal archive and consider the voices and actions of Black women in both slavery's archive and freedom's archive.⁷ In the lives of enslaved women, for example, the patriarchal state was personified in the figure of the enslaving patriarch (or, in some cases, enslaving female patriarch), to whom the institutional state granted and extended its powers.⁸ Few Black women formally petitioned state legislatures or the courts in the same way that white women did; this, however, does not mean that free and enslaved Black women did not petition the patriarchal state in advocacy of themselves and their families in other ways. Deeds of emancipation, which are often written by enslavers, can uncover the otherwise invisible antislavery activism of those people—including women—who were held in bondage. Legal sources like deeds of emancipation, then, provide evidence of Black women's petitioning efforts.

These important sources reveal that gendered familial roles circumscribed the ways in which Black women navigated their legal status in the revolutionary era. As was the case with Carolina Lamboll and his wife, Jane, Black men and women often worked together in their quests for freedom. Black husbands and fathers performed the role of protector of and provider for their wives and children in exceptional ways, especially relative to white husbands and fathers already discussed in this work. Likewise, Black women fulfilled wifely and motherly duty in their interactions with the patriarchal state, despite the legal, economic, and social limitations imposed on them by their racial identity and status of enslavement.

Significantly, Black women's capacity to grant freedom and unfreedom to their children was literally embodied within them. Because of the law of *partus sequitur ventrum*, a child's legal status of freedom or slavery would follow that of their mother at birth. Numerous scholars have analyzed the ways in which Black women's reproductive capacity bolstered the white patriarchal state by facilitating the natural increase of the enslaved population, both institutionally and literally, as numerous enslavers raped enslaved women and subsequently held their own biological children in slavery.⁹ Yet, by the same framework of law, Black women's bodies could also grant freedom to their children, and importantly, to subsequent generations of free Black Americans.¹⁰

The stakes of Black women's efforts in testing and exploiting the boundaries of patriarchal power, therefore, were higher than those of white women.[11] The latter petitioned the state in the revolutionary era for relief and assistance because of the upheavals of war and daily life, on certain occasions doing so as a matter of survival. Regardless of the intent or need of these white women petitioners, these rhetorical strategies reinforced white patriarchs' expectations of dependent women's behavior and attitudes. Free and enslaved Black women, on the other hand, resisted the patriarchal state in a more explicit way, seeking to free themselves and their progeny from enslavement forever, performing the utmost measure of devoted motherhood. Yet notably, they too conformed to the terms of patriarchal law to codify that freedom, out of extreme necessity.

Black Women and the Traditional Legal Archive

Unlike those relatively numerous petitions white women filed through state legislatures or local courts in the revolutionary era, Black women's voices are largely silent in the "traditional archive."[12] This is especially true in the traditional *legal* archive, which privileges patriarchal voices and power structures. The project of recovering the words and experiences of free and enslaved Black women and their own perspectives on their interactions with the patriarchal state is, thus, immensely difficult. Legal records produce, at first glance, a deafening silence where Black women's voices ought to be heard. Records of their bodies and their labor—property to be bought, sold, and exploited—however, are omnipresent in the traditional archive. A few petitions filed directly by Black women do exist, but they are relatively rare. This does not mean, however, that Black women—free and enslaved—did not petition the state.

The traditional legal archive leaves few records written explicitly from the perspective of Black women. Black women almost never directly petitioned state legislatures for assistance. In Boston, for example, there were just two successful petitions submitted to the Massachusetts legislature by Black women between the years 1750 and 1820, and one petition for divorce submitted by a Black woman during the same period. A few others exist, as some women chose to petition the governor and council of Massachusetts; three of those have been identified.[13]

One such petition was submitted by a woman identified in the record as "Daphne, an African." Daphne's plea spoke tersely about her life of enslavement. "She was born in Africa," the document began, "and upon her being brought into the Country, was purchased as a Slave by Henry Barnes Esqr." Daphne made no attempt to further elucidate the horrors she experienced in slavery. Instead, she quickly moved on, perhaps understanding the limited patience of members of the General Court for critiques of slavery. Daphne instead noted that Massachusetts leaders had confiscated Barnes's property after he fled the state during the Revolution, and that the legislature itself "ordered the Agent on the said estate to support your Petitioner (she being unfirm & wholly unable to support herself in a very advanced age)."[14] Daphne outlined the legal right she had to such financial support. Yet, she gently reminded the body that it had "discharged" the agent who oversaw Barnes's estate: "Ever since that time your unhappy Petitioner has been put to the most distressing expedients for her subsistence and has become indebted to sundry persons, who from motives of humanity & in expectation that she would receive an allowance from your Honors to make her comfortable during the short time which probably she has to live, have exerted themselves, to support her."[15] Daphne's petition, submitted in late 1790, demonstrated that she had gone without this payment and support for more than a year.

Daphne's language, like that in all other women's petitions, was a gendered performance. Her situation "unhappy," Daphne resorted to "distressing expedients" to survive, though what those were remains unclear. In her attempts to mitigate her situation, she depended on others who were driven both, it seems, by a moral sense of obligation to a pitiable figure like Daphne and also by the assumption that they would eventually be repaid the debt out of the state's allowance. Perhaps in an attempt to convince the patriarchal state that such financial support—to be clear, support that they had already assented to provide—would be minimal, Daphne suggested that she might not have been long for this life. The General Court seems to have recognized Daphne's lamentable situation, granting her "suitable Provision"—notably, an unspecified amount—"for her Comfortable support, untill the further Order of the General Court."[16]

Daphne, however, also had to consider how to perform her racialized dependence as it intersected with her gender identity. Daphne's experience of enslavement, for example, amounts to a footnote in her plea for support. She mentions only briefly her capture and subsequent bondage, though certainly this would have been a defining experience of her life, and a compelling justification for petitioning the state for support. The bulk of the petition dissected her current and unfortunate circumstances, as well as her intense need for financial support. Other than its first sentence and her lack of an identifiable surname, Daphne's words did not explicitly provide any clarity as to her race or former status of enslavement. In all likelihood, this was strategic. Daphne and those assisting her in drafting the petition might have assumed that the legislature would not take kindly to being lectured about the deleterious effects of slavery. Instead, she followed the model for successful petitions submitted by other women: supplicating the legislature as a humble dependent in need of protection and care from the patriarchal state.

Because of the inherent power of the patriarchal state and of gendered norms in revolutionary America, free and enslaved Black Americans often did not deviate from expectations prescribed to white spouses. A woman named Lydia Sharp, likely a free woman of color, had been married to an enslaved man named Boston, owned by Joseph Belknap, a prominent Boston printer. The two had been married in 1767 by Samuel Mather, a minister and son of noted Congregationalist leader Cotton Mather.[17] Aside from this introduction into the identities of both Sharp and Boston, the remainder of the petition follows the common, performative language of divorce suits. Sharp complained of her husband having abandoned her for three years and having slept with "divers other women of infamous Character," from whom he became infected with venereal disease. Sharp insisted that Boston "lives in the constant violation of every marriage Duty to the great Grief misfortune and almost absolute Ruin of your Petitioner."[18]

The case is significant for a number of reasons. It is the only extant divorce petition involving a Black woman suing her husband in the city of Boston between 1750 and 1820. It is notable, too, that such a marriage was sanctioned by Mather, and that Boston evidently had enough freedom of movement both to be married to a free woman and to enable him to commit adultery regularly. Finally, what is perhaps most remarkable is Sharp's exploitation of the mechanisms of the patriarchal state to free herself from this marriage. She leveraged language and strategies that had become commonplace among white Bostonian women in the revolutionary era, providing evidence that Black women did not assume such marital protections were the exclusive privileges of white women.

Notably, Sharp was, legally, *more* free than her husband, yet in order to extricate herself from her marriage, she needed to submit herself as his dependent, positioning herself in the status of subordinate wife. In this way, she elevated Boston to the status of family patriarch in order to demonstrate the ways in which he had failed to uphold those solemn vows of care and protection. But the situation was, of course, more complex than this. Boston could not possibly fulfill the role of family patriarch; his enslavement meant that he would not be able to provide financially for his wife and any children the two might have together. That task would fall to Sharp.

Like other women in her position, Sharp probably at least recognized the power inherent in expressing this form of dependence on paper, legitimating women's unequal status before men while simultaneously challenging the consequences of that system. It is possible, too, that Sharp preferred such a status. Twenty-first-century feminist readers may bristle at a woman's desire for such legal protections, which required submission to male authority. Yet, as a free Black woman married to an enslaved Black man who had been consistently unfaithful and who, if he remained enslaved, would never be able to provide for his family as a free man would, Sharp may have found more safety and comfort in the status of female dependence traditionally experienced by middling and elite white women. Recognizing the intersectionality of dependencies requires us to see that a situation viewed as oppressive by one group may be coveted as a privilege by another.[19]

Though Black women's petitions to the state were scant in the revolutionary era, there is evidence to show that Daphne's and Sharp's strategy was not the only one employed by Black women in similar situations. A woman named Belinda had been enslaved by Isaac Royall Jr., a prominent Bostonian who fled to Nova Scotia during the Revolution, and later settled in England.[20] Belinda petitioned the state of Massachusetts a number of times for a pension out of Royall's estate, and used patriarchal assumptions about protecting dependents to make her case.[21] Yet she also condemned slavery in no uncertain terms, and persisted repeatedly—submitting and resubmitting petitions for years—when the state refused to follow through on its own recognized obligation to Belinda's care and maintenance.

Belinda's first petition contains masterful prose detailing her former life in Africa, the place from which white slave traders had kidnapped her. Belinda's description of her capture and subsequent enslavement paints a vivid picture of the visceral reality of slavery and the slave trade: "She was ravished from the bosom of her Country, from the arms of her friends—while the advanced age of her Parents, rendering them unfit for servitude, cruelly separated her from them forever!"[22] Belinda's petition also noted the inherent irony of the American Revolution. American colonists fought that war—ostensibly, as she noted—"for the preservation of that freedom which the Almighty Father intended for all the human

Race," yet it was the "terror of men armed in the Cause of freedom" that forced Royall to flee Massachusetts. Presenting a critique of those patriarchs who held power over her desperate situation—however veiled it appeared—was certainly a risk.

Belinda endangered her petition again by suggesting that as an enslaved person, she was rightly due a portion of Royall's wealth. "Her frame feebly bending under the oppression of years," Belinda bemoaned that she was "denied the enjoyment of one morsel of that immense wealth, apart whereof hath been accumulated *by her own industry*, and the whole *augmented by her servitude*."[23] Other free white women made similar cases for their worthiness for relief, having provided domestic and productive labor in their households and families that went uncompensated, and for the fruits of that labor to which, under coverture, they had no legal rights. Belinda's case was, of course, distinct; enslavement and *feme covert* status were vastly different legal conditions and lived experiences. Yet they both existed on the continuum of unfreedom to which all women in the revolutionary era were subject.

Not ignorant of the prescriptive behavior required of the state's supplicants, Belinda demonstrated humility at the feet of those powerful patriarchs who constructed laws to reinforce this continuum of unfreedom upon women and people of color alike. Despite her sweeping critiques, Belinda asked for very little from the state. All Belinda requested was an "allowance made . . . out of the estate of Colonel Royall," which would "prevent her and her more infirm daughter from misery in the greatest extreme, and scatter comfort over the short and downward path of their Lives." Royall had provided for such an allowance in his will dated 1778. The House of Representatives resolved and the Senate concurred on February 19, 1783—just five days after Belinda's petition was dated—to provide her with an annual pension out of Royall's confiscated estate of fifteen pounds twelve shillings "for reasons set forth in said Belinda['s] petition."[24]

Notably, Belinda signed this and all subsequent petitions she submitted to the state with an "X"—her mark—indicating her inability to write. She therefore had assistance in crafting this petition, as was the case with numerous other women who submitted pleas to the patriarchal state. Yet this should not diminish the power of Belinda's words, the images constructed in the petition, nor her own involvement in strategically deploying particular language to make her case to the state. Certainly, another friend, family member, or acquaintance of Belinda's would have helped; some scholars suggest that Prince Hall, a notable member of Boston's

free Black community, may have assisted Belinda in crafting the petition.[25] But undoubtedly, this was Belinda's story, a record of her lived
experience, one that provides a window into the experience of enslaved
women in the revolutionary era whose words have been either purposefully erased or silenced by the mechanisms of the patriarchal state and
of historical study.

Was Belinda, in this case, asserting a claim to reparations for her
enslavement, to rights to such dues, or was she instead claiming a legally
sanctioned pension in her intersectionally dependent status? Historian
Margot Minardi speculates that the latter explanation is most likely.[26]
Certainly, Belinda's 1783 petition is replete with forceful language befit-
ting an antislavery position. Yet, Belinda also focused on her own feeble-
ness, her age, and her daughter's sickness—all tokens of dependence
claimed by those who relied on the goodwill and sympathy of patriarchs
in power. And, Belinda's petition can also be interpreted as an insistence that the law be followed—the law that patriarchs constructed to
reinforce their own power. Perhaps, then, the piece of Belinda's petition
that was most convincing and effective for the patriarchal state was not
her forceful condemnation of slavery and the slave trade but instead the
brief two sentences with which she closed her plea, presenting herself as
a dependent in need of protection, support, and care.

It seems rather unlikely, however, that Belinda would have self-
identified in that way. Unlike the hundreds of cases of white women's
petitions analyzed thus far, we can be more certain of Belinda's opinions
of freedom and unfreedom, of independence and dependence, because
of her own experience in and written opinions about slavery. The very
construction of her petition provides evidence of this. Poetic harangues
against the violence, viciousness, and greed of white men who separated
innocent children from their families and unjustly enslaved them for
decades occupied the most space in her petition, and she firmly believed
herself to be owed compensation for decades of bound labor (and
asserted as much in this document). It is clear what her opinions on the
matter were. Yet Belinda also seems to have recognized that she would
not be able to tear down the figurative master's house under the circumstances, and the best she could hope for would be the pension she was
legally owed out of the estate of her late enslaver. Here again was a push
for immediate, individual action, rather than sweeping collective and
institutional change.

Unfortunately, the Massachusetts General Court failed to follow
through on their promise to the beleaguered Belinda. Two years after the

body approved Belinda's annual pension, she submitted another petition, this time requesting back pay for the amount that the legislature had already consented to provide her; she submitted a copy of the original resolve as proof of her complaint.[27] She tried again in 1787, noting that the body had already granted a "Resolve in her favor" and that she was "thro' age & infirmity unable to support herself" and humbly requesting the maintenance that she had already been granted.[28] Another of her petitions that did not pass as an act of the assembly in 1795 indicates that more than a decade after the body's initial approval of her pension, Belinda Sutton had never received any of the compensation legally owed to her.[29]

So, what do we make of Belinda's repeated failed attempts to compel the legislature to abide by their own resolutions? Did they fail to follow through because she was a free Black woman? Did they assume Willis Hall, the executor of Royall's estate, would manage her pensions? Did the economic turmoil of the 1780s prevent them from doling out such pensions, and did they decide that those due to a free Black woman were not a priority? The answer to these questions is unclear. When the General Court failed to pass measures, they frequently did not provide a reason for doing so.[30] Even less clear is the source of disconnect between their assent to the pension and action on her first petition and their failure to follow through on either. In this case, the patriarchal state rhetorically recognized that Belinda's dependence merited her an annual pension, yet failed to provide such protection. In many ways, the patriarchal state's promises and expectations for the care of dependents did not match reality, as many of these women knew all too well.

Absent these few cases, finding evidence of Black women's interactions with the patriarchal state poses particular challenges. Scouring legal records and attempting to uncover the lives of free and enslaved Black women often requires combing through the extant materials detailing the lives of powerful white people (most often, white men) and tracing Black women's relationship to them. When those records do exist, the traditional legal archive exhibits evidence of violence against Black women not only in its content but in its very organization. The extant judicial records for Suffolk County, Massachusetts, provide a case study. The indices and docket books record evidence of numerous revolutionary-era Bostonians being warned out of the city. Warning out often affected the most vulnerable members of society, particularly dependent women and children: those who could not otherwise provide for themselves, and who were often reliant on public support. Unsurprisingly, women of color made up a disproportionate number of these individuals who were warned out of Boston.[31]

This warning-out process likewise further erases Black women from the record. The extant documents that provide evidence of their warning out are often maddeningly vague. A woman named Dido Benson, for example, was told to leave Roxbury, just outside Boston, and go to her previous place of residence, which is unnamed.[32] Benson, however, was at least identified with a surname. In other cases, free people of color were simply listed by their first name and told to leave the city, and the extant documentation leaves no indication of how scholars might trace them in the historical record. These women experienced the dual violence of being banished both from their towns and from the historical record.

By far the most frequent occurrence of a Black woman's presence in the Suffolk County legal archive was in the documentation detailing the inquisition into her death. These coroners' reports appeared on printed forms in which the clerk would fill in blank spaces, identifying the location and date of the report along with the name of the deceased and witnesses. "Phillis, a Negro Woman," for instance, died on August 5, 1770, "By Some Accident." Having slipped from the wharf, she fell into the water and drowned. The witnesses testified that Phillis had been washing her feet at about eleven o'clock when the "Accident" happened.[33] Even less detailed was the record of Sarah's death; the short form indicated that she had died after "accidentally falling into the water & was drowned."[34]

These records display a frustrating lack of effort on the part of officials to truly investigate the deaths of these Black women. Yet another woman, Margarett, died after she "accidentally fell from a wharf in the Town of Boston" and drowned. Those who gave witness to this account claimed that this was the cause of death "as appears to us by the best Evidence we can get."[35] "The loss of stories," Saidiya Hartman writes, "sharpens the hunger for them. So it is tempting to fill in the gaps and to provide closure where there is none. To create a space for mourning where it is prohibited. To fabricate a witness to a death not much noticed."[36] We can deduce little if anything about Margarett's life, about Sarah's, about Phillis's, about the numerous other Black women whose presence in the patriarchal archive occurs only on the occasion of their death, with little else about their lived experiences being evident.

Black women's intersectional dependencies are subject to this very violence—in history, and in the archive. Black women, under law, were in a state of dependence in slavery, and in freedom were subject to sexist and racist restrictions on their behavior in many ways. But evidence of their lives, their own expressions of agency and power, their lived experience, is often predicated on—dependent upon—the lives of powerful patriarchs. Scholars can often garner more substantive evidence and glean more information on Black women's lives in the revolutionary era by examining sources written by the white men who held enormous power over them—the personifications of the patriarchal state. In this way, we as scholars are beholden to and dependent on white patriarchs of the past to understand and draw meaning from the lives of society's most vulnerable people.

Yet hidden within the words of enslavers, deep in the ink that penetrates the parchment, is the otherwise invisible activism of free and enslaved Black women negotiating their own freedom and the freedom of their descendants. Studying Black women's history must go beyond the simple (if heartbreaking) act of recovering the violence they experienced during their lives. Importantly, as Fuentes and Hartman advise, we must also refrain from replicating the violence perpetrated against Black women by their historical experience and by the archive itself.[37] The available sources—those preserved for generations in archives— mimic the patriarchal state's power; they privilege the voices of enslavers; they exist in "an archive structured to erase them."[38] Attuned to this knowledge, we must thus read primary sources in the traditional legal archive from an anti-patriarchal perspective, resist the reconstruction of violence perpetrated against Black women in historical memory, and challenge the power that the traditional archive holds over dispossessed people of the past: a difficult but worthy task.

Redefining Petitioning

The paucity of legislative and judicial petitions penned by enslaved and free Black women in the revolutionary era's traditional archive should not be mistaken as a lack of Black women's activism in their interactions with the patriarchal state. The traditional legal archive prohibits our full understanding of Black women's lived experience and intersectional dependence. In order to get a full and complete record of the ways in which Black women advocated for themselves and their families in their interactions with the patriarchal state, we must reframe our understanding of what constitutes a petition as well as the act of petitioning itself. We must actively seek out an inclusive legal archive that will allow us to recover the voices and agency of Black women, both free and enslaved.

Sources like emancipation deeds, for example, can be seen as evidence of the arduous work of enslaved women's petitioning. The language in manumission deeds was, of course, largely crafted by white enslavers whose rhetoric met legal requirements set by the patriarchal state. But these deeds stand as evidence of enslaved women's persistence, in whatever degree it manifested, in claiming their freedom from bondage.[39] Petitioning, therefore, was not just the act of taking pen to paper, of outlining (with or without assistance) one's plight to a sympathetic body of patriarchs. The act of petitioning—of activism in favor of one's own liberation from enslavement—is hidden between the lines of the deeds and legal documents in which enslavers consented to the freedom earned by formerly enslaved people. Enslaved women's words are largely invisible in the traditional legal archive, but when we broaden our conception of the archive of revolutionary-era petitions, Black women's acts of petitioning are clearly evident.

Free and enslaved Black women's petitioning through manumission deeds demonstrates their subtle and overt forms of resistance to patriarchal authority amid a massive system of oppression. Black women exploited the terms of their intersectional dependencies, but in ways that were distinct from white women's rhetorical strategies. Cate Ollier's plea demonstrates the complex nature of these efforts. In a petition she penned to the Pennsylvania Abolition Society (PAS) in 1809, Ollier recounted a dramatic story in her quest for freedom. Born in St. Domingo, Ollier first came with her father to Philadelphia in 1784, where she "has resided constantly" since that time. Ollier argued that "she was always considered a free person" by "all people of [her father's] and her acquaintance." After her father's death, however, Ollier's status of freedom came into question.

Having recently married a free Black man named Joseph Pine, Ollier moved to New Orleans with her husband "in hopes of enjoying their situation." Her father's widow, however, had other intentions. Ollier held that her late father's wife had "laid a plan for claiming your Petition[er] as her Slave & property & which but for her secret and speedy flight, would have been carried into execution." This plan having failed, Ollier noted that her father's widow—the unnamed woman whom Ollier labeled her "Enemie"—filed a charge against Ollier's husband, who spent "several days in Gaol."[40]

Ollier's petition demonstrates her attempts to seek protection from a variety of patriarchs and patriarchal institutions. Her father, in his lifetime, had protected her from enslavement; her husband, duly employed as a silversmith, promised protection in their "lawful Marriage"—a privilege of free couples. When circumstances prevented both of these men from maintaining Ollier's freedom—her father having passed away and her husband having been jailed—she took it upon herself to seek assistance from the PAS, asking them to legitimate her free status, guaranteed by deed from her father.[41] Ollier explicitly sought to "invoke [the] assistance & protection" of the organization, and inquired of the society as to "whether the Laws of the United States can afford them [Ollier and her husband] sufficient protection for their safe residence at New Orleans."[42]

It seems clear that Ollier knew well what the laws dictated. Earlier in her plea, she noted her "constant" residence in Philadelphia for the majority of her twenty-four years, save for six months that she spent in St. Domingo. Since she had sought out the intervention of the PAS, she obviously knew of the organization's work and its ability to seek enforcement of the laws, as it had done for numerous others. The society's diligent advocacy in favor of the freedom of Black men and women in the revolutionary era and beyond made it an ideal group for Ollier to consult.[43] She recognized the association's penchant for protecting free and enslaved women like her, and framed her plea in such a way as might elicit the sympathies of the group to intervene on her behalf.

Significantly, though, in the very same document Ollier also demonstrated her own capabilities to care for herself. Ollier provided all the evidence the PAS would have needed to protect her; presumably, she had multiple witnesses who could have attested to her long residence in Pennsylvania. She had done the work necessary to advocate for herself to the PAS, in the same way that numerous white women did when they petitioned state legislatures or local judicial bodies. Likewise, she provided evidence that she would not be a financial burden on her community. Ollier offered that "her means of support have been supplied from her Work as a Seamstress" until she was married, and her husband was also gainfully employed.[44] She and Pine had marketable skill sets, and had proven their willingness to work to support themselves and each other.

Many enslaved women's petitions in the form of manumission deeds provide evidence that these women attempted to comply with certain standards of comportment assigned to them by the patriarchal state. A woman named Molly earned her freedom from enslavement from George Young in September 1800, as a "reward," as Young characterized it, "for her faithful and constant attention and services to him during his life."[45] Another enslaved woman named Sarah evidently performed her role as an enslaved woman dutifully, earning her manumission with her "unmerited obedience & fidelity" as well as "her merit and intigrity." Yet John Bull, who enslaved Sarah until her manumission in April 1801, also promised the state of South Carolina that, in order that "she may never become or burthen or expence to the state," he would pay her ten pounds annually, which he extended as a financial obligation to his heirs after he died.[46] The patriarchal state's fear of dependents—particularly women and, in this case, free Black women—becoming financially reliant on the public dole was very real, and petitioners across the spectrum of dependence sought to prove their self-reliance in their pleas for aid.

These acts of petitioning show evidence of some enslaved women doing just that: demonstrating that they would be capable of providing for themselves if manumitted.[47] The state of South Carolina altered the process and requirements for emancipating enslaved people in 1800, requiring a certain measure of security guaranteeing that newly freed people would not become a burden on the patriarchal state's financial coffers.[48] Diana, a woman enslaved by Samuel Theus, labored as a nurse. She earned her freedom, along with the freedom of her six children, through the payment of ten shillings to Theus, and the signed testimony of two men in the community. These men testified that they had been provided with "Satisfactory proof," presumably by Diana herself, that she was "not of bad Character" and that she was "capable of gaining a lively hood for herself and said Children by honest men" (remarking, too, on the respectability of Diana's sexual history). Diana, being "by profession" a nurse, had learned and mastered a skill to the degree that she would, according to these men, be able to provide for herself and six children—certainly no small feat.[49]

We do not hear Diana speak directly for herself in this source. She did not pen these words on her own, nor was she even permitted to leave her mark, the sign of an illiterate person advocating for themselves and assenting to the terms of the agreement in these legal documents. But that does not mean that we cannot observe Diana's activism in the implicit content of the source. She learned a trade; she mastered that trade; she paid for her own freedom and the freedom of her six children; and she proved to several local, patriarchal authorities that she would not need their help to survive in freedom. By reading between the lines, we can witness Diana's drive, her motherly devotion, and her hard work to guarantee the freedom of her children and subsequent generations of her family. She labored assiduously to meet the standards for freedom of Black women set by the patriarchal state.

Interdependent Unions

The traditional legal archive provides a clear record of the ways in which Black women faced significant obstacles to freedom and independence relative to white women. Despite this, Black men and women often came together to resist the oppression of the patriarchal state. Free and enslaved Black spouses employed the ideals and expectations of the marriage contract (even in cases in which their marriage was not recognized under law) to claim legal protections, and in some instances, to claim their freedom as well.[50] Certain gendered expectations of comportment and marital duties were common in the revolutionary era regardless of spouses' racial identities, yet obviously slavery and the power of the enslaver complicated those roles.[51] Regardless of the marital limitations imposed upon them by the patriarchal state, Black men and women exploited contemporary gendered tropes of marriage in their quests for freedom. In interactions with the patriarchal state, Black marital unions served as an equalizing force in which Black women and men cited their mutual love and obligation to each other in their petitions for freedom.

The common law custom of coverture along with Anglo-American expectations of masculinity and femininity were only meant to apply to elite and middling white men and women, yet Black men and women still performed gendered marital roles, even in slavery or in their unequal status.[52] Black men, for example, often fulfilled the expectations of masculine protector and provider, if not in the precise way that elite white men did.[53] Black husbands who provided the monetary sum needed to manumit their wives, in effect, fulfilled both of those roles. John Mills gave Jonas Phillips 130 pounds in exchange for the freedom of Mills's wife, Phillis.[54] One hundred and thirty pounds was a substantial sum, and it would have taken significant labor to accrue such an amount. Mills proved himself capable of earning a living for himself and providing an adequate maintenance for his wife, thereby playing the ultimate role of protector in providing the funds necessary to rescue her from bondage.

It is clear from manumission deeds that love and spousal devotion motivated free and enslaved Black men to purchase their wives' freedom. Archibald Davis, for example, wrote that because of the "great Love I bear to Phebe late Phebe Thompson (my Wife) . . . I hereby declare her altogether a free woman."[55] A man named Neo purchased the freedom of his wife, Dinah, for the sum of five shillings (which likely indicates either a degree of empathy on the part of Thomas Irwin, Dinah's enslaver, or some other arrangement between Irwin and Neo).[56] Sampson Williams purchased the indenture of his wife, Phillis, and immediately released her from it.[57] Most remarkably, a man named Andrew sacrificed his own freedom for that of his wife; he negotiated her release from indenture by offering up himself in bound labor instead.[58] Arguably, enslaved or free Black men in some cases performed the role of loving husband better than the white male ideal professed was possible. The love and devotion required to amass an often substantial sum of money for the purchase of one's spouse's freedom, especially given the additional barriers of systemic racism—and in some cases, slavery—were exceptional.

These efforts at spousal protection occasionally saw Black men suing white patriarchs in court. In one particularly egregious instance, Philip Lairy brought suit against William Hollingshead, who unlawfully enslaved Lairy's wife. The court served two writs against Hollingshead in mid-September of 1792, alleging that Hollingshead owed Lairy thirty-nine pounds Pennsylvania money *and* that he had been unlawfully enslaving Lairy's wife, Ann, for years. The Lairys had been married for four years at the time when Philip brought suit against Hollingshead. Lairy contended that Ann was "born a free Woman," though Lairy had been told otherwise until recently. A few weeks after the suit, William Hollingshead issued a deed of manumission, and thanks to the efforts of her husband, Philip, Ann was able to seize her freedom from Hollingshead's clutches.[59]

The structures of the patriarchal state and its deeply embedded systemic racism dictated the terms by which enslaved and free Black men could go about protecting their wives and children. Abraham Willing arranged for the purchase of his wife, Dinah, and their son, Abraham, in 1784, presumably to free them. The language of the deed of purchase—written by Dinah and the younger Abraham's enslaver, Christopher Elliott—is revealing. Upon purchasing Dinah and the couple's son from Elliott, Abraham Willing was "to have and to hold the said Negro woman and child unto him the said Abraham Willing his Executors and assigns forever."[60] Willing, naturally, would free his family members from slavery, but before he could do that, he owned them in accordance with the law as Elliott had done before him. In this way, white enslavers dictated the terms through which Black men could protect and free their own wives.[61]

Free and enslaved Black Americans exploited whatever mechanisms of the patriarchal state they could both to preserve their marital unions and to seek freedom.[62] One curious case lays bare the great lengths to which these men and women had to go to achieve these goals. Boston's sheriff arrested a woman identified as "Peggy, a negro" in February 1782. He brought her to jail after neither she nor her husband paid "security" for the writ of habeas corpus filed against her and one unnamed other (later identified as Peg's husband, Roger).[63] Additional documents reveal that a man named Thomas Walker had filed suit against the couple. Walker submitted a petition to the Court of Common Pleas, demanding that authorities "attach the goods or Estate of Roger"—who was identified as a "negro man" and a "Labourer"—the value of such property being appraised at five hundred pounds. If the property could not be secured, Walker insisted, local officials should "take the body of the said Roger & peg" and hold them until the matter could be settled by the local judiciary. The crime Walker alleged Roger and Peg to have committed was trespass.[64]

In his petition to the court, Walker detailed his relationship with the couple, which began in March of 1771. Walker had been traveling in Montreal, Quebec, where "a discussion was had between" Walker, Roger, and Peg. Walker soon learned that a man named Jacob Thomas, a "negro Jockey," intended to perpetrate, as Roger told Walker, "the greatest evil that could befall them": Thomas intended to separate Roger and Peg from each other, to sell Peg to a man "who had refused to purchas[e]" Roger as well, a common moral crime that only compounded the horrors of chattel slavery and occurred all too frequently in American history.[65]

The language that follows, in Roger's voice via Walker's reiteration of the story, is significant. "To be parted from each other" would mean that the two would be "deprived of all the comfort & enjoyments of the married State."[66] If we assume that this language was a reflection of Roger's own sentiments as remembered by Walker, it tells us that Roger and Peg clearly understood marital tropes of gendered comportment, or of the social expectations of husbands and wives. The petition continues by identifying Peg as a "loving & obedient wife" who would suffer "great grief loss & damage" when "separated for ever" from her husband. Isolating this language from the context of Roger and Peg's potential or continued enslavement, we see a familiar strategy: the loving and obedient wife would suffer immense damage in the absence of her husband or a lack of intervention by patriarchal authorities. Yet we might also reasonably assume that Walker independently employed such language himself. In his suit, Walker may have wanted to present himself as a benevolent enslaver, the kind of sympathetic patriarch to whom numerous women petitioned for redress in the revolutionary era. Doing so would reinforce his own power along the stratified spectrum of independence and dependence by elevating him to the role of benevolent patriarch.

Whether the petition's rhetoric belonged to Roger and Peg or to Walker, the narrative frames Roger and Peg's marriage as a way to convince Walker—a patriarchal authority to whom they pled for assistance—to protect them from Thomas's actions. In this retelling, the two beseeched Walker to purchase both of them, which he did, for 131 pounds. Roger, Peg, and Walker then struck a deal of sorts. Roger and Peg would labor for Walker and his wife, Martha, "for twenty years without any elopement or refusal whatsoever," and any children that Roger and Peg might have would also be enslaved to the Walkers, but freed upon reaching adulthood (at twenty-one years for any male children and eighteen for any female children). The bargain struck among members of the group, however, was striking. In exchange for decades of Peg's, Roger's, and their potential children's contracted labor, Walker promised to "give them reasonable Liberty & find them good & Comfortable meat drink washing lodging & Cloathing & take due care of them both in sickness & in health & would take due care of their offsprings should they have any & give them the said offsprings or Children all the good & wholesome Instructions that should be necessary to make them good & capable house Servants feed & Cloth them & take care of them also in Sickness & in health."[67] This language, of course, mirrors that found in marital vows. Walker agreed to provide the family with food, clothing, and shelter; he would care for Peg, Roger, and their children "in sickness & in health." In exchange, Roger, Peg, and their children "would truly & faithfully serve" the Walkers.[68] The enslaved family offered labor, obedience, and submission in exchange for care and protection, reflective of the mutual duties of husband and wife, of uneven and unequal dependencies in marriage. In this case, however, it was the enslaved family who were subordinates of the enslaver, rather than a wife who was a subordinate to her husband. Roger and Peg were truly operating as one, unified entity in this arrangement.

The group having agreed to these terms, Walker brought Roger and Peg to Boston. In his petition, Walker suggested that he complied with his end of the bargain. Here, Walker's language mirrors that in divorce petitions, emphasizing the contractual nature of the relationship: "Thomas Walker further saith & avers that he hath fully & truly performed his said promis to the said Roger & his wife Peg." He then detailed the list of obligations he owed to the couple under the terms to which they had agreed before leaving Montreal, including providing the same for their

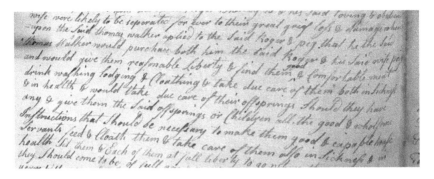

FIGURE 6.2. Thomas Walker's promises to Peg and Roger in their enslavement echo the language in marital vows. Source: Petition of Thomas Walker to Court of Common Pleas, 1 January 1782, #102787, *Suffolk Files Collection*, Supreme Judicial Court, Judicial Archives, Massachusetts Archives, Boston, Massachusetts.

only child, a girl named Kate. Yet, Walker asserted, Roger and Peg "not regarding the said promis," instead "defraud[ed]" Walker. They had absconded between September 19, 1776, and May 19, 1781, a period of "four years & eight months," as calculated by Walker. Apparently having returned to Boston for a few months, the family then left, again, in December 1781. After their second absconding, Walker filed suit with the court because Peg and Roger "now refuse to return to their duty & service" and thus, he claimed, owed him "thirteen years ten months & twenty one days" of bound labor.[69]

The remaining extant documentation details little about how the situation was resolved. As we already know, Peg was arrested and held in jail. The sargent judge of the Suffolk County Court of Common Pleas sent notice to the jail to bring Peg to court on the third Tuesday of February, 1782.[70] The jailer complied, bringing her to the court on February 20.[71] The last document contained in this file, however, is a note of discharge, simply stating, "Habeas Corpus for Peg In Supreme Judicial Court Suffolk Feby Term 1782 Peg within named Discharged in Court." There is no record of any case involving Peg, Roger, and Walker ever making it to the docket for this term.

The judge overseeing cases at that time was a man named William Cushing. Cushing is well known to early American historians as the judge whose 1781 decision in *Brom and Bett v. Ashley* and 1783 decisions in *Walker v. Jennison* and *Commonwealth v. Jennison* effectively ended legal slavery in the state of Massachusetts.[72] William Cushing served as the Supreme Judicial Court's chief justice for all of these momentous cases, and likewise served in the same position when Peg and Roger's case would have come before the court. Could it be that Cushing, having already decided in favor of an enslaved woman named Mum Bett who brought a freedom suit to the court in 1781, knew that Thomas Walker's suit was moot after his ruling? Or was there simply not enough evidence to try the case? The record is maddeningly quiet on these points, despite an assiduous search for any conclusion.[73]

Regardless of the inability to be certain of the way in which this case was resolved, several things are clear. Roger and Peg went to great lengths to earn their freedom, first negotiating with Walker to avoid being separated from each other, and then absconding on two occasions from Walker himself. Notably, while the patriarchal state did not recognize the legitimacy of enslaved marriages, this extensive file does just that. The language of marital obligations figures heavily in this series of documents, too, though not in the traditional sense. Roger and Peg were presented as one unit in their marriage, and as the submissive entity in the patriarch/dependent relationship. Both Roger and Peg were dependents in this scenario; dependence was not only gendered but also racialized. But, they were dependents *together*. Roger and Peg's freedom emerged not from their intersectional mutual dependence on the state but rather from their dependence on each other.

Freedom as a Matrilineal Inheritance

The legal system that patriarchs constructed to retain their power and wealth through generations was built upon the exploitation of Black women's bodies. The colonial American doctrine of *partus sequitur ventrum* dictated that a child's status of freedom or enslavement would follow that of their mother. This was, of course, a race-specific departure from patrilineality in English common law, which applied to white Britons. Patriarchs intended this deviation from precedent to increase their wealth, their power, and their property in enslaved people, in addition to providing legal sanction for them to abuse enslaved Black women while profiting from the bound labor of their own progeny. This monumental legal choice—intentionally implemented by white men hellbent on retaining power and subjugating enslaved Africans and their descendants—has shaped American race relations from the colonial period through to the present day.[74]

Black women's reproductive capacity thus figured prominently in their quests for freedom. In negotiating for her freedom from enslavement, a woman named Teeny assented to work for her former enslaver, William McMurtrie, for a period of ten years. Included "under the following conductions expressly agreed to by herself" was one clause in particular that stood out from the language of many similar deeds of indenture. Teeny agreed, per the document, "that she will behave herself diligently as a servant; Sober & Honest, and that *she shall have no more children*; on failure of those conditions this agreement to be void."[75] Teeny's tenuous freedom was contingent on her consent to refrain from bearing children.[76] Importantly, an enslaver would not have compelled an enslaved woman in his household to agree to such a stipulation; on the contrary, Teeny's reproductive capacity as an enslaved woman could only enhance an enslaver's wealth and power. Yet in freedom—a relative, tenuous freedom in her status as an indentured servant—Teeny's potential children would only be a burden on McMurtrie's finances, as he would not legally be able to enslave them. Teeny thus assented to McMurtrie's control over her reproductive capacity in exchange for a marginal degree of freedom.

Like Black men who performed the role of masculine protector through the purchase of their wives' and children's freedom, Black women also performed the consummate feminine role in seizing freedom for their children: that of mother. Black women who were able to purchase their children's freedom, for example, did so as an extension of motherly love and devotion. Freedwomen who purchased and subsequently manumitted their children detailed the express power of love as a motivating factor for their emancipatory efforts. Abigail Lee freed her daughter "in Consideration of the Natural Love and affection" she felt for Rosetta.[77] A mother's love was a central component of the networks and alliances women built in the revolutionary era, and racial difference did not diminish the significance of this woman-centric advocacy.

Black mothers' activism in intervening to free their children occasionally manifested in courtroom battles. A woman named Marcie sued Maria Anne Collier Ferqueau to claim freedom for herself and her two children. Four witnesses testified on their behalf, providing evidence that Ferqueau had brought Marcie and her children from the West Indies to Philadelphia in March of 1795, and had stayed until October—beyond the six-month window that mandated formerly enslaved people be freed.[78] The final hearings of the case took place precisely ten years to the day after Marcie and her children set foot in Philadelphia for the first time, though under the law they had been free nine and a half years prior. The judge in the case decreed that Marcie and her children were thus "no Slaves agreeable to the Laws of this State."[79]

These records sometimes provided direct evidence of an enslaved woman's intervention in facilitating her children's freedom. A twenty-five-year-old woman named Lise earned her freedom along with that of her three daughters: Eugiene (also known as Jenney, seven years old), Babet (five years old), and Claudien (three years old). The family's former enslaver, Anthony Peter Provenchere, expressly wrote that his consideration of Lise's and her daughters' manumission was, in part, in exchange for "the faithful services rendered me by the said Lise."[80] Likewise, Marinette accumulated the sum of 130 silver US dollars to facilitate the purchase of her own freedom and that of her young son, Alcindor.[81] Importantly, mothers' purchase of their children reveals a paradox, simultaneously necessitating their recognition of an enslaver's legal ownership of their own children while also working from within the confines of the law constructed by the patriarchal state to free their children from bondage, and in turn, resist its strictures.

While acknowledging that the patriarchal state used Black women's reproductive capacity to enslave a race of people in perpetuity, we must also be attentive to the ways in which freedom was conversely embodied in Black women. Their bodies literally birthed their children, and by extension, their descendants, into a status of perpetual freedom or servitude.[82] In seeking to prove the free status of her son, Richard, for example, Margaret Gough first testified that she herself was born of a free white woman (a Mrs. Esther Wrand), and swore to the fact that Richard was "begotten on her [Margaret's] body," which thus granted him the status of freedom under the law.[83] In the deed of manumission freeing a woman named Eunice from enslavement by Thomas Elliott, the latter noted specifically that he guaranteed legal freedom both for Eunice and for any "future Issue of her body."[84] Certainly, the knowledge that by virtue of their gender, their reproductive capacity, and their status of enslavement, Black women could bring their progeny into eternal bondage was unbearable. Their ability to bestow freedom on scores of African Americans through their bodies, however, could be empowering. And a number of women seized on that power.

Women passed on knowledge of their embodied freedom to generations of their descendants, particularly their daughters.[85] In 1793, Rachel Williams appeared before the Philadelphia alderman with her two daughters, Rachel and Charlotte Williams, to certify proof of their freedom. Rachel the daughter sought to legally record the freedom of her own daughter, Mary. Mary had recently married "a french Man named—Anthony," and brought with her proof of the union from Kent County, Maryland. The elder Rachel confirmed that Mary Anthony "is her Grand Daughter," and thus was "a free Woman, her Mother Rachel having been manumitted as aforesaid." The certificate required that "all Persons" recognize this freedom, and be "forwarn[ed]" against "illegally molesting the said Mary, as they will be dealt with as the Law directs."[86] It seems clear that the women of the Williams family sought to create a paper trail of their inherited freedom; in this case, one could reasonably assume that in this instance, Rachel, Rachel, and Mary also instigated this action to protect the future children that Mary and her husband wished to be born in freedom. These women worked together to ensure the future freedom of all of their descendants.

Just as white women exploited the terms of their varied dependencies, free Black women also turned the patriarchal framework of the law on its head. They ensured their own freedom in a society that saw their race as a mark of inferiority and a justification for enslavement, turning the confines of the law—*partus sequitur ventrum*—into an instrument guaranteeing freedom for generations to come. This was a power that neither Black nor white men had. Such a power is confirmed in a deed certifying the status of freedom of Hannah, John, and James, the children of Dolly Owens. Enslaver John Gordon testified that Owens was herself "a free Black person . . . who I employed as a domestic." Hannah, John, and James were born of the relationship between Owens and Cyrus, an enslaved man "belonging to" Gordon.[87] It was thus Owens's status of freedom—not the children's father's status of enslavement—that defined their own legal identities, and thus it was Owens's body that literally guaranteed their freedom.

Owens's advocacy for her children is largely invisible in the explicit language of this legal document, though certainly she would have pressed Gordon to attest to her own freedom and therefore her children's. She must have done so vehemently, too; all three children were born on Gordon's estate (according to his own testimony), and Gordon still claimed ownership over the person and labor of Cyrus, the children's father. He would have significant financial reason to ignore Hannah's, John's, and James's status of freedom. Yet the fact that he testified on their behalf speaks to the lengths to which Owens must have gone to secure her children's future, and of the power she possessed by virtue of her own status of freedom to bequeath to them the same.

For decades, scholars of women in the American Revolution have elucidated the central role of motherhood for white women, in terms of both their gender identity and their role as citizens in the new republic. Republican mothers were tasked with passing on the values of republicanism to their sons—who were the nascent nation's future leaders—and to their daughters—who would, like their mothers, pass on these values to their children.[88] Yet a focus on these assumptions of elite white women's domestic and maternal contributions to American nation building obscures the significant role of free and enslaved Black mothers in the revolutionary era and limits conversations about the meaning and legacy of American independence.[89] As evidenced by their tireless efforts to seek freedom for their children, and their embodied capacity to pass freedom on to their children if they themselves escaped enslavement, Black women were the truest arbiters of the values purported to be expressed by white, republican mothers.[90]

Importantly, too, republican mothers were not a threat to the patriarchal state. By contrast, Black mothers fighting for the freedom of their children were. In assuming the mantles of freedom and independence, the ostensible values of the Revolution, Black women taught to, passed on to, and imbued these values in their children. Numerous scholars have noted the ways in which Black Americans—free and enslaved—heard or read, understood, and imbibed the rhetoric of the Revolution, and in many cases, waged their own wars against enslavement.[91] Notably, free Black mothers could do more than just pass along an intellectual understanding of the true value of freedom to their children; they could pass along legal freedom from bondage, and a protection from enslavement for their descendants born of the maternal line.

I do not want to diminish and thus must acknowledge the abject difficulty of Black women succeeding under these circumstances. Freedom proved exceptionally elusive, particularly for enslaved mothers, and millions remained in bondage while a relatively small percentage of women, like those cited in this chapter, earned their freedom for themselves and/ or their descendants. Even in cases where mothers did earn freedom for their children, that freedom was never guaranteed so long as the institution of slavery was still legal in the United States. Regardless of the relative paucity of this experience, it is central to understanding the power of these women's actions, their defense of and devotion to their children, and the ways in which they were paragons of motherhood and of the Revolution's most central ideals of freedom and independence. The values of the American Revolution were, in most cases, sheerly aspirational for all but those already in power, namely, white men of means. But what Black mothers did in these cases was to enact these aspirational values and the principles of the nation in a truer way than any "founder" or "framer" whose actions have inspired infinite hagiographical treatments and whose portraits adorn the halls of power to this day.[92]

Notably, however, their efforts present a paradox. Certainly, the freedom that Black mothers bestowed upon and bequeathed to their children in these cases was remarkable, and has been wisely interpreted by scholars as a form of resistance.[93] They claimed their humanity as mothers—a humanity otherwise denied them under chattel slavery and the white-supremacist legal structure. They rejected their ostensible "social death" imposed upon them by the law.[94] They shaped and redefined the meaning of freedom for themselves and their progeny on their own terms.[95] They made "self-conscious choices" in making claims to freedom.[96]

But at the same time, their petitioning, their practicing and enactment of manumission for themselves, their spouses, and their children was done within the patriarchal structure. Black mothers recognized the (albeit slight) opportunities within the terms of *partus sequitur ventrem* to free their children and their descendants; these actions run parallel to those rhetorical strategies adopted by white women who engaged and exploited the terms of their dependence in their quests for aid and intervention from the patriarchal state. Black mothers abided by the offensive, degrading, and discriminatory terms of the patriarchal state because they *had* to. If they wanted to free their children through legal means, they were required to assent to the terms set forth by the patriarchal state. They *had* to at least tacitly acknowledge that their children were legal property in order to liberate them from that status under law. And ultimately, it is a marvel that in these cases, they succeeded. Even in working with the terms of racist, patriarchal laws that commodified their bodies and lives—and those of their children—they fought back against and undermined this very system.

* * *

Black women's intersectional experience of dependence was dictated by expectations of gender and race foisted upon them by the social, economic, and legal infrastructures constructed and perpetuated by the patriarchal state. The traditional legal archive is a trail of violence perpetrated against the bodies, lives, and historical memory of Black women. Traditional modes of exchange with the patriarchal state—petitions and court filings, for example—were limited and in certain cases prohibited for Black women. Free and enslaved Black women, therefore, had to find alternative means of petitioning the overbearing power of the patriarchal state. This labor is often invisible in the explicit words of the traditional legal archive, but visible when scholars consider the evidence of Black women's activism in legal sources drafted by white men. Likewise, Black men and women worked in tandem, through their marital unions, to undermine the authority of the patriarchal state and seize their freedom together.

In some cases, the result of formerly enslaved Black women's work of petitioning was to break the literal and metaphorical chains of that patriarchal institution. They worked in tandem with their husbands to secure their freedom for themselves and future generations of their family. Whether they used their reproductive capacity to earn freedom for their children or advocated for themselves and their family members in emancipation efforts, formerly enslaved women who earned their legal freedom and fought for the freedom of others explicitly used the constraints of the patriarchal structure to break free from them. Like their white counterparts, Black women paradoxically exploited the legal structure meant to keep generations of African Americans enslaved instead to guarantee the freedom of their descendants. In so doing, they were among the truest advocates of American freedom in the revolutionary era.

7 /   The Rights Revolution

The war was over, at least on paper. Powerful men from Britain and the newly independent United States made it so by inscribing their names on parchment in September of 1783. The Treaty of Paris established peace between these lately fledgling colonists and their former king, a man previously revered and beloved in his role of protector of his subjects.[1] The agreement solidified the words Jefferson had etched into parchment seven years prior, and legitimated American independence.

The war was over on paper, but in many ways, and for many Americans, it continued to occupy their lives. Like others at the margins of society, white women bore a disproportionate burden of the war's consequences. For these women, the war—*their* revolution—continued. They took to paper, penning petitions to patriarchal legislators, in defense of their families, their property, and themselves. The upheavals of war created the circumstances by which women were compelled to demand aid, assistance, and protection from the state. Because of the war and the brutality it wrought, women petitioned their legislators in increasing numbers. The Revolutionary War tore apart their lives, so they took to paper in an attempt to piece them back together. This significant, in some cases exponential, increase in the number of petitions women submitted from the revolutionary period onward demonstrates that the war and its consequences ultimately politicized women.[2] Women themselves believed they were entitled to certain rights and protections under the legal structures of the patriarchal state. To be clear, these rights were not new; what *was* new was women's individualized activism in claiming them, in seeking out aid from the state due to them under law.

The increase both in petitions and in the politicization of women was not the only consequences of the war for women. The language, the very words that women chose to commit to paper, began to change as well. During the later years of the imperial crisis and throughout the war and its aftermath, women began to ground their petitions in the language of rights, particularly in their suits seeking divorce. No different from any other American colonist who lived through the conflict, white women absorbed the language of rights that saturated so many conversations in their homes, in the streets, and, of course, on paper.[3] Despite the ways in which the Constitution's framers had formally excluded many from the rights of full citizenship, these women internalized the American Revolution on their own terms, and asserted their rights on paper.

The dictates of the patriarchal state governed the ways in which women exercised and claimed these rights. The war compelled Americans to process the implications of the "unalienable" rights that they had so vehemently championed during the conflict. Ostensibly inherent to all humans, natural rights threatened to disrupt the clear social hierarchy and the power and authority of white male property owners in the new republic. Some white women and free and enslaved Black Americans seized upon the language of the Revolution and insisted upon a vision of universal equality that included them, and undermined the social, legal, and economic foundations of the American patriarchy.[4] Some rights of Black Americans would be legitimated in northern states, which abolished the institution of slavery either outright or at a gradual rate.[5]

Women's rights were slow to expand over the course of American history, and in this period, seemed to stagnate on the basis of an Enlightenment vision of the natural differences between men and women. Both men and women possessed certain rights, but rather than being equal, they were, instead, "parallel." Women's rights were benefits, "expressed in the performance of duties to society." A woman drew her rights from her role as a wife and mother.[6] These duties, however, came with benefits: men, too, owed certain obligations to their wives.[7] Although the stubbornly entrenched patriarchal system kept women from attaining full political rights in the wake of the Revolution, the emergence of "rights talk" had a powerful, and perhaps broader effect on the types of rights women claimed, and how they actively claimed them.[8] White women firmly demanded the rights and entitlements that were central to their legal, social, and economic statuses as dependents. If women fulfilled

FIGURE 7.1. Rate of divorces filed by women in Boston. See "A Note on Sources" for an explanation of the limitations of the data.

FIGURE 7.2. Rate of divorces filed by women in Philadelphia. See "A Note on Sources" for an explanation of the limitations of the data.

their roles as submissive and subordinate wives, mothers, daughters, and good female citizens of the new republic, they could, in turn, claim a right to certain protections and benefits from their spouses, sons, and fathers.[9] In asserting these rights, women laid claim to certain entitlements, such as widows' pensions, the legal capacity to own and sell property, and even divorces and alimony.[10] They did so in increasing numbers during and after the Revolution, often armed with a new sense of themselves as rights-bearing individuals.

Studies of the political rights of women during and after the American Revolution have, for the most part, been focused on answering questions that cannot illuminate the most complete picture of women's rights in this period: Did the Revolution benefit women? Did the Revolution change the status of women? If so, how? If not, why?[11] These questions are grounded in a masculine interpretation of the Revolution, a normative version engraved in textbooks and a triumphalist narrative serving the interests of American exceptionalism. In order to understand the impact of the Revolution on women's lives, we should question the ways in which they internalized its meaning and made it their own. Doing so requires taking a fresh perspective on what constitutes women's rights, and paying closer attention to women's own perception of their rights distinct from our own contemporary vision. Analyzing the period this way ensures that we see the picture of women's rights more fully, on women's own terms, and in their own words.

"Entitled to Be Provided for by Law"

The Revolutionary War created the circumstances that compelled women, most of them out of necessity, to petition the state for various forms of assistance. Many women regurgitated the language of female dependence, but the Revolution shifted women's views and understanding of their rights. Likewise, the politics of the conflict figured prominently in women's petitions. Some women, for instance, sought property, compensation, the right to dower, and other forms of relief by making distinctions between their own political views and those of their husbands, asserting themselves as independent political actors despite the enduring confines of coverture. Women had to be cautious in their demands for rights, though, as asserting a political opinion apart from their husbands' could unravel the very fabric of coverture and thus, one of the structures holding the patriarchal state in place. Choosing their language carefully, women separated themselves politically from their husbands, or demonstrated their own performance of female patriotism, while still using the language of dependence in their claims for rights. These women, in effect, balanced the notion of women's rights with their status as the dependents of men.

Nearly thirty years after the passage of South Carolina's Confiscation Act, for example, Ann Valk petitioned for a portion of her late husband's property in an assertion of her dower rights. Ann claimed that, as a result of the 1782 law, her husband Jacob's property had been confiscated, and a portion of it had been bought by others. In 1811, when Ann finally submitted her petition, a house and plot of land still remained unsold, "and now remain as Part of the Estate of the said Jacob Valk deceased." Petitioning on behalf of herself, her child, and her grandchild—a long line of dependents—Ann pled for the General Assembly to nullify the law in her particular case, and vest the remaining property in her name. She highlighted her condition as a "helpless widow depending on her son for Support," while also being "wholly deprived of her dower" as a result of the Confiscation Act.[12]

Significantly, Ann expressly made a distinction between her husband's property rights and her own. Not squandering any ink in defense of her husband's politics or in questioning the justice of the state's confiscation of his share of the property, Ann instead petitioned only for a part of the estate, which she was owed as Jacob's widow—her dower portions. This right—her right as a dependent widow and wife—was clearly separate from her husband's claim (and therefore, forced forfeiture) on the property. Ann never once made any distinct political statements in her petition, yet the implication of her tone was clear: while her husband erred, she did not. Jacob's property could justly be confiscated by the state, but her portion could not. Despite her late husband's political missteps, Ann Valk declared her right to this property: a right necessarily separate from Jacob's, yet ironically steeped in her dependence on him. Her role as Jacob's wife remained steady. Astutely judging the expectations of her audience, Ann's silences in political matters indicate that she wished herself to be perceived by the state as an apolitical being.

The state seemed, at least on occasion, to be a more sympathetic patriarch than women presumed it to be, conferring property rights on women who appeared to be victims of their husbands' politics. Freelove Scott, whose husband's loyalist sympathies compelled Massachusetts authorities to confiscate his property, petitioned the legislature for a sum of money that could provide her with adequate means to support her family in her husband's absence (he absconded from the state as a result of the changing political tides). In her petition, she emphasized the "helpless" situation in which she found herself "distressed," with five children for whom she was responsible. "Only" having received 150 pounds from the Committee of Sequestration, Scott had no hope of maintaining her family. Notably, Scott also differentiated her own politics from those of her husband. In lieu of falling further into debt and destitution, Scott demanded relief from the body so that she might avoid being reduced to extreme want.[13]

The Massachusetts state legislature, however, interpreted Scott's petition much more broadly, perhaps, than she had originally intended.[14]

In her case, the state viewed Scott as a dependent woman, but a rights-bearing dependent woman whose politics, separate from those of her husband, warranted her separate consideration.[15] While she originally sought a stopgap measure to overcome her family's financial hardships, the state granted Scott one-third of her husband's estate, thereby effectively guaranteeing her dower rights while her husband was still alive.[16] Significantly, too, the legislature used this moment as an opportunity to set a precedent for future politically abandoned wives in similar situations. They authorized the Committee of Sequestration "to settle in like manner with any other of the s[ai]d Absentees Wives." In equating Joseph Scott's desertion with death, in these instances, the Massachusetts state legislature empowered wives of absentee husbands to invoke their right of dower in order to support themselves, and often their children, by becoming independent property owners.

While on the surface, it may seem that the patriarchal state was pre-emptively extending benefits and property rights to some of its most vulnerable citizens, in all likelihood it did so to protect itself, with the intention of avoiding having these women depend on the state for assistance.[17] Scott's case certainly demonstrates the state's willingness to extend the benefits of its paternalist sympathies to those they viewed as the worthiest objects. She presented her best case, working within the framework that governed women's comportment, and in effect, her petition provided protections for other women living through similar conditions and consequences of war. But the state also clumsily showed its hand here; officials had no intention of fixing the catastrophic financial circumstances clearly wrought by the patriarchal state and the conventions of coverture. Instead, they were keen to institute provisional and spontaneous assistance on an individualized basis, rather than address the systemic problems underlying Scott's and other women's lives. In so doing, these legislatures solved Scott's immediate problems, and while her property rights were protected, ultimately, the powers of these patriarchs remained fully secured.

While many women demonstrated humility, submissiveness, and deference to authority in their petitions, others took a much bolder, more assertive approach, demanding, rather than requesting, their right to their banished husbands' property. Those who found success wrapped these demands in the trappings of feminine dependence. Isabella Kingsley's petition, though brief, is illustrative of such attempts. Kingsley, like other women, complained of "being deprived of her Husbands Estate," after he was banished from the state of South Carolina in the wake of the war. Isabella only weakly requested her husband's return and instead expended more energy in emphasizing her need for the return of Zephaniah's estate in order to care for her "helpless innocent family" and prevent them from succumbing "to misery and want." Never trying to deny her husband's problematic political attachments, Isabella instead pleaded for the state to consider the plight of her children, "who are most of them natives of this Country and Citizens of the State." Most significantly, Isabella boldly proclaimed herself "entitled" to the "patronage and protection" of the newly formed government. Not only did Isabella Kingsley stress the dependence of herself and her children on the return of her husband's property, but she "humbly" demanded—if such a thing was possible—that the state of South Carolina give her *both* Zephaniah's estate and government support.[18]

Like Isabella Kingsley, those who attempted to exercise property rights sometimes resorted to using their maternal roles to persuade the state of the worthiness of their situation. They used their children as objects of sympathy and their roles as devoted mothers to convince the court that their claims to rights and entitlements were valid. Judith Scott's late father bequeathed her an estate in his will, yet Scott and her husband copetitioned the state of Massachusetts to allow her to sell the land, specifically for Judith's benefit and that of her infant son, Peter. Although Judith's husband, John, signed the petition along with his wife, he was identified nowhere else in the document, and the two framed the plea from Judith's point of view. The petition claimed that the house on the land had been destroyed by a fire, so selling the remaining brick walls along with the land would bring a greater profit than retaining the land herself (held, of course, by her husband). Judith's primary argument asserted that the income garnered from the sale of the land "would be a support to the said Mrs. Scott during her life, agreeable to the intention of her dec[ease]d Father."

Interestingly, nowhere in Judith's petition did she mention her husband's inability to care for her as a reason for her need of this support; instead, she insisted that it was her father's intention that she receive the support from his estate.[19] Likewise, Judith implied that the sale of the property would benefit her young son, by proxy. It was only with her husband's signature that she was able to declare her intentions to convey her late father's estate, demonstrating that women's right to property in these cases was often contingent upon their husbands' consent, even if receipt of the property was for the benefit of her child and in accordance with the wishes of her father.[20]

Elizabeth Freeman, however, did use her husband's lack of support as the central argument to assert her right to convey property for the benefit of her children. Elizabeth's husband, Isaac, left Boston about five years prior to her petition, "& hath not since been heard of." In the span of these five years, she had been left to care for, support, and educate five children "without adequate means to do it, of which her husband, the said Isaac, was well aware before he last left her." In lieu of her husband's support, and as a direct result of his failure to provide for his family adequately before his departure for the West Indies, Elizabeth petitioned the legislature to sell land held in her husband's name. Not only, Elizabeth claimed, did she and her children desperately need the money, but selling the land would be more financially beneficial to her family than would keeping it. Her husband had left her with the power of attorney over the estate before his departure, yet she still needed the legislature's approval to convey the land in her own name as a *feme covert.*[21] Here, Elizabeth emphasized the state's duty to advocate for her when her husband failed to provide for her, and insinuated that it was the state's duty to step in as surrogate patriarch tasked with protecting her in her covered status. The state obliged.[22]

Despite the assumptions of coverture, women did attempt to separate their husbands' financial activity from their own beliefs and actions in their petitions to exercise property rights during and in the wake of the war. Sometimes, the value of property husbands left their widows did not exceed the debts they incurred in life, thereby leaving their wives in dire financial straits when they died. Richard Hood left his wife, Susanna, a "very large provision," yet she discovered that his estate was insolvent because of the numerous debts he owed. She was forced to sell the majority of Richard's estate to pay for his debts, yet she retained her dower: a small wooden house on a tiny plot of land on Cow Lane in Boston. Thirty years later—in the earliest years of the republic—Susanna petitioned the legislature in desperation that she be able to sell the land provided to her by her dower rights, which she may have been able to do in another state without the express permission of the legislature.

Because of the limits that the state of Massachusetts placed on women's rights in the laws of conveyance, Hood felt compelled to petition the legislature for redress. She focused her plea on her destitute situation, highlighting the "very unfit residence" in which she lived, and how "she lives upon the Charity of her daughters who themselves depend for a support on keeping a small school."[23] Susanna emphasized her own dependence on her daughters, who could barely support themselves, and in so doing, obtained the right to sell her property.[24] Where the laws of the state of Massachusetts failed to provide the same freedoms in the laws of conveyancing as did South Carolina, women like Susanna Hood claimed their right to protection and support from the state as its duty to dependent women.[25] After thirty years of widowhood, Hood finally asserted her right to her late husband's property.

War widows found themselves in a unique situation. Often faced with the death or the severe disability of her husband as a consequence of war, a widow turned to the state to provide her, and often her family, with support. In some cases, wives linked themselves to patriotic service in defense of their nation by virtue of their marriages. Their claims enumerated and detailed the various ways in which their husbands, and therefore *they*, sacrificed for the cause. This patriotism by proxy, they argued, entitled them to certain material benefits and, in most cases, a pension. By virtue of their marriage, widows often petitioned their state legislatures as well as other governing bodies or committees for remuneration as compensation for the loss of their husbands and for their own sacrifices to the nation.

In a number of cases, women insisted that their husbands' death or incapacity, brought on by the state, inhibited their survival. It was then the responsibility of the state—the surrogate patriarch—to provide for and support its dependents. This, in these women's views, was their right, endowed by virtue of their subordinate status as wives. Supported by various laws and engaging the sympathy of state and local governing bodies, mothers, daughters, and wives claimed the right to their sons', fathers', and husbands' pensions and salaries earned as a result of these men's service in the military.

It is essential to see widowhood in this period as a semi-autonomous yet still dependent state.[26] While widowhood came with certain legal, social, and cultural measures of independence, these were inherently tied to the dependent status of wife.[27] The difference between wives and widows was, in many ways, "more a matter of degree than kind."[28] With this essentially dependent identity, however, came a number of rights of protection afforded to widows in particular.[29] The courts, for example, exercised a kind of "judicial paternalism," as social custom implied women's dependence, regardless of economic or marital status, and hence established the need of their protection.[30] In this way, widows "wore the clothes of feminine dependence," yet they were able to carve out a measure of agency and independence in their new role as unmarried women because of this somewhat convoluted social and economic status.[31] Their ability to do so was contingent upon their careful and deliberate declaration of rights in this semi-dependent state.

The war created an opportunity for women to attach themselves to the "American cause" through men's military service, as they argued for certain rights endowed to patriotic wives, mothers, and daughters. Through fulfilling their obligations and duties in these roles, women claimed the rights of dependents, which included widows' pensions and soldiers' back pay earned during these men's service. Major Brown petitioned the Pension Committee to receive a pension due her because of the death of her late husband, who had served during the Revolutionary War. Her petition does not survive; only the report of the committee tasked with addressing her complaint remains. Despite its brevity, the language of the report reveals a great deal about how the state thought about and treated war widows. The committee members decided that "the Petitioner, is Entitled to be provided for by Law," and thus furnished her with an annual pension "during her Widowhood," in addition to five pounds annually for each of her children until they reached the age of twelve. Between 1803 and 1812, Major Brown received $628.76 from the state of South Carolina due to her status as a widow dependent on the state for support.[32] A number of other women were granted the same pensions on account of their entitlement as widows as well.[33]

Implicit in widows' petitions was women's right to the money their husbands earned during their service. Ann Tatnall, for instance, declared that her husband had an "undoubted Right" to back wages, which were likewise due to *her* upon his death. In her petition, Ann demanded that she be able to draw from his account his pay and his rations from the time of his capture and imprisonment through the date of his death. Presuming the Pennsylvania Council of Safety would find her petition justified, she "makes no Doubt your hon[ora]ble Board will take her melancholy Situation into your Serious Consideration." Tatnall's subtle but pointed engagement with the sympathies of the state combined with her assertion of her husband's—and, implicitly, *her own*—right to back wages compelled the council to grant her request for compensation and rations for her family.[34]

By virtue of their positions as wives or widows of Continental soldiers or militiamen, some women claimed that they *themselves* were owed certain entitlements, rather than centering their pleas around their husbands' rights. In her petition, Hannah Ellis requested the "Relief which is due *to her.*"[35] Further, Hannah complained that she had not received any relief from the "Publick," which she was owed as a result of the law passed for widows and children of fallen Revolutionary soldiers. While she prioritized her own entitlement to these veterans' benefits, Hannah explicitly connected herself—albeit belatedly—to her husband's service. She emphasized her husband's having "bled and died" at the Battle of Monmouth "in Defence of the Rights of Mankind, and in Support of the Freedom and Independance of the United States of America." Here, her petition presented her husband's service in explicit connection with her own experience of the war and its aftermath.[36] Hannah was widowed, effectively, by the fight for American independence, which in turn gave her the right to compensation for her losses.

Women whose husbands went missing—either as prisoners of war or missing in action—during the Revolution often petitioned the government for compensation for lost earnings, while employing a language of entitlement particular to their status as wives of American prisoners. Mary Booth's husband, John, for instance, was impressed on board a British man-of-war, and was later taken captive by the French, under whom he "suffered greatly." Besides this brief mention of his suffering, in her petition Booth seemed to have little concern for her husband's well-being, and instead focused her plea on requesting the "Sum of Money allowed by the Government to those Persons who were on board said Vessel when taken." The money, Booth recognized, was owed to her husband, yet it was Mary who felt herself entitled to the ten pounds' compensation, as the committee put it, "for her Husband's suffering and Captivity."[37] The implication of the committee's language, spurred by Mary's petition, is that the state owed her the earnings of her suffering husband, to which she was entitled under her covered status.

Some petitioners completely bypassed the recognition that their husbands or other male family members were owed wages. Instead, these women insisted that back payments and pensions belonged *to them* in *their own right*, because of the additional labor they had assumed in their husbands' absence. Elizabeth Shelton's husband and son both served the revolutionary cause; both had been captured during the war. As the British imprisoned both of her pillars of financial support, Elizabeth's situation compelled her to petition the state legislature in order to provide for her "poor family." Significantly, though, she requested that "she may have *her* same Wages paid her for her support."[38] In Elizabeth's mind, the wages earned by her husband and son did not belong to them; they were *her* wages, by virtue of the burdens and suffering *she* had endured as a wife and mother of veterans. Elizabeth used her position as a dependent of her male family members to claim a right to and the ownership of wages earned by her husband and son.

Other women deployed their younger, dependent children strategically in these claims to war widows' rights. Sarah Tucker Simons cited her husband James's service under the command of Colonel Hastens. She not only declared her dependence on her late husband's pay but highlighted the plight of her own children, in addition to John's children from another marriage for whom she was caring. She demonstrated not only that she had a right to these back payments but that it was poor, innocent children who would suffer if the state did not step in as a surrogate patriarch. Sarah successfully won compensation for "revolutionary services of her late husband" in the form of a three-thousand-dollar payment.[39]

Margret Clendening even used her children to argue for the right to compensation beyond what the state recognized as lawful.[40] Margret attempted to settle up her late husband John Barnet's account with the state of South Carolina. For these services, he was paid only five hundred pounds "of the then Depreciated paper Currency" in compensation.[41] Here, Margret presented two implicit critiques of the state: that it failed to manage its books capably, and that it failed to preserve the integrity of the economy, such that its currency would provide any value to its citizens. Playing on the sympathy of the state, Margret insisted "that her case is Exceeding hard being Reduced to necessitous Circumstances by the Ravages of the warr & the Loss of her husband." She also drew the committee's attention to her "number of Small Children whose support & Education depends wholly upon the Industry of your petitioner." As a widow, Clendening was entitled to one-third of her late husband's estate, but clearly, she believed this was insufficient, as she petitioned the commission for just a "small pitence that their father so hardly Earned."[42] She used her status as a mother and a dependent widow to claim a right to compensation owed to her late husband, all the while using these positions as a cover for her critiques of the state.

Effectively, these women framed their domestic duties as an expression of their patriotism. Their roles as wives of veterans made them patriots by proxy, through their union with their veteran husbands and their own continued devotion to these men, and therefore, their country. Mary Bell's husband was wounded during the Revolution and thus was paid an annuity of $21.42 until March of 1797, at which point the payments inexplicably stopped. Her husband, James, died in January of 1801, so Mary sought payment of the balance of these annuities that then, as his widow, belonged to her. The committee directed the comptroller of South Carolina to pay Mary the remaining annuities owed to James, amounting to three years and ten months' worth of payment to which she was "Justly Entitled."[43] Mary's request was granted, demonstrating that women's connection to the memory of their husbands' service provided a clear reminder to state legislators of their rights as the dependents of both the state and their husbands.[44]

Women used their place as widows in the shadows of their husbands' service to demand a right to more from the state than it was offering. Mary Avery's husband, John, served for thirty years as secretary to the state of Massachusetts before his death. She claimed that though she believed her husband's work was to the "general satisfaction of the Government & people," the "allowances" he received during his lifetime "were at no time adequate to the support of his family." If it were not for his patrimonial inheritance, she suggested, surely the family would have fallen into great debt. This minimal patrimony, however, was hardly sufficient to support Mary and her three daughters, especially after the family had lost John's income. Mary focused her petition heavily on the sacrifices her husband made to the state, mirroring the language some women chose to present in their petitions requesting veterans' pensions: "So large a portion of the life of the husband of your petitioner has been wholly devoted to the public service." His dedication to the state prohibited him from seeking financial gain in private business, she claimed, and their family's finances suffered. John seemed not to complain about his salary in life, but his wife did so after his death. For her, it was a matter of her family's survival, and the state ought to attend to that.

Mary's petition illustrates that she believed the state had a duty not only to recognize her right to protection but also to provide the entitlements she was owed as a widow of a state employee. She took it upon herself to request an allowance that might compensate for her husband's service and likewise relieve her of the onerous burden of supplying her family with "necessities" without his financial support. Mary presumed that she was incapable of providing these "necessaries" without her husband and that the state should supplant his role as provider by relieving her financial distress. Apparently, this presumption was mutual; the legislature obliged, granting her one thousand dollars "in Consideration of the public services of the late John Avery Esq."[45] As she was no longer able to depend on her husband, Mary Avery successfully painted a wretched picture of her destitute life in widowhood, tugged on the heartstrings of the legislative body, and invoked her husband's memory as well as her helplessness in order to receive significant financial relief from the state. Because she fulfilled her duties as a wife, and John fulfilled his duties to the state, Mary Avery claimed a right to support from the government, and expected the state to recognize that right.

The assumption that the state would provide for war widows seems to stand in stark contrast, discursively, to their assertion of rights. Yet women's carefully constructed petitions reveal that their rights were firmly grounded in their status as dependents, first on their husbands, and then on the patriarchal state. Elizabeth Chatham used her husband John's service to argue for compensation from the Pennsylvania state legislature. She detailed John's immense difficulties during his service, highlighting that "he suffered great hardship" after being taken prisoner and detained for a year. Upon his release from imprisonment, John was sent to Baltimore and unfortunately drowned, and since his death, Elizabeth had been unable to support herself and her four children. Elizabeth presented herself as entitled to financial support, based on "the Merit of her late Husband's service, and the losses he sustained by his Attachment to the cause of the United States," hoping that she and her children would "obtain some relief" from the state. In Elizabeth's view, she was owed compensation both for the loss of her husband and also for the sacrifices he made—sacrifices in which she shared by association—and the suffering that she continued to endure after his passing.[46]

Other women whose husbands returned from war similarly experienced hardship as a result of their husbands' military service, and looked to the state to alleviate their distresses. Anna Christiana Labar's husband had been wounded in the war, taken prisoner a number of times, and spent nearly seven years serving as a soldier for the American cause. As a result of his service, however, he was "rendered thereby utterly incapable to get his living by hard labor." Because of "affliction and other circumstances such as a total derangement of his reasonable powers," John found himself "utterly incapable of doing any thing either to support himself or your petitioner his wife." Anna similarly demonstrated her own inability to work for the support of her family, because she was "obliged" by her duty as John's wife "to attend him every moment" so that he would not injure himself or even another. Anna's petition, signed and legitimated by eight men who attested to John's condition, underscored her vulnerability and need for assistance from the state in this "most distressing & melancholy case."[47] The legislature granted Anna's request.[48]

In her petition, Anna stressed her loss of her husband as her financial support system, but also demonstrated how faithfully she carried out her role as John's wife. By stressing her own adherence to spousal duty despite her husband's physical incapability of fulfilling his, Anna Christiana Labar undermined her husband's masculine authority while simultaneously declaring her own right to these funds based on her dependent status as John's wife and the familial role she fulfilled in his stead. According to Anna, the hardship she endured as the wife of a man who could not support her endowed her with the right to certain compensation, which she claimed in her petition to the South Carolina state legislature.

The war and these interactions with the state politicized women in important ways, often in the context of their domestic roles. Yet their demands on the state animated them with a sense of boldness, as some seized the opportunity not only to demand pensions and back pay from the state but also to criticize their husbands, undermining the authority of those on whom these rights depended.[49] Hannah Durant cited the service of her husband, Ephraim, who was in several artillery corps during the Revolution, and later enlisted in the Continental Army and served until the end of the war.[50] He never received payment, however, for his time in Colonel Revere's corps. He had been away from home for nearly two years, leaving his dependents to fend for themselves, so Hannah petitioned the General Court of Massachusetts for the money he was owed based on his service. During this time, it appears, Hannah argued that Ephraim neglected to provide proper care and support for his wife, having not "afforded your Petitioner any relief whatever" even though she was "in great want having been sick along time & hard by the Common necessarys of Life & three Child[re]n to Support."

Implicit in Hannah's request was her dependence on an absent husband, as well as a critique of her husband's failure to fulfill his spousal duties. Ephraim may have served his country and the cause of liberty, but he had neglected to provide adequately for his family in his absence. His duty to country distracted him from his duty to his wife and children, so Hannah's petition also served as an implicit critique of the war and the state. Since Ephraim did not follow up on the back payments owed to him in his lifetime, Hannah took it upon herself to do so. She used her husband's service in congruence with her performance of wifely duty and her husband's failure to provide for his family to argue that money owed to him was likewise owed to her, and was necessary for the support of their family.[51]

Women's assertion of their property rights in petitions could also evolve into more overt critiques of state policies. Catherine Tolley, for example, made her frustrations with the state's policies toward alleged loyalists clear in her 1778 petition to the Supreme Executive Council of Pennsylvania. Catherine's husband, John, had left Philadelphia before the British evacuated the city, and at the time of her petition, lived and traded in New York. Because of her husband's political affiliations and his failure to surrender to the state, an order of the Executive Council confiscated the Tolleys' property, much of which, Catherine asserted, was acquired with "the hard Earnings of her own honest Industry." With no property and no husband, she was "reduced (she must say she thinks on her part undeservedly) to this pitiable situation." In Catharine's view, it was the state itself that instigated "this pitiable situation."

Remembering her audience and the gendered expectations of comportment that governed the behavior of eighteenth-century Anglo-Americans, Tolley did "supplicate" to the authority of the council in her request to travel to New York. There, she insisted, she would be able to assert her "just Claim upon whatever property he yet possesses" and then would return to Philadelphia without her husband.[52] Catherine's assertive claims to the right to her husband's property were rooted both in his obligation to provide for his wife and in her own contribution to the family economy. Clearly, Catherine Tolley had lost her patience with the system that claimed that women were to be dependent and reliant upon men for support despite the frustrating reality that the system often failed to fully provide for these women. The Revolution, and the state, put her in this situation, yet she subtly censured both in her attempts to work her way out of it. Women petitioners balanced expectations of feminine comportment and their domestic roles with their own increasingly assertive demands that the state recognize their rights as dependents.

The Right to Divorce

Beyond the increased rate at which women petitioned the state during and after the Revolution and the ways in which this process politicized them, some women began to alter the language of petitions they had long made to the state by invoking their "right" to divorce in the revolutionary era. In their divorce petitions, some women began to maintain that divorce was a right provided to them by law during and after the war. Certainly, many women believed this, as they used the law and the terms of their marriage covenant to argue for justice against their adulterous, absent, or unsupportive husbands. They invoked the "right" to divorce in cases in which husbands proved unfaithful, refused or were unable to provide financial support, or did not protect their wives properly.

Importantly, though, women's invocation of the "right" to divorce was presented within the context of their dependence. A husband owed fidelity to his wife in exchange for her dependence on him, both legally and financially. Similarly, a husband was required to provide the necessaries of life to his dependents, including his wife and children; when a man deserted his family, he abandoned this crucial duty. Finally, a husband had an obligation to provide his wife with certain protections, which included being a safeguard from physical harm. Men who neglected their marital obligations while their wives remained dependent upon them could be taken to task for their behavior.

The emergence and circulation of "rights talk" provoked a shift in the strategic language women employed in their suits for divorce during and after the Revolution. Sally Jones Wilson, for example, used the language of rights to present her case to the Supreme Court of Judicature in Massachusetts. Sally married Robert Wilson on October 7, 1799, at which time, she claimed, Robert "became obliged to be faithful and true to the bed of the said Sally and not to commit the crime of adultery." Sally described Robert's fidelity not just as a reasonable expectation for their marriage, but as a precondition for its validity. Because Sally and Robert entered into the marriage contract together, each owed the other the performance of certain behaviors, and among these was fidelity. Robert, however, "regardless of the laws and his marriage vows," committed adultery with "divers[e] African women," which a cook witnessed on board the sloop *Polly*. In so doing, he not only broke his marriage vows but also "destroyed" Sally's "happiness."

Significantly, she argued that "*a right accrues* to the said Sally to be loosed from the bonds of matrimony with the said Robert." Because of his failure to uphold the duties imposed upon him as a husband, Sally claimed a right to a divorce, and likewise, alimony from her husband.[53] Women like Sally Jones Wilson demonstrated how they acquiesced to their submissive role as wives by performing their expected duties, even when they had not received just treatment in their dependent roles. Therefore, Sally and other women were able to use the terms of the marriage contract and their positions of dependence to argue for their right to divorce their husbands, and in Sally's case, receive alimony as well.

Other women also combined the language of marital duty, obligations, and rights in their petitions for divorce. Nancy Robinson, for instance,

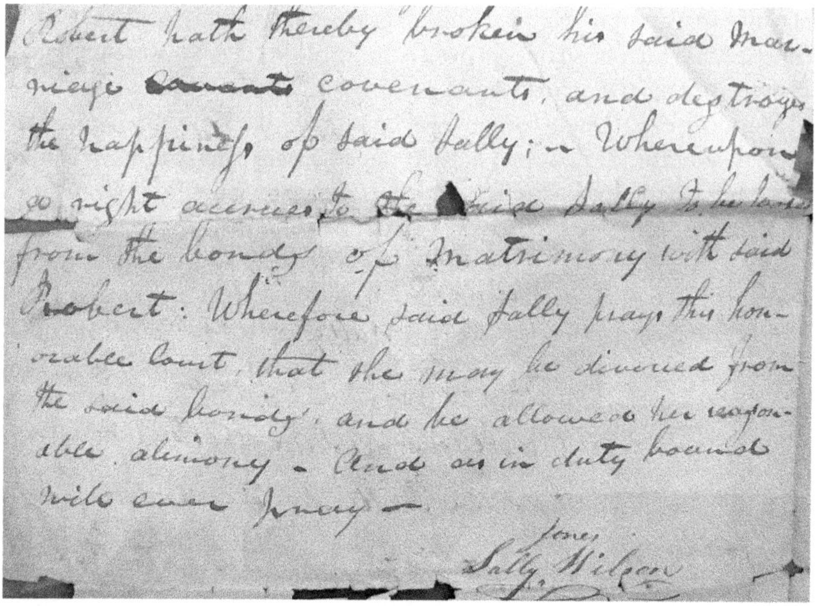

FIGURE 7.3. Sally Jones Wilson's petition for divorce demonstrates that she, along with other women, claimed a right to divorce in the wake of the American Revolution. Source: Petition of Sally Jones Wilson, n.d., Wilson divorce, Docket #112, November Term 1803, Judicial Archives, Massachusetts Archives, Boston, MA.

said that when her husband "William became the lawful husband of the said Nancy," he also became "by his marriage covenants" and "the law of the land . . . obliged to be true and faithful to the bed of the said Nancy." Like Sally Jones Wilson, who propounded her right to divorce her husband, Nancy Robinson noted how her husband William's actions had "destroyed" her "peace and felicity," and accordingly, "a right accrue[d] to the said Nancy, by the laws of this Commonwealth, to be loosed from the bond of Matrimony."[54] Elizabeth Winneck also invoked this "right" to divorce by emphasizing her husband's failure to be faithful to her despite her submission to his authority and identity. She asserted that at the time of their marriage, she "took the name of Elizabeth Winneck," thereby forgoing her former identity and voluntarily submitting her individual, legal personhood to that of her husband, John. In her new role as Elizabeth Winneck, she argued, she was endowed with the right of protection and care provided by the man whose name she now bore. Despite this ostensibly willing sacrifice of her own identity, John neglected his "marriage Covenant" and likewise his "Duty" to be "true & faithful" to his wife. This, in turn, justified Elizabeth invoking her right to a divorce.[55] Based on their husbands' inability to be faithful to their wives, both Nancy Robinson and Elizabeth Winneck presented their requests for divorce in terms of rights that were owed to them as dependent wives.

In addition to the right to divorce that some women asserted in their petitions, others invoked their right to certain property held by their husbands. This included property that may or may not have belonged to these women prior to their marriages. Sarah Dix, for example, accused her husband of adultery, and affirmed the "right" to divorce that "accrues" to her by virtue of his misdeeds. Similarly, Sarah requested that a certain amount of alimony be provided to her because of her dependence on her philandering husband for financial support. In response, the Supreme Judicial Court of Massachusetts stipulated that Sarah be provided with "all real estate, which . . . is held by said John in right of said Sarah."[56]

Clearly, these jurists took seriously Sarah's assertion of her "right" to a divorce. She insisted that as compensation for John's wrongdoing, and his failure to protect and provide for his dependents, Sarah have returned to her the property that she had held in her own right prior to their marriage. Additionally, the court required that in compensation for the personal estate that Sarah brought to their marriage, John was to pay her an additional three thousand dollars. Finally, the court required that John pay her 150 dollars annually in alimony to provide her with "reasonable and comfortable support" for the rest of her life.[57] Sarah therefore remained perpetually dependent on John for regularly distributed alimony payments, but at the same time, became possessed again of a huge sum of money and a portion of real estate in her own name, completely independent of her husband's intervention. In exercising these rights, Sarah vacillated between financial security and relative independence on the one hand, and perpetual dependence on her husband for a regular maintenance on the other.

Women's cognizance of their right to divorce extended to their requests for alimony. Like most women seeking divorces, wives who petitioned for alimony from their husbands emphasized the contractual obligations of husband and wife, and how their husbands had broken these vows. While wives were obligated to submit to their husbands' authority and turn over the right to any property these women might have held in their own right prior to their marriage, husbands were likewise duty-bound to provide financial support to their wives "as compensation . . . for their losses."[58] Because of the legal framework of coverture, women were not entitled to their own separate wages or financial resources. Women used this ostensible legal crutch—the assumption that they could not possibly provide adequately for themselves, which was indeed the case under the law of coverture—to argue for support and alimony, even after they had already achieved independence from their husbands and their marriages.

In their petitions for divorce—regardless of the cause—many wives demanded alimony.[59] The Massachusetts divorce statute of 1786 provided that wives whose husbands committed adultery would be assigned their dowers "in the same manner as if such husband was naturally dead."[60] Similarly, women in Massachusetts could receive alimony if they demonstrated their husbands' extreme cruelty in their divorce petition.[61] Pennsylvania provided that alimony should be provided to wives in cases of divorce *a mensa et thoro*, or from bed and board, amounting to legal separation but not full divorce.[62] The courts could award the wife up to one-third of her husband's earnings indefinitely for the remainder of her life.[63]

Although women who obtained divorces *a mensa et thoro* from their husbands remained *femes covert* and were not able to remarry, their continued dependence on their husbands allowed them a measure of financial security while they legally obtained the right to live separately from their spouses. A number of women, it seems, preferred to receive support from their husbands in the form of alimony rather than seek a divorce *a vinculo matrimonii*, or an absolute divorce.[64] In order for women to receive financial support from abusive or adulterous husbands, it remained critical for them to assert their dependence on the men who had wronged them while simultaneously asserting their need to be independent from these men through a divorce *a mensa et thoro*.[65]

Of women in Boston, those who accused their husbands of cruelty were the most frequent recipients of alimony. This meant that the courts took seriously a husband's duty to protect as well as provide for his wife. Women who petitioned for alimony understood their right to support from their husbands even after their marriages had ended. Mary Appleton detailed that although she had "performed all acts and things" required by a wife, her husband, William, had abused her. As a result, the court granted her a divorce *a mensa et thoro* and required William to pay Mary an annuity of eighty dollars for the remainder of her life. Eliza Morgan requested "an allowance" from her husband William's estate, after she alleged that he did not provide "the common & ordinary necessities of life" for her and their children during their marriage.[66] Elizabeth Orrock requested alimony on the basis of her husband's abusing her despite his obligation to be a "faithful & tender husband" to her; the court required Alexander Orrock to pay his wife one thousand dollars in the divorce.[67] The courts used these regular maintenance payments to prevent abused women's dependence on the state, despite their legal separation from their husbands.

Women's petitions for alimony, however, were not entirely about financial need. Even women who demonstrated that they were capable of supporting themselves without their husbands' assistance petitioned for alimony on the basis of their rights as dependents of their husbands, defining alimony as a sum they were owed by virtue of their legally subordinate status as a wife. Catherine France, for instance, supported herself and her five children by taking in washing as her husband hoarded his paltry earnings for himself and frequently demanded funds from his wife to fuel his alcoholism. Although her petition (and the depositions of three of her neighbors) clearly demonstrated that she was capable of providing for her family without John's meager and often nonexistent assistance, she still requested that the state grant her alimony in her divorce. This indicates that Catherine believed alimony to be more of a right given to wives after their divorces than an allowance granted merely out of necessity and under certain circumstances.[68] Although the decision of the court is unclear, it is unlikely that Catherine would have received any alimony from John even if the court mandated it, as he had been unwilling and unable to provide for her when they were married. Still, Catherine's request for alimony underscores her understanding of this maintenance as a right guaranteed to her by virtue of her dependence on her husband, and her shrewd understanding of the state's view of women's seemingly inherent inability to provide a maintenance for themselves.

Notably, there was at least one case of a woman who herself broke the marriage contract, yet still believed that she deserved support from her husband. Martin Blake divorced his wife, Mary, after he petitioned the court to end their marriage because *she* committed adultery. Not sixth months later, Mary petitioned the same court (which had already found her guilty of committing adultery) for a regular alimony from her husband.[69] The very fact that Mary Blake assumed that her husband, William, should still provide for and support her financially despite her own failure to be faithful to him demonstrates the extent to which women believed they were owed economic protection and financial support from their husbands.

Underscoring the powerful assumptions of women's need for this protection, the state sometimes took matters into their own hands in their attempts to protect wives from profligate and abusive husbands. After Ann Gardner accused her husband of extreme cruelty, the courts decreed the Gardners divorced *a mensa et thoro*, compelling David to pay Ann a sum of money for her maintenance and support. The courts, however, went a step further, guaranteeing that should Ann outlive her ex-husband, she would still be entitled to her "right of Dower in the Estate of the said David," despite their being divorced. Divorces from bed and board legally separated spouses, but as they did not permit either the husband or the wife to remarry, husbands were often compelled to provide their ex-wives with regular alimony payments, as an extension of their financial obligations in the marriage contract. Sometimes, the courts, as in the case of the Gardner divorce, went so far as to extend a woman's divorce rights to include her dower, as if she were a widow and had never divorced her husband in the first place.[70] Here, of course, the state was protecting its own interests, too, attempting to ensure that Ann might never become dependent on the state.

Importantly, women claimed this protection as a right, particularly in defense of themselves against their husbands' cruelty. Elizabeth Finney, for instance, endured physical abuse and regular threats to her life at the hands of her husband. She requested a divorce because "all that Comfort & hapiness which she had a right to Expect in a State of Matrimony" was "wholly subverted" by her husband's actions.[71] Mary Lobb likewise described the abuses she suffered at the hands of her husband, George, in vivid detail. He "beat and bruised your proponent in the most cruel and merciless manner . . . leaving her almost lifeless on the floor." He "denied her almost all the necessaries of life," often kicking her out of their home, or locking her in their house and refusing to let her leave.

Mary's narrative, replete with details of her suffering, likely would have been sufficient to convince jurists that her husband abused her. Nevertheless, she went further in her petition, focusing instead on how her husband violated her rights to protection and care as a wife. In so doing, Mary asserted, George not only flouted the "tender obligations of that connubial life" but by his actions was "in violation of the rights of humanity and the laws of the land." Her petition, above all, was meant to "appeal for Protection to that power which the Constitution has wisely lodged in the hands of your Excellency and Honrs." When she suffered under the abusive hands of the patriarch in her home, she turned to the patriarchs in the courtroom to provide the "protection" to which she had a right under the law. Despite George submitting two responses contrary to Mary's account, her assertion and her appeal advocating for her rights as a dependent convinced the courts that she deserved to be divorced from her husband.[72]

These cases also served as an opportunity for women to subtly critique the patriarchal structures of marriage that brought them to court in the first place. Some women used their petitions for divorce to express their frustration with the laws that restricted women's rights over property that they brought to marriage, especially in cases in which husbands proved unwilling or unable to manage the family finances. Sarah Parker exploited her husband's financial failings and criminal activity to argue for an end to their marriage. While she conceded that her husband, David, had not violated the marriage contract in their first seven years of marriage, the two years prior to her petition saw his desertion, adultery, and transmission of venereal disease—*twice*—to his wife. Additionally, he abused her, was convicted of theft, and sold their home and all their household goods, which included items she had brought with her to their marriage. David turned her out of their home, refused to support her, and had also "forbidden any others to do it."

Beyond a reasonable doubt, Sarah Parker demonstrated how her husband failed to provide her with the obligatory support, necessities, and love that she was owed as a *feme covert*, his dependent wife. Sarah's tone indicates a distaste for David's behavior and for the law, both of which forced her into this position. Despite having a husband who had violated her rights as a wife, she still was forced by law to acquiesce to his sale of the property that *she* had brought to their marriage. For these reasons, she sought a divorce from her thieving, profligate husband, which was granted in 1781.[73] Sarah Parker's divorce petition highlighted the paradoxes inherent in the laws of coverture while demanding that the court provide the rights and privileges due to her as a dependent wife, even after her divorce.

Women ultimately faced the threat of having their rights as wives violated with potentially no legal recourse to protect these rights. Katherine Mayhew, for instance, asserted that her husband, Joseph, "ill requited her good conduct for many years" and likewise "did but little to support her." Joseph abandoned her, and although he "supported her tolerably well" until five years before his departure, he later "became a bad husband and did no work to support his said wife or himself, and was a meer vagabond." According to witness testimony, Katherine "conducted" herself "without blame" and during those five years supported her husband and their five children by her own labor. Since Joseph Mayhew's absconding, however, Katherine and her children had fallen into dire straits, forced to petition for the right to sell her tenth of her late father's estate, the profit of which would go "towards the necessary maintenance of herself & children."[74] Katherine Mayhew's petition used the language of dependence to illustrate the failure of property law in Massachusetts to protect women whose husbands did not live up to the standard set by society, thereby subtly undermining the state's disregard for women's property rights.

Not only did women who petitioned for divorce invoke their right to do so, but some wives exposed the hypocrisy of their husbands' property rights remaining intact despite these men's failures to uphold their duties within the marriage contract. Susannah Mitchell's divorce petition proclaimed her right to be provided for by her husband during their marriage. In addition to physically abusing Susannah, throwing her out of the house, and treating her with general cruelty, John Mitchell deserted his wife and daughter, "neglecting to afford either of them any support, except one hundred Dollars in paper money"—likely the significantly devalued Continental currency—from the time he left in 1779 through the time of Susannah's petition, in 1795. This, she asserted, violated their marriage contract, and thus provided ample grounds for divorce. Yet, she had waited more than fifteen years after John's departure to sue for a divorce, and her petition makes clear the reason why: she feared that she and her daughter would suffer further indignities because of John's "right which her said husband may have by means of his marriage contract . . . to controul her person or to deprive her of any property she may acquire by her labour and industry."[75]

Susannah Mitchell's petition exposed one of the greatest hypocrisies and complications inherent in the assumptions of coverture. Although husbands were obligated by law to provide financial support to their wives and families, often these men fell short of their responsibilities—or neglected them entirely. As a result, wives and children were forced to labor or depend on the charity of family, friends, the community, or the state. Yet these profligate, delinquent husbands still had a right to the money these women earned, regardless of their cruel behavior, their adulterous habits, or even their absence. Women like Mitchell used the very language of women's subordination to argue for a reason to be freed from the constraints of their marriages, all while subverting the court's understanding of rights. In her exercise of her right to divorce, Susannah

Mitchell undercut her husband's right to claim the fruits of her own independent labor. That women asserted the right to divorce husbands who refused or became unable to protect them or support them financially reveals the particularly gendered nature of this claim to rights, and the distinct advantage women could employ in seeking separations from their husbands.

* * *

As women were the legal, social, and economic dependents of men, their rights were contingent upon the obligations and duties they owed their husbands and state officials. Women in revolutionary America used these assumptions to employ the language of helplessness and submission in their claims for certain rights endowed to them on the basis of their dependent status. Women demonstrated their right to certain protections and support based on the obligations they performed as wives, mothers, and daughters. From the right to protection and support, these women claimed entitlements in the form of relief, care, the ability to convey land, and even the ability to divorce and receive regular alimony payments from their former husbands. War widows emphasized their patriotism through their relationships with deceased veterans, thereby claiming their rights to pensions and back pay. Other women proved themselves patriots in their own right, performing the duties of "female patriots" worthy of relief and support. Some resisted property restrictions against women while simultaneously emphasizing their rights as the dependents of men. Importantly, women invoked the responsibility of the state to intervene in such cases, in order to guarantee their feminine right to protection and support.

In these cases, the Revolutionary War clearly provided the circumstances and the language that enhanced women's ability to declare their rights in petitions to state legislators and county court officials. Despite its ostensible disadvantages, women's dependent status provided them with a particular outlet to assert rights contingent upon this dependence, demonstrating that "rights talk" was present not only in the traditional political realm but in the private lives of women as well. The rights these women declared were framed firmly within the context of their status as the dependents of men. The Revolution, its upheavals, and its accompanying rhetoric provided the framework from within which women could assert and argue for old rights in new ways. In the late eighteenth and early nineteenth centuries, women found themselves newly emboldened to declare themselves endowed with certain rights on the basis of their dependence as a direct result of the war. Despite the fact that the patriarchal state may not have recognized an expansion in women's rights, women themselves did.

Paradoxically, these petitioners assumed the mantle of dependents, which required them to at least tacitly accept the terms of the patriarchal state and its assumptions about women's subordinate status. In these cases, women asserted their rights on an individualized basis, often to great success, while simultaneously accepting the terms of their own dependence, which in turn legitimated the power of the patriarchal state. The rights revolution that early American women claimed did not question or challenge their dependent status writ large. Instead, the movement exploited the deep-seated and entrenched gendered assumptions inherent in American society during the revolutionary era, perhaps strengthening those very assumptions in the process. Women did not attempt to rise up and challenge the power of the patriarchal state. In the new world the Revolution made, women's status changed very little. Yet, in one seemingly small but significant way, *they* were changed. They saw themselves as rights-bearing individuals, a necessary foundation for the long push for women's equality that still persists today.

Conclusion: On Collaboration and Collective Action

This book began in early 2015 with a loaded question: Why didn't the American Revolution bring about significant changes in women's lives? I have already outlined the ways in which this line of inquiry is problematic, and how following it provides an incomplete understanding of women's lived experiences in the revolutionary era. We have also seen the ways in which women did make the Revolution—its rhetoric and the disruptions it caused—work for themselves and their families. They managed as best they could with the tools at their disposal, even when it meant buying into patriarchal norms that undermined their own power.[1] But these discoveries provoked another question that haunted me: Is it possible that revolutionary-era women acted as collaborators in bolstering the patriarchal structure, and thus were party to their own subjugation?

The word "collaborator" has a double meaning. It signifies at once one's contribution to, or partnership in, work with others, but it also carries deeply negative connotations, suggesting cooperation with the enemy.[2] This latter form of collaboration can be performed either voluntarily or involuntarily, done out of necessity or deep ideological commitment, or chosen out of survival or self-interest. There are a multitude of "collaborationists," just as there are a myriad "dissidences."[3] Collaboration, like other concepts discussed in this work, exists on a spectrum. From this framework of understanding, we can certainly say that women collaborated in their own legal, social, and economic subjugation—at least inadvertently, or out of necessity—but at times they overtly supported the logic behind white patriarchal power.

Most women in the revolutionary era did not have the time, capacity, or inclination to pursue collective action to fight against the oppressive forces of the patriarchal state. Their collaboration—their tacit acceptance of their own unequal status—was motivated by the need to survive, by managing the consequences of men's choices in war, in politics, and under the law, among other things. So perhaps we can qualify that even in their collaboration, most women were not complicit—i.e., acting as willing accomplices participating in the nefarious work of their own subjugation. In their collaboration, they did not, or could not, prioritize countering the suppression of their sex by men, instead pursuing the more feasible goal of expressing agency and power over their own individual lives.[4] Ironically, when women engaged with, employed, and exploited the terms of their dependence as a strategy for survival, advancement, and empowerment, the unintended result of that method was to perpetuate their inequality.

This strategy may have retarded women's ability to collectively organize and push for the rights and freedoms that eluded them during and in the wake of the American Revolution. Without collective action, with only short-term resistance to individual abuses in particular situations for specific women, the system of oppression—the white patriarchal power structure—flourished. Patriarchy thrives when the problem identified, as was the case in revolutionary-era women's petitions, is individual men who did not conform to the system. When women identified singular abusive husbands, negligent providers, or derelict male leaders as the obstacle to their safety and survival, these men appeared as aberrant cogs in an otherwise functional machine. The real problem, however, was a hierarchical structure crafted according to deficient and erroneous presumptions that could only ever truly protect those already in power. Guaranteed protection for dependents was—and is—merely a veneer to hide the failures of a flawed system that could never live up to its promises.

The fight for women's rights in American history has been uneven, disunited, and torturously slow. Perhaps collective action took so long to materialize because so much of women's survival in the patriarchal system necessitated their accepting its premises in exchange for limited protections. The language of women's petitions, too, remained relatively consistent throughout this period. Women regularly employed the tactic of emphasizing the tropes of feminine helplessness in petitions to the patriarchal state. To a certain degree, women did not modify the language or use of their dependent status during the extent of the period studied in this work. In this way, they collaborated in reinforcing the power structure of the patriarchal state, which kept all women, free and enslaved people of color, and poor Americans subjugated to elite white male authority.

In other ways, however, women's strategies in employing the tools of petitioning changed as a result of the American Revolution. The upheaval brought about by the war created scenarios in which women who likely had had little contact with their government prior to the war were compelled to request relief, assistance, or redress for a variety of grievances in petitions to state legislatures. The number of women's petitions increased significantly during and after the Revolution, demonstrating that the war and its aftermath at the very least created situations in which women felt compelled to demand assistance from the state. Likewise, the reasons for which they sought redress from the state also changed as they responded to the upheavals brought about by the war. The American Revolution, therefore, had an impact on the content and the quantity of women's petitions, shaping and increasing their interactions with the patriarchal state.

Most importantly, the Revolution altered the ways in which women thought about rights they already enjoyed as the dependents of men. A number of women seized upon the opportunity brought about by the Revolution to petition their state legislatures and county courts for their rights as dependents. These rights were not given to them as a result of the war, yet the ubiquitous "rights talk" surrounding the conflict and its aftermath provided women with the impetus and a new linguistic framework with which they could demand their rights. After the Revolution, women framed their demands more in terms of "rights" than they had done prior to the war. They invoked their right to property, to pensions, to compensation, to divorce, to alimony payments, and even to freedom, all within the context of their dependence.

Significantly, then, although there may not have been an overt change in women's collective rights as a result of the Revolution, there was a change in women's perception of their own individual rights, as they developed a new consciousness of and confidence in their ability to demand these rights from the state. This seemingly small and almost imperceptible shift in women's individual consciousness raising as rights-bearing persons was an integral first step in the long and continuing women's rights movement in the United States. Women's reform movements of the antebellum era, especially the push for abolition and suffrage, depended on these petitioning efforts. The early collectivized women's rights movements of the mid-nineteenth century and beyond, then, grew out of women's submission of individual petitions during the revolutionary era. Women could not come together and fight for legal changes to property rights, the right to divorce, the right to vote, reproductive rights, equal employment access, and the right to equal pay (among many other rights) without first understanding and believing that they were endowed with rights as American citizens.

Even so, American women have still not achieved full equality with men under the law. In some ways, especially regarding reproductive rights, the state has forced a regression in women's legal status. Dismantling the patriarchal structure is difficult work, especially when women themselves are collaborators—willingly or unwillingly—in bolstering its power. Women who enjoyed racial and class privileges have exerted those advantages in their efforts to expand (and curtail) women's rights throughout American history. Scholars have shown the ways in which white, antebellum plantation mistresses, for example, emphasized their racial identity to enjoy the advantages that came with it, rather than empathizing with the suffering of women more broadly, especially enslaved Black women.[5] After the Fifteenth Amendment guaranteed voting rights to Black men, white suffragists engaged in racist tactics in their attempts to secure the vote, thus giving credence to white-supremacist assumptions about Black men.[6] Among the biggest adversaries of the Equal Rights Amendment (ERA) were women themselves; Phyllis Schlafly, the antifeminist leader of the STOP ERA campaign, argued that women ought to be full-time wives and mothers in order to preserve a conservative vision of American society.[7] Like many of the subjects of this book, Schlafly performed patriarchal assumptions about women's positions in American society, while herself a lawyer, author, and political leader who toured the country doing work that belied her own public-facing ideology. The history of American women is deeply fraught with paradoxes.

The American women's rights movement is far from over. It continues to be plagued with conflicting visions and exclusionary practices while facing formidable foes. It has not always marched forward; it has hardly ever marched forward with all of its participants in unity. Sometimes, it has marched backwards. As this book was in production, the Supreme Court of the United States handed down its earth-shattering decision in *Dobbs v. Jackson Women's Health Org.* in late June of 2022, thus overturning the nearly fifty-year-old legal precedent established in *Roe v.*

Wade. In their dissent, Justices Breyer, Kagan, and Sotomayor argued that the decision "says from the very moment of fertilization, a woman has no rights to speak of. A State can force her to bring a pregnancy to term, even at the steepest personal and familial costs."[8] In one act, the patriarchal state stripped constitutional rights from more than half of the population.

Yet abortion rights activists—and women's rights activists more broadly—have been galvanized in this historical moment. For activists hoping to restore these stolen rights, the past can provide lessons of both success and failure. Revolutionary-era American women seized their historical moment using the tools they had at their disposal to claim the rights of dependents, recognizing themselves as rights-bearing individuals, even if the state did not. But for the most part during this period, they worked alone; they focused on their own individual struggles (often understandably), and in the process, gave a measure of credence to the discriminatory power underlying American patriarchy. In order for the long arc of the women's rights movement to bend towards justice, activists must unify—collectively—around a common purpose, regardless of gender, race, class, or creed. Perhaps then, future generations can dismantle, and perhaps eventually smash, the patriarchy.

Even for those women who sought to remedy only the injustices of their own statuses, their individual persistence created significant cracks in the foundation of the patriarchal system. Power is not always a matter of tearing down walls and breaking through barriers. It is not always loud, visible, or paradigm shifting. It is often slight and subtle, quiet or silent, careful not to disturb the vast machinations of subjugation against which it resists in order to make small but meaningful gains (and, in some cases, assenting to components of that subjugation as a means to an end). Power, in many cases, is evidenced by that persistence amid deep and structural disadvantage built into systemic discrimination and oppression. That persistence is the through line among all instances of the fight for rights, freedom, and independence in American history.

ACKNOWLEDGMENTS

Having spent a number of years enmeshed in studying and writing about the various facets of early American women's dependence, I have not failed to notice that I myself have become dependent upon so many friends, family members, colleagues, and mentors to whom I owe a tremendous debt of gratitude. I do not have sufficient words—or space—to demonstrate my appreciation for the countless people who have made this project possible, but I shall try anyway.

This work has benefited immensely from feedback from panel chairs, copresenters, and attendees at the various conferences in which I presented earlier versions of most of the book's chapters. Especially helpful were the astute comments made by Ben Carp, Holly Mayer, Mary Beth Sievens, Sheila Skemp, and the participants both at SHEAR's 2017 annual meeting and the "Petitions in the Age of Atlantic Revolutions" conference held in Lisbon in February of 2019. Many scholars and friends have read portions of this manuscript—some in its earliest draft form, some in its entirety, and some more than once. For their thoughtful critique, I would like to thank Ian Beamish, Lindsey Bestebreurtje, Jane Turner Censer, Sara Collini, Judy Giesberg, Catherine Kerrison, Cindy Kierner, Charlene Boyer Lewis, Maria Seger, David Squires, and Rosie Zagarri. My furiously supportive writing group—Kristen Beales, Lauren Duval, and Shira Lurie—deserve a special shoutout for having read most of these chapters multiple times, and for meeting virtually long before it was cool or necessary. Additionally, I would like to thank NYU Press's anonymous reviewers for their keen suggestions and encouragement for the project, as well as anonymous reviewers from the *South Carolina Historical Magazine* and the University of Virginia Press who provided feedback on previously published work that appears in this book. Clara Platter at NYU Press has been everything I needed in an editor: an enthusiastic advocate for the project, a sounding board in demystifying the publication process, and an assiduous email correspondent.

A number of archivists at various repositories across the East Coast helped me to navigate their vast collections and answered my incessant questions about locating source material. I would like to thank especially Charles Lesser and Steve Tuttle at the South Carolina Department of Archives and History; Katie Gray and Nik Butler at the Charleston Archive; Libby Bouvier, Martha Clark, Jennifer Fauxsmith, John Hannigan, and Caitlin Jones at the Massachusetts Archives; the staffs at the Massachusetts Historical Society and the Widener Library at Harvard University; Aaron McWilliams at the Pennsylvania State Archives; Jim Green, Connie King, and Linda August at the Library Company of Philadelphia; and Sarah Heim at the Historical Society of Pennsylvania. Thanks, also, to Riley Sutherland, who took last-minute photos of sources that appear in this book and saved me a long trip down and back up I-95.

Portions of chapters 2 and 3 have appeared in a previously published article: Jacqueline Beatty, "Privileged in the Patriarchy: How Charleston's Wives Negotiated Financial Freedom in the Early Republic," *South Carolina Historical Magazine* 119 (July 2018): 168–90. Portions of chapters 1, 4, and 5 were previously published in another form in "Complicated Allegiances: Women, Politics, and Property in Post-Occupation Charleston," in *Women Waging War in the American Revolution*, Mayer, Holly A. © 2022 by the Rector and Visitors of the University of Virginia. Reprinted by permission of the University of Virginia Press.

I have received generous financial support for this project from a number of institutions, including the Department of History and Art History, the Provost's Office, and the Graduate and Professional Students' Association at George Mason University; the Library Company of Philadelphia and the Historical Society of Pennsylvania; and the Faculty Development Committee at York College of Pennsylvania, which provided funding for research travel and, happily, a microfilm reader so that I could complete research from the comfort of my home office during the early months of the COVID-19 pandemic.

Academia can be a lonely vocation, but I am lucky to have found great friends in my career who have supported my work and injected my professional life with more than a bit of fun. Although my stint at the University of Louisiana–Lafayette was brief, the friendships I made there have lasted beyond my short contract. To Ian Beamish and Maria Seger: thank you for your encouragement, sharing your takes (even the bad ones, and the *really* bad ones), and your love of Top Chef. Conversations with Elise Franklin helped me navigate the insanity of academia (and still do), and I am grateful for our shared love of certain (not to be named) reality television programs. It is rare for an academic department to run so smoothly, but my colleagues in the Department of History and Political Science at York College of Pennsylvania have cultivated an exceptionally collegial workplace, of which I am truly glad to be a part. I would like to thank Corey Brooks and Nick Anspach for helping me understand the college's funding bureaucracy, Deb Staley for running the department like a well-oiled machine, and Peter Levy, especially, for being my next-door office buddy and tolerating my interruptions and harangues about politics (and beyond) for the few years our paths crossed at YCP. Thanks to Emily Arendt, Kristen Beales, Mark Boonshoft, Lauren Duval, Alexi Garrett, Lindsay Keiter, Shira Lurie, and Alyssa Wade for making conferences more fun than they have any right to be. I am most grateful to have met Rachel Walker in Paris in the summer of 2016. Since then, our paths have crossed so many times in the most hilarious fashion (especially, when vying for many of the same jobs, we chatted for a bit in an airport bar as she left and I arrived for the same campus visit!). Luckily, I found the most supportive, encouraging, and fun "job market buddy" I could have ever asked for—I wouldn't have made it to the other side without you.

My friends outside of academia have reminded me of what is most important in life. I am grateful to Bri, Maria, Marin, and Meg for our friendship that always picks up right where it left off; to Maggie, my go anywhere, do anything travel buddy and future Amazing Race partner; to Allie, for being my friend since before you could talk (Shady Lane forever); to Mel, Caitlyn, and Ivonne, for regular Beyoncé dance parties in the kitchen; and especially to Lindsey, the Amy to my Tina, the Abed to my Troy, and the Nick to my Schmidt (insert gifs here).

I have been more fortunate than most, I think, to have had a cadre of dedicated mentors throughout my educational and professional career, without whom this book would not be possible. Cynthia Lynn Lyerly ("Prof L.") has always been a tireless cheerleader, unwavering in her support of my work from the moment she suggested I go to graduate school and long after she was obligated to do so. I thank her especially for her courageous model of optimism and strength in adversity, and for many invitations to BC basketball games. I am grateful to Team Awesome—Judy Giesberg, Lynne Hartnett, and Catherine Kerrison—not just for their professional guidance, constant encouragement, and completely *objective* support (ahem), but most of all, for their friendship. From "Summit" dinners to Zoom happy hours to the endless text thread that has taken on a life of its own, I'm so glad that I (rather fortuitously) ended up at Villanova so many years ago. For more than a decade, Rosie Zagarri has been the consummate mentor, teaching me how to be a better writer and historian, believing in me even when I didn't believe in myself, and sneaking human food to my dog when we come down to Virginia to visit.

My family deserves the most credit for buoying me throughout the long process of writing this book. Extra credit goes to Neen for never having to feign interest in my work, for volunteering to read chapter drafts whenever I had them ready, and for accompanying me on a cold, January research trip to Harrisburg. A few months after I started at YCP, I (rather impetuously) brought Dot home; in the years that followed, she has devotedly snored by my feet as I wrote, kept me company during quarantine, and always taken me away from my desk at just the right time thanks to her deep love of long walks (I must also mention Delilah, who would grow jealous if Dot were the only dog to be mentioned in these pages). I am thankful to my brother, Jeff, who can provide levity and laughter in any situation and who makes the amount of Parmesan cheese I put on my pasta look normal. My parents have not only loved me unconditionally (which is no small feat!) but have always encouraged me to express my opinions and insisted that I do what I love. Throughout my life, I have been completely dependent upon Mike and Nancy Beatty for their love and support, and it is because of that dependence that I have been able to finish this herculean task and compose the pages in this book. I dedicate this work to my parents in an attempt to thank them for, well . . . everything.

A Note on Sources

Completing a comparative rhetorical analysis and sociolegal study of three cities in three different jurisdictions that, over the course of seventy years, were under the control of three different forms of government necessarily leads to a range and variety of source material. It was, in many cases, impossible to use completely comparable source material, and thus likewise impossible to accumulate completely comparable data among these three cities. I want to be open about the conclusions and analysis I draw from the source material, recognizing its limitations in particular. I do not want the data provided in this book to obscure more than it reveals, or even to obscure the reality of women's lived experiences. I have spent the bulk of this book doing close readings of women's often terse and repetitive petitions to illuminate larger patterns among these sources, particularly the rhetorical choices women petitioners made, what this language revealed about the gendered power dynamic between women and the patriarchal state, and how these choices may have impacted women's status during and in the wake of the Revolution. When possible, I have provided limited graphs that I think can prove helpful, when and where the data is most complete. I include here this note on sources to illuminate where and why there are gaps in the data.

Regarding petitions women submitted to their state legislatures, the most consistent data comes from Massachusetts. The General Assembly recorded acts and resolves from individual subjects' and citizens' petitions that the legislature approved for the entirety of the period under study. Separate files exist in the archive of unpassed petitions, though these records are not complete; additionally, those collections do not begin until 1775. Nevertheless, Boston provides the most fruitful jurisdiction in which to study change over time between 1750 and 1820 relative to Philadelphia and Charleston.[1] Because the petitions are separated by those confirmed in the *Acts and Resolves* volumes and those unpassed either in the House or Senate, it is easier to conclude with a degree of certainty the rate at which Boston women's pleas were recognized by their state legislators.

Philadelphia's and Charleston's petitions records, however, are far more inconsistent. The Pennsylvania State Archives in Harrisburg has an entire collection entitled "Pennsylvania's Revolutionary Governments," which houses all extant materials related to the function of the Whig legislature during that period (1775–1790). Additionally, "Petitions and Miscellaneous Records" covers the same period within the records of the General Assembly. Outside of that chronological time frame, extant records are far more inconsistent. In some cases, petitions submitted after that period can be traced through the minutes of legislative journals (of both the House and the Senate) and then located in the House or Senate files; prior to 1775, few if any petitions from the colonial assembly survive.[2] The South Carolina Department of Archives and History in Columbia has a well-indexed collection entitled "Petitions to the General Assembly, 1776–1883." The consistency of access to extant petitions from the period 1776–1820, then, is ripe for analysis. Prior to that period, the limited number of petitions filed by Charleston women from 1750 to 1776 come from a search of the index of the journals of the Commons House of Assembly of South Carolina. In a number of cases both in terms of Philadelphia and Charleston women's petitions, it is impossible to know with any certainty whether their petitions were approved.

Divorce records produce fewer challenges, though limitations in quantitative analysis of these records persist. The Judicial Archives housed in the Massachusetts Archives in Boston contain divorce records throughout the period studied in this work. Some, however, are incomplete. Especially after the 1780s, cases sometimes appear in the record books, but not in the docket books; if they appear in both of these places, file papers may not exist; and even if file papers exist, a record as to the decision of the court does not always survive. The Pennsylvania State Archives in Harrisburg hold extant records of divorce papers from 1786 to 1815 within the records of the Pennsylvania Supreme Court, but as with records related to Boston women's divorces, the judges' rulings in Philadelphia women's divorce suits are also often unknown.

One of the reasons why I chose to do a comparative *urban* study instead of a more representative statewide study was so that I could get a sense of women's experiences in their interactions with the patriarchal state across class as well as regional lines. Records of institutions dedicated to poor relief were more numerous in cities, where concentrations of impoverished early Americans were likewise higher. The Philadelphia and Charleston almshouses and workhouses left copious records that survive in archives in both cities; institutions there kept prodigious notes on admissions, day-to-day lives of residents (or "inmates," as they were sometimes called), as well as notations as to why certain applicants were denied various forms of aid. The most complete record of the comparable Boston institution is available in *The Eighteenth-Century Records of the Boston Overseers of the Poor*, available in print and online.[3] These records, however, consist of tabular data of aid recipients and inmates—that is, demographic data and quantities of aid provided to applicants. To compensate for the lack of narrative primary source material of the Boston overseers' records relative to those in Philadelphia and Charleston, I have engaged with secondary source analysis on the subject.

Finding women in the traditional legal archive during this period is challenging. It is exponentially more difficult to identify Black women, as I briefly discuss in chapter 6.[4] Not only were the legislature and the courtroom patriarchal spaces, in which women—Black and white—needed to perform certain prescribed behaviors on the basis of their gender and race to gain the protection of patriarchs in power, but so too is the archive a patriarchal space in the way it is organized, in the sources that have been collected, in the people whose stories are most accessible to scholars and to the public.

The Massachusetts Archives provides examples of these challenges. The coverage of the Judicial Archives during the revolutionary period is vast. The way in which the archives are organized—on the basis of case numbers and file names instituted by the patriarchal state—obscures the presence of women, but especially women of color. In order to locate instances in which Black women interacted with the patriarchal state in the revolutionary era, it is necessary to comb the index of this collection. Here, the clerk recording and organizing cases before the Suffolk County judiciary systems would, on occasion, note the race or status of enslavement of a plaintiff or defendant. The index shows notations such as "Parthenia, negro slave," "Inquisition, on negro woman," or "Briton, slave Johna. Webb, case of." This was the case *only* for Black and Indigenous people; white was the normative race according to the standards of those recording the court's business, and thus required no specification. The clerk, however, was not consistent. He did not always note that a man or woman was a "Negro" or an "Indian." As enslaved people were subject to the capricious cruelty of their enslavers, so too were free and enslaved people of color in revolutionary-era Boston subject to the fickleness of the clerk recording the cases. The only way, then, to fully recover Black Bostonians' experiences in the legal record would be to read every last case file and meticulously read tens of thousands of documents on microfilm.

In an attempt to find each instance of Black women's interactions with the patriarchal state in legal records *without* reading every last legal document over the span of seventy years, I followed the whims of the clerk. I read through every relevant index, searching for notations where he deemed it necessary to denote the race of any parties involved. I also made a case for reading alternate source materials, like emancipation deeds found in the records of the South Carolina Department of Archives and History as well as the Pennsylvania Abolition Society Papers, as evidence of Black women's petitioning efforts. When we read sources in the traditional archive "along the bias grain" and actively seek out Black women's voices and views in traditional sources where they otherwise appear silent, a more full picture of their power and agency emerges.[5] Illuminating Black women's interactions with the patriarchal state provides evidence that gendered dependence and women's strategies in both deploying this construct and effectively exploiting its presumptions were contingent upon one's intersectional identities, particularly relative to race and gender. We must always be cognizant of the ways in which the archive is, itself, at least a byproduct of the patriarchal state, if not another institution acting in service of strengthening it and its interests. In order to dismantle these structures, we must think critically about who the archive serves; who retains power under its current structures; who is silenced in the process; and how we might recover the voices and experiences of those lost in the silences.

Abbreviations

GCM, MA General Court of Massachusetts, Massachusetts Archives, Boston, MA

HSP Historical Society of Pennsylvania

JA, MA Judicial Archives, Massachusetts Archives, Boston, MA

"JOURNALS," CHARLESTON ALMSHOUSE RECORDS, CCPL "Journals, Records, and Minutes, 1800–1917," in Charleston (SC) Commissioners of the Almshouse, *Records of the Commissioners of the Alms House (Poor House), 1800–1923*, Charleston Archive, Charleston County Public Library

MA Massachusetts Archives, Boston, MA

MAGDALEN SOCIETY MINUTES, HSP Magdalen Society of Philadelphia Records, Collection 2016, Series 1: Administrative, 1800–1919 (Boxes 1–10) a. Minutes, 1800–1916, p. 1, Historical Society of Pennsylvania, Philadelphia, PA

MAN. BK., PAS PAPERS, HSP Manumission Book, Papers of the Pennsylvania Abolition Society, Historical Society of Pennsylvania, Philadelphia, PA

MISC. RECORDS, SCDAH *Miscellaneous Records*, South Carolina Department of Archives and History, Columbia, SC

PAS PAPERS, HSP Papers of the Pennsylvania Abolition Society, Historical Society of Pennsylvania, Philadelphia, PA

PGA, SCDAH *Petitions to the General Assembly,* South Carolina Department of Archives and History, Columbia, SC

RG27, A2, PSA Record Group 27 Pennsylvania's Revolutionary Governments, Subgroup A Committee of Safety 1775–1776, 2 Executive Correspondence and Petitions, 1775–1776, undated, Pennsylvania State Archives, Harrisburg, PA

RG27, E17, PSA Record Group 27 Pennsylvania's Revolutionary Governments, Subgroup E Supreme Executive Council, 17 Applications for Passes, Pennsylvania State Archives, Harrisburg, PA

RG27, E25, PSA Record Group 27 Pennsylvania's Revolutionary Governments, Subgroup E Supreme Executive Council, 1777–1790, 25 Clemency File, 1775–1790, undated, Pennsylvania State Archives, Harrisburg, PA

RG27, E28, PSA Record Group 27 Pennsylvania's Revolutionary Governments, Subgroup E Supreme Executive Council, 1777–1790, 28 Executive Correspondence and Petitions, 1777–1790, undated, Pennsylvania State Archives, Harrisburg, PA

RG 33, A41, PSA Record Group 33 Supreme Court of Pennsylvania, A Eastern District, 41 Divorce Papers, 1786–1815, Pennsylvania State Archives, Harrisburg, PA

RG 35, PCA Record Group 35 Guardians of the Poor, Philadelphia City Archives, Philadelphia, PA

SCDAH South Carolina Department of Archives and History, Columbia, SC

SUFFOLK FILES, SJC, JA, MA *Suffolk Files Collection,* Supreme Judicial Court, Judicial Archives, Massachusetts Archives, Boston, MA

Notes

Introduction

1. Elizabeth Graeme Fergusson's intellectual career and tumultuous personal life are chronicled in a biography by Anne Ousterhaut. See Ousterhaut, *The Most Learned Woman in America: A Life of Elizabeth Graeme Fergusson* (College Park: Pennsylvania State University Press, 2004).

2. The state's Supreme Executive Council operated as Pennsylvania's executive branch of its revolutionary-era government. Alternatively known as "the Executive Council" or merely "the Council," the body was comprised of members and led by a president and vice-president with explicit powers guaranteed by the Pennsylvania Constitution of 1776. It operated in this way from 1777 through 1790, at which point the governor replaced the authority of the council. At the time of Elizabeth's petition, Joseph Reed, the council's president, harbored a grudge against her for the part she played in advocating for an acquaintance of hers, and it negatively affected the outcomes of her petitions to the body for years. See Ousterhaut, *Most Learned Woman*, 215–58. See also "Pennsylvania Constitution of 1776," *Our Documentary Heritage*, Pennsylvania Historical and Museums Commission, August 26, 2015. Accessed June 29, 2021. Available at www.phmc.state.pa.us.

3. Except where otherwise noted, I have retained all original spelling, capitalization, and punctuation in quotations from primary sources. Changes from the original are only made when the original impedes clarity.

4. Petition of Elizabeth Graeme Fergusson, 20 February 1781, Gratz Collection, Mss., Case 14, Box 16, Folder 9, Elizabeth Graeme Fergusson Correspondence, 1737–1794, HSP.

5. Emphasis added. Letter from Andrew Robeson to Elizabeth Graeme Fergusson, 12 July 1778, Gratz Collection, Mss., Case 14, Box 16, Folder 22, Elizabeth Graeme Fergusson Correspondence, 1737–1794, HSP.

6. Letter from Joseph Reed to Mrs. Stockton, 14 June 1779, Gratz Collection, Mss., Case 14, Box 16, Folder 22, Elizabeth Graeme Fergusson Correspondence, 1737–1794, HSP.

7. The historiography of revolutionary-era women is vast, but among the most notable works are Carol Berkin, *Revolutionary Mothers: Women in the Struggle for America's Independence* (New York: Vintage Books, 2005); Ruth H. Bloch, "Republican Virtue: The Gendered Meanings of Virtue in Revolutionary America," in *Gender and Morality in Anglo-American Culture, 1650–1800* (Los Angeles: University of California Press, 2003), 136–53; Linda Grant DePauw, *Founding Mothers: Women of America in the Revolutionary Era* (Boston: Houghton Mifflin, 1975); Joan R. Gundersen, *To Be Useful to the World: Women in Revolutionary America* (Chapel Hill: University of North Carolina Press, 2006); Linda K. Kerber, *Women of the Republic: Intellect and Ideology in Revolutionary America* (Chapel Hill: University of North Carolina Press, 1980); Susan Klepp, *Revolutionary Conceptions: Women, Fertility, and Family Limitation in America, 1760–1820* (Chapel Hill: University of North Carolina Press, 2009); Jan Lewis, "The Republican Wife: Virtue and Seduction in the Early Republic," *William and Mary Quarterly* 44, 4 (October 1987): 689–721; Mary Beth Norton, *Liberty's Daughters: The Revolutionary Experience of American Women, 1750–1850* (Ithaca, NY: Cornell University Press, 1980); Mary Beth Norton, "The Evolution of White Women's Experience in Early America," *American Historical Review* 89, 3 (June 1984): 593–619; Barbara B. Oberg, ed., *Women in the American Revolution: Gender, Politics, and the Domestic World* (Charlottesville: University of Virginia Press, 2019); and Rosemarie Zagarri, *Revolutionary Backlash: Women and Politics in the Early American Republic* (Philadelphia: University of Pennsylvania Press, 2007).

8. Notable exceptions include the brief window in which certain propertied women from New Jersey exercised their right to vote for a short time in the early republic as well as shifting divorce laws—particularly in Pennsylvania—by Whig governments. See Zagarri, *Revolutionary Backlash*, 31–34; and Kerber, *Women of the Republic*, 181, respectively. On the stagnation of women's rights and women's legal status, see, for example, Marylynn Salmon, *Women and the Law of Property in Early America* (Chapel Hill: University of North Carolina Press, 1987); and Joan Hoff Wilson, "Illusion of Change: Women and the Revolution," in Alfred F. Young, ed., *The American Revolution: Explorations in the History of American Radicalism* (DeKalb: Northern Illinois University Press, 1976), 383–95. Linda Kerber ultimately observed the "conservatism of the legal revolution" for women. See Kerber, *Women of the Republic*, 9. On the law and women's lives in the long eighteenth century more broadly, see Norma Basch, *In the Eyes of the Law: Women, Marriage, and Property in Nineteenth-Century New York* (Ithaca, NY: Cornell University Press, 1982); Norma Basch, *Framing American Divorce: From the Revolutionary Generation to the Victorians* (Berkeley: University of California Press, 2001); Thomas E. Buckley, *The Great Catastrophe of My Life: Divorce in the Old Dominion* (Chapel Hill: University of North Carolina Press, 2002); Lee Virginia Chambers-Schiller, *Liberty, a Better Husband: Single Women in America, the Generations of 1780–1840* (New Haven, CT: Yale University Press, 1987); Richard H. Chused, *Private Acts in Public Places: A Social History of Divorce in the Formative Era of American Family Law* (Philadelphia: University of Pennsylvania Press, 1994); Nancy F. Cott, *Public Vows: A History of Marriage and the Nation* (Cambridge, MA: Harvard University Press, 2002); Cornelia Hughes Dayton, *Women before the Bar: Gender,*

Law, and Society in Connecticut, 1639–1789 (Chapel Hill: University of North Carolina Press, 1995); Clare A. Lyons, *Sex among the Rabble: An Intimate History of Gender and Power in the Age of Revolution, Philadelphia, 1730–1830* (Chapel Hill: University of North Carolina Press, 2006); Kerber, *Women of the Republic*; Norton, *Liberty's Daughters*; Lisa Wilson, *Life after Death: Widows in Pennsylvania, 1750–1850* (Philadelphia: Temple University Press, 1992); and Karin Wulf, *Not All Wives: Women of Colonial Philadelphia* (Philadelphia: University of Pennsylvania Press, 2005).

9. Elizabeth Anthony Dexter first elucidated the "declension thesis" in 1924. Elisabeth Anthony Dexter, *Colonial Women of Affairs: A Study of Women in Business and the Professions in America before 1776* (Boston: Houghton Mifflin, 1924). Other more recent and notable works whose arguments mirror Dexter's declension are Dayton, *Women before the Bar*; and Elaine Forman Crane, *Ebb Tide in New England: Women, Seaports, and Social Change* (Boston: Northeastern University Press, 1998).

10. Linda K. Kerber, "The Republican Mother: Women and the Enlightenment—an American Perspective," *American Quarterly* 28, 2 (Summer 1976): 187–205; Klepp, *Revolutionary Conceptions*; and Norton, *Liberty's Daughters*.

11. Berkin, *Revolutionary Mothers*; Kerber, *Women of the Republic*; Holly A. Mayer, *Belonging to the Army: Camp Followers and Community during the American Revolution* (Columbia: University of South Carolina Press, 1996); Alfred F. Young, *Masquerade: The Life and Times of Deborah Sampson, Continental Soldier* (New York: First Vintage Books, 2004); and Zagarri, *Revolutionary Backlash*.

12. On the ways in which loyalists—real and accused—navigated the political landscape during and after the American Revolution, see Rebecca Brannon, *From Revolution to Reunion: The Reintegration of the South Carolina Loyalists* (Columbia: University of South Carolina Press, 2016); Lauren Duval, "Mastering Charleston: Property and Patriarchy in British-Occupied Charleston, 1780–82," *William and Mary Quarterly* 75, 4 (October 2018): 589–622; Maya Jasanoff, *Liberty's Exiles: American Loyalists in the Revolutionary World* (New York: Vintage, 2011); and Donald F. Johnson, "Ambiguous Allegiances: Urban Loyalties during the American Revolution," *Journal of American History* 104, 3 (December 2017): 610–31.

13. Mary Kelley argues that access to education for women in the early republic was critical to their eventual move to public life in the antebellum United States, and Lucia McMahon demonstrates how these women grappled with the potential for gender equality through education while living in a world deeply grounded in sexual difference and inequality. Mary Kelley, *Learning to Stand and Speak: Women, Education, and Public Life in America's Republic* (Chapel Hill: University of North Carolina Press, 2008); Kerber, "The Republican Mother"; and Lucia McMahon, *Mere Equals: The Paradox of Educated Women in the Early Republic* (Ithaca, NY: Cornell University Press, 2012).

14. Abigail Adams to John Adams, 31 March 1776, *Adams Family Papers* (Massachusetts Historical Society), accessed September 2, 2020. Available at www.masshist.org.

15. The American system of race-based chattel slavery can serve as an example in this case. The revolutionary-era American patriarchal system was reliant upon unfree human labor as capital and wealth. Slavery, though incompatible with the rhetoric of the Revolution, was only torn apart in a piecemeal, drawn-out, and incomplete way; there would be no federal prohibition on the institution of slavery until the Thirteenth Amendment to the Constitution (which, of course, includes the significant stipulation

that allows for unfree, forced labor of incarcerated people). Not only did the founding generation fail to eradicate slavery, but they further embedded and protected it within the United States Constitution. See Paul Finkelman, *Slavery and the Founders: Race and Liberty in the Age of Jefferson* (New York: Taylor & Francis, 2014), 3–45; and David Waldstreicher, *Slavery's Constitution: From Revolution to Ratification* (New York: Hill and Wang, 2009).

16. The "First Wave" of the American feminist movement refers to the push for suffrage beginning formally in the mid-nineteenth century and extending through (though unevenly) the ratification of the Nineteenth Amendment in 1920. The "Second Wave" of the American feminist movement generally connotes the women's rights movement begun in the 1960s and extending through the 1980s, at which point it was met head-on by an increasingly powerful and revived conservative movement. Scholars have debated whether using "waves" as a metaphor of the stages of the women's rights movement in US history is a useful device. See, for example, Linda Nicholson, "Feminism in 'Waves': Useful Metaphor or Not?" *New Politics* 12, 4 (Winter 2010), accessed September 2, 2020. Available at https://newpol.org.

17. I came to this realization, in part, after attending a roundtable and engaging in the discussion at the 2018 Annual Meeting of the Society for Historians of the Early American Republic (SHEAR). Much of the conversation centered around investigating women's intellectual worlds in the early republic, and some participants questioned the degree to which they existed. The standards to which these women were held were explicitly those crafted by men to suit the opportunities only available to elite white men. It is unfair, unrealistic, and ahistorical to presume that women, collectively, were capable of creating and participating in such an intellectual world themselves because patriarchal society and culture explicitly prohibited them from doing so. Rosemarie Zagarri, Tom Cutterham, Sara Georgini, Lucia McMahon, and Sarah Pearsall, "Roundtable: New Intellectual Histories of Early American Women" (roundtable discussion: 40th Annual Meeting of SHEAR, Cleveland OH, July 21, 2018).

18. On the lives of these three remarkable women, see Edith Gelles, *Abigail Adams: A Writing Life* (New York: Routledge, 2002); Sheila Skemp, *First Lady of Letters: Judith Sargent Murray and the Struggle for Female Independence* (Philadelphia: University of Pennsylvania Press, 2009); and Rosemarie Zagarri, *Mercy Otis Warren and the American Revolution: A Woman's Dilemma* (New York: Wiley Blackwell, 2015).

19. On the long history of patriarchal oppression, see Gerda Lerner, *The Creation of Patriarchy* (New York: Oxford University Press, 1986).

20. Scholars who have studied early American urban culture and politics, particularly in the revolutionary era, have similarly focused their work on these cities. See, for example, Benjamin Carp, *Rebels Rising: Cities and the American Revolution* (New York: Oxford University Press, 2009). Recently, in their comparative urban studies, Kristen Beales and Lauren Duval have also focused on these cities. Kristen Beales, "Thy Will Be Done: Merchants and Religion in Early America, 1720–1815," PhD diss. (College of William and Mary, 2019); and Lauren Duval, "Landscapes of Allegiance: Space, Gender, and Military Occupation in the American Revolution," PhD diss. (American University, 2018).

21. See, for example, Joan R. Gundersen, "Independence, Citizenship, and the American Revolution," *Signs* 13, 1 (Autumn 1987): 59–77; and Barbara Clark Smith,

The Freedoms We Lost: Consent and Resistance in Revolutionary America (New York: New Press, 2010).

22. Gundersen, "Independence, Citizenship, and the American Revolution," 60.

23. Gundersen, "Independence, Citizenship, and the American Revolution," 62.

24. This concept caused considerable complications for women, particularly in the wake of the war when the United States investigated women's loyalties. Linda Kerber examines these issues in greater depth. See Kerber, "The Paradox of Women's Citizenship in the Early Republic: The Case of Martin vs. Massachusetts, 1805," *American Historical Review* 97, 2 (April 1992): 349–78.

25. Gundersen, "Independence, Citizenship, and the American Revolution," 62. Smith makes a similar point about the link between dependence and femininity: "Patriots maintained a critique of femininity, for the feminine epitomized in many minds a certain natural dependence, a weakness of will in the face of tea or expensive laces, susceptibility to the sorts of social pretensions that brought households into excessive consumption and devastating debt." Smith, *The Freedoms We Lost*, 107.

26. I am adapting this theoretical construction of a spectrum or continuum of dependence and independence from Jared Hardesty's study of freedom and unfreedom in the lived experience of Black Bostonians. Hardesty argues that "rather than the traditional dichotomous conception of slavery and freedom, colonial-era slavery should be understood as part of a continuum of unfreedom." Hardesty, *Unfreedom: Slavery and Dependence in Eighteenth-Century Boston* (New York: NYU Press, 2016), 2.

27. Feminist scholar Elizabeth Janeway analyzes the "powers of the weak," particularly those exerted by women, in "Women and the Uses of Power," in Hester Eisenstein and Alice Jardine, eds., *The Future of Difference* (New Brunswick, NJ: Rutgers University Press, 1985), 327–28. See also "power, n.1," *OED Online* (Oxford University Press, March 2015), accessed May 6, 2015. Available at www.oed.com.

28. Kimberlé Williams Crenshaw coined the term "intersectionality" in 1989 to describe the multilayered subordination that Black women face in the United States. She complicated notions of feminism by highlighting women's divergent experiences of sexism based on their race, class, and gender. Crenshaw, "Demarginalizing the Intersection of Race and Sex: A Black Feminist Critique of Doctrine, Feminist Theory, and Antiracist Politics," *University of Chicago Legal Forum* 1989, 1, article 8 (1989): 139–67. Intersectional feminist theory has challenged scholars to observe race, class, and gender as layered, interconnected social categories that generate "overlapping and interdependent systems of discrimination or disadvantage." "Intersectionality, n.," *OED Online* (Oxford University Press, June 2016), accessed August 26, 2016. Available at www.oed.com.

29. Hardesty, *Unfreedom*.

30. Catherine Adams and Elizabeth Pleck, *Love of Freedom: Black Women in Colonial and Revolutionary New England* (New York: Oxford University Press, 2010), 12–14.

31. Smith, *The Freedoms We Lost*.

32. Jennifer Morgan's *Laboring Women* is the founding tome analyzing how Black women's reproductive labor built and sustained the system of slavery in the New World. Sasha Turner's work explores the ways in which abolitionists simultaneously sought an end to slavery while also rationalizing their case by suggesting that Black women's reproductive labor would still suit the labor needs of sugar plantations in Jamaica. Jessica Marie Johnson examines the complex position of Black women in

the African diaspora, who practiced and claimed freedom through intimacy and kinship ties and were very much defined by constructions of their reproductive capacity. See Jessica Marie Johnson, *Wicked Flesh: Black Women, Intimacy, and Freedom in the Atlantic World* (Philadelphia: University of Pennsylvania Press, 2020); Jennifer Morgan, *Laboring Women: Reproduction and Gender in New World Slavery* (Philadelphia: University of Pennsylvania Press, 2004); Sasha Turner, *Contested Bodies: Pregnancy, Childrearing, and Slavery in Jamaica* (Philadelphia: University of Pennsylvania Press, 2017).

33. Because of the ways in which the Anglo-American patriarchy viewed Black women's bodies, these women existed outside of the confines of those whom white society considered to be protected, helpless dependents. See Johnson, *Wicked Flesh*; and Morgan, *Laboring Women*.

34. The literature on Black women's experience within and adjacent to American slavery is vast. Canonical works include Elizabeth Fox-Genovese, *Within the Plantation Household: Black and White Women of the South* (Chapel Hill: University of North Carolina Press, 1988); Jacqueline Jones, *Labor of Love, Labor of Sorrow: Black Women, Work, and the Family from Slavery to the Present* (New York Basic Books, 1985); and Deborah Gray White, *Ar'n't I a Woman? Female Slaves in the Plantation South* (New York: Norton, 1985). See also Daina Ramey Berry, *The Price for Their Pound of Flesh: The Value of the Enslaved, from Womb to Grave, in the Building of a Nation* (Boston: Beacon Press, 2017); Stephanie M. H. Camp, *Closer to Freedom: Enslaved Women and Everyday Resistance in the Plantation South* (Chapel Hill: University of North Carolina Press, 2004); David Barry Gaspar and Darlene Clark Hine, eds., *More Than Chattel: Black Women and Slavery in the Americas* (Bloomington: Indiana University Press, 1996); Thavolia Glymph, *Out of the House of Bondage: The Transformation of the Plantation Household* (Cambridge: Cambridge University Press, 2008). On the experience of free Black women in the revolutionary era, early republic, and antebellum period, see Erica Armstrong Dunbar, *A Fragile Freedom: African American Women and Emancipation in the Antebellum City* (New Haven, CT: Yale University Press, 2011); Amrita Chakrabarti Myers, *Forging Freedom: Black Women and the Pursuit of Liberty in Antebellum Charleston* (Chapel Hill: University of North Carolina Press, 2011); Jessica Millward, *Finding Charity's Folk: Enslaved and Free Black Women in Maryland* (Athens: University of Georgia Press, 2015); Johnson, *Wicked Flesh*; and Loren Schweninger, "Property-Owning Free African-American Women in the South, 1800–1870," *Journal of Women's History* 1, 3 (1990): 13–44.

35. Though the terms "power," "autonomy," and "agency" have some overlap in meaning, it is useful to codify the difference. I have already discussed my interpretation of power earlier in this chapter. In the context of this work, "autonomy" signifies "liberty to follow one's will; control over one's own affairs; freedom from external influence, personal independence." Women of all statuses and identities experienced various degrees of and limitations on their autonomy during the revolutionary era. "Agency" denotes, quite simply, the "capacity to act," which all early Americans possessed in some capacities, albeit with significantly different capacities to act freely. See "autonomy, n.," *OED Online* (Oxford University Press, June 2021), accessed July 1, 2021. Available at www.oed.com; and "agency, n.," *OED Online* (Oxford University Press, June 2021), accessed July 1, 2021. Available at www.oed.com. On the challenges inherent in using agency as a framework of historical analysis, particularly regarding the

resistance of enslaved people, see Walter Johnson, "On Agency," Special Issue, *Journal of Social History* 37, 1 (Autumn 2003): 113–24.

Historians of American slavery have examined the complex relationship among power, agency, and oppression in important ways. Steven Hahn, for instance, argues that enslaved African Americans were able to build the foundations of grassroots mobilization from within the institution of slavery; this groundwork paved the way for political activity that would follow in the post-emancipation landscape. John Blassingame illustrates how slaves resisted the authority of their masters by retaining pieces of their culture and family life while also amalgamating older traditions with new ones. Deborah Gray White demonstrates the resourcefulness and strength of African American women in the antebellum South who found themselves in a particularly oppressive position within slavery due to their gender. See Steven Hahn, *A Nation under Our Feet: Black Political Struggles in the Rural South from Slavery to Migration* (New York: Belknap Press, 2005); John Blassingame, *The Slave Community: Plantation Life in the Antebellum South* (New York: Oxford University Press, 1979); and White, *Ar'n't I a Woman?*

36. Recently, scholars have sought to understand how dependent persons and groups in early America resisted their subordinate status. Kelly Ryan's work, for example, illuminates the ways in which legal and social dependents—namely, Black Americans, white women, and servants—promulgated stories of their violent oppression to advocate for themselves, and in so doing gave birth to a nascent human rights movement. See Ryan, *Everyday Crimes: Social Violence and Civil Rights in Early America* (New York: NYU Press, 2019). Gregory Downs identified a similar pattern of political power inherent in the invocation of dependence during the American Civil War and Reconstruction, a phenomenon he dubs "American patronalism": "I examine dependence not just as a structural condition but as a tool that people used to mediate politics for their own benefit." My work, in part, seeks to find the origins of this paradigm much earlier in American history, as well as the ways in which the particularities of gendered dependence functioned in women's relationship to the state. Downs, *Declarations of Dependence: The Long Reconstruction of Popular Politics in the South, 1861–1908* (Chapel Hill: University of North Carolina Press, 2011), 1, 228 n. 2.

37. Tera Hunter, *Bound in Wedlock: Slave and Free Black Marriage in the Nineteenth Century* (Cambridge, MA: Harvard University Press, 2019), 64.

38. Laura Edwards's groundbreaking *A People and Their Peace* explores the centrality of "ordinary" people in shaping local legal practices. Edwards makes distinctions between the development of local and state laws, their varying influence over civil and criminal law, and historians' attention—or lack thereof—to the primacy of these separate systems. Laura Edwards, *The People and Their Peace: Legal Culture and the Transformation of Inequality in the Post-Revolutionary South* (Chapel Hill: University of North Carolina Press, 2009), 3–25. See also Ryan, *Everyday Crimes.*

39. "The Character of a Good Husband, and a Good Wife," *Free-Masons Magazine* (London), January 1795, 44–45.

40. A good husband was one who treated his wife "with delicacy as a woman" and "with tenderness as a friend." He would recognize his wife's inherent inferiorities, and deal with them patiently. All of his efforts were to be geared toward her welfare. He did not abuse his wife, physically or otherwise, but rather, he accepted her "natural softness and sensibility" and treated her with compassion. Ultimately, a good husband

provided "support and protection" to his wife. "The Character of a Good Husband, and a Good Wife," *Free-Masons Magazine* (London), January 1785, 16.

41. On the application of coverture in women's lives, see Kerber, *Women of the Republic*, 120–21. For an example of the practical limitations of coverture in early American women's lived experience, see Kirsten Sword, *Wives Not Slaves: Patriarchy and Modernity in the Age of Revolutions* (Chicago: University of Chicago Press, 2021), 5–7.

42. See *Blackstone's Commentaries on the Laws of England*, book 1, chapters 421–33, "Of Husband and Wife," available online at http://avalon.law.yale.edu.

43. I am indebted to participants at the 2019 Petitions in the Age of Atlantic Revolutions Conference hosted by the University of Lisbon. The work of each contributor and commentator broadened my understanding of the impact of petitions in the revolutionary Atlantic world and helped to clarify my theoretical approach to these important sources. For work that examines the political dynamics of early American women's petitions, see, for example, Kristin Collins, "'Petitions without Number': Petitions and the Early Nineteenth-Century Origins of Marriage-Based Entitlements," *Law & History Review* 31, 1 (February 2013): 1–60; Kerber, *Women of the Republic*, 85–99; Cynthia A. Kierner, *Southern Women in Revolution, 1776–1800: Personal and Political Narratives* (Columbia: University of South Carolina Press, 1998); Elizabeth R. Varon, *We Mean to Be Counted: White Women and Politics in Antebellum Virginia* (Chapel Hill: University of North Carolina Press, 1998); and Zagarri, *Revolutionary Backlash*.

Chapter 1. Sympathy and the State

1. The state of Massachusetts had assessed several legal penalties against Tarbell and his property; he seems to have remained in Newport to avoid paying the fines he owed to the state. See, for example, Resolve Directing Perez Morton to Bring Forward a Process on the Bond Given by Samuel Tarbell, 23 April 1778, ch. 998, *The Acts and Resolves, Public and Private, of the Province of the Massachusetts Bay*, vol. 20 (Boston: Wright & Potter Printing Co., 1918), 385.

2. On women's status as refugees of war and the political implications of requesting passes to be reunited with their husbands, see Kerber, *Women of the Republic*, 47–53.

3. Petition of Rebecca Tarbell, 15 February 1779, *Felt Collection*, vol. 170, p. 228; vol. 221, p. 447, MA.

4. On the significance of sympathy, fellow feeling, and the culture of sensibility in early America, see, for example, G. J. Barker-Benfield, *The Culture of Sensibility: Sex and Society in Eighteenth-Century Britain* (Chicago: University of Chicago Press, 1992); "'The Turnings of the Human Heart': Sympathy, Social Signals, and the Self," in Nicole Eustace, *Passion Is the Gale: Emotion, Power, and the Coming of the American Revolution* (Chapel Hill: University of North Carolina Press, 2008), 253–84; and Sarah Knott, *Sensibility and the American Revolution* (Chapel Hill: University of North Carolina Press, 2009). Kirsten Sword notes a similar pattern in elopement notices published by women in local newspapers beginning in the 1760s. In those cases, women placing ads sought both to appeal to the public's sense of empathy and also to match the increased demand for sentimental literature. See Sword, *Wives Not Slaves*, 181.

5. Petition of Rebecca Tarbell, 15 February 1779, *Felt Collection*, vol. 170, p. 228; vol. 221, p. 447, MA.

6. Resolve on the Petition of Rebecca Tarbell, 13 April 1779, ch. 633, *Acts and Resolves*, vol. 20, p. 663.

7. Historian Linda Kerber defined the experience of petitioning thus: "The petitioner is inherently a prepolitical being. The formulation of a petition begins in the acknowledgment of subordination; by definition the petitioner poses no threat. The rhetoric of humility is a necessary part of the petition as a genre, whether or not humility is felt in fact." Yet, as Kerber also notes, humility was not a given. Kerber, *Women of the Republic*, 85. On petitioners who neglected or refused to supplicate the state in the way in which Kerber details, see chapter 5 of this book.

8. "Gender trouble" is a term I am borrowing and modifying from Judith Butler's foundational text of the same name. In this formative work, Butler argues that gender is performed, and that there is no one category of "woman" or "women," for example. Ideas about gender and gender performance are complicated by race, class, and sexual orientation. Butler also holds that sex itself is a social construct, not gender alone. For the purpose of this project, I employ the term "gender trouble" or "gender troubling" to signify early American women's ability to play with tropes of femininity and masculinity to work to their advantage. This understanding assumes a widely held range of practices of comportment for middling and upper-class white revolutionary-era Americans regardless of gender, and argues that despite the rigidity of these socially, legally, and economically prescribed roles, gender performance was malleable. Judith Butler, *Gender Trouble: Feminism and the Subversion of Identity* (New York: Routledge, 2006). On the application of this contemporary gender theory to eighteenth-century subjects, see Greta LaFleur, "Sex and 'Unsex': Histories of Gender Trouble in Eighteenth-Century North America," *Early American Studies* 12, 3 (Fall 2014): 469–99.

9. In her 1980 work, Mary Beth Norton indicates that early American women and men did accept the subordinate position of women—at least until the Revolution—and uses women's diaries and private correspondence to come to that conclusion. While I would argue that women's petitions demonstrate the performative nature of these tropes, the question of whether women truly believed in or accepted these various frameworks of their dependence is not the focus of this study. See Norton, *Liberty's Daughters*, 110–24.

10. LaFleur, "Sex and 'Unsex,'" 471.

11. Petition of Mary Peronneau, 22 February 1783, no. 279, PGA, SCDAH.

12. Petition of Mary Peronneau, 22 February 1783, no. 279, PGA, SCDAH.

13. Michael E. Stevens and Christine M. Allen, eds., *Journals of the House of Representatives, 1787–1788* (Columbia: University of South Carolina Press, 1981), 399–400, 424–25.

14. Petition of various Subscribers on behalf of Margaret Baker, 23 February 1787, RG27, E25, PSA.

15. Petition of Ann Sutter, n.d., punishment remitted, and Petition of Sundry Inhabitants of Philadelphia in the case of Anne Sutter, 30 October 1786, RG27, E25, PSA.

16. Petition of Margaret Baker, n.d., RG27, E25, PSA.

17. Petition of various Subscribers on behalf of Margaret Baker, 23 February 1787, RG27, E25, PSA.

18. Margaret Baker fine remitted & punishment at hard Labor remitted, 4 March 1788, RG27, E25, PSA.

19. Women's intellectual capacity was often seen either as unequal to men's or as a tool of masculinization that likewise became a threat to domesticity. See, for example, Kerber, *Women of the Republic*, 193–99, 226–27.

20. Petition of Ann Cannon, 1 May 1794, File of William Cannon, no. 1044, *Revolutionary Accounts Audited*, SCDAH.

21. The assembly required that after that date, she reapply to the legislature for additional funds in the future per the recent change in the application process. Report of the Committee on the Petition of Ann Cannon, 1794, File of William Cannon, no. 1044, *Revolutionary Accounts Audited*, SCDAH.

22. Petition of Elizabeth Toussiger, 5 April 1781, File of Peter Toussiger, no. 7869A, *Revolutionary Accounts Audited*, SCDAH.

23. Report of the Committee on the Petition of Elizabeth Toussiger, 6 December 1793, File of Peter Toussiger, no. 7869A, *Revolutionary Accounts Audited*, SCDAH.

24. Petition of Mary Dunton, 19 January 1783, RG27, E17, PSA.

25. Petition of Sarah White, 15 October 1782, granted 17 January 1783, RG27, E17, PSA.

26. Petition of Catherine Richards, 18 November 1782, granted 19 November 1782, RG27, E17, PSA.

27. Petition of Anna Roberts, 13 October 1779, granted 16 November 1779, RG27, E17, PSA.

28. Petition of Mary Badger, 18 April 1778, *Felt Collection*, vol. 218, p. 296, MA.

29. Petition of Abigail Gallop, 23 June 1777, *Felt Collection*, vol. 182, p. 266, MA.

30. Petition of Mary Anderson, 4 April 1784, RG27, E17, PSA.

31. Petition of Mary Smith, 3 October 1785, RG27, E25, PSA.

32. Sarah mentioned her family's "distresses" four times in her petition. Petition of Sarah Scott, 3 February 1783, no. 186, *PGA*, SCDAH.

33. Petition of Sarah Scott.

34. Theodora J. Thompson and Rosa S. Lumpkin, eds., *Journals of the House of Representatives, 1783–1784* (Columbia: University of South Carolina Press, 1977), 552.

35. Petition of Mary Brown, 15 February 1783, no. 220, *PGA*, SCDAH.

36. On the complicated nature of women's political positions, power, and authority in the revolutionary era, see Kerber, *Women of the Republic*, 73–136.

37. Petition of Mary Brown, 15 February 1783, no. 220, *PGA*, SCDAH.

38. Petition of Mary Brown.

39. Petition of Mary Brown.

40. Thompson and Lumpkin, eds., *House Journals, 1783–1784*, 552.

41. Petition of Eliza Clitherall, 16 February 1784, no. 23, *PGA*, SCDAH.

42. Cynthia A. Kierner, *Southern Women in Revolution, 1776–1800: Personal and Political Narratives* (Columbia: University of South Carolina Press, 1998), 127.

43. Kierner, *Southern Women in Revolution*, 94.

44. Petition of Mary Inglis, 15 February 1783, no. 229, *PGA*, SCDAH.

45. Petition of Sarah Capers, 22 February 1783, no. 264, *PGA*, SCDAH.

46. Petition of Mary Crippe, 16 October 1779, RG27, A2, PSA.

47. Petition of Mary Johnson, 16 September 1778, RG27, A2, PSA.

48. Petition of Mary Yard, December 1785, RG27, E25, PSA.

49. Mary Yard's fine remitted, 10 December 1785, RG27, E25, PSA.

50. Petition of Mary Lincoln, n.d. (between 1775 and 1792, likely c. 1792), GCM, MA.

51. The "republican mother" is Linda Kerber's designation for a woman in the post-revolutionary era who was tasked with the responsibility to raise republican sons for citizenship and republican daughters to be republican mothers for the good of the nascent nation. Kerber, "Republican Mother," and Kerber, *Women of the Republic.*

52. Resolve on the Petition of Mary Lincoln, 8 June 1792, ch. 7, *Acts and Laws of the Commonwealth of Massachusetts,* vol. 28 (Boston: Wright & Potter Printing Co., 1895), p. 147.

53. Petition of Sarah Lewis, 27 April 1780, *Felt Collection,* vol. 186, p. 191, MA.

54. Emphasis added. Petition of Sarah Lewis, 27 April 1780, *Felt Collection,* vol. 186, p. 191, MA.

55. Resolve on the Petition of Sarah Lewis, 29 April 1780, ch. 1038, The *Acts and Resolves, Public and Private, of the Province of the Massachusetts Bay,* vol. 21 (Boston: Wright & Potter Printing Co., 1922), pp. 467–68.

56. The law defined fatherless children as orphans. See Kirsten E. Wood, *Masterful Women: Slaveholding Widows from the American Revolution through the Civil War* (Chapel Hill: University of North Carolina Press, 2004), 61.

57. The state generally preferred to grant dependent women requests that would ensure these petitioners (and likewise, their children) would not become *public* dependents. In so doing, however, they assented to women's lack of "political obligations to the state," which often contradicted their treatment of loyalist or loyalist-adjacent women. Kerber, *Women of the Republic,* 123.

58. Petition of Sarah Bonsall, 27 December 1782, Petition Granted 31 December 1782, RG27, E17, PSA.

59. Emphasis added. Petition of Dorcas Hutchins, 17 October 1776, *Felt Collection,* vol. 210, p. 460, MA.

60. Resolve on the Petition of Dorcas Hutchins, ch. 466, The *Acts and Resolves of the Province of the Massachusetts Bay,* vol. 19 (Boston: Wright & Potter Printing Co., 1918), pp. 632–33.

61. Petition of Ruth Gay, n.d., *Felt Collection,* vol. 226, p. 65, MA.

62. Resolve on the Petition of Ruth Gay, 13 January 1780, ch. 775, *Acts and Resolves,* vol. 21, p. 356.

63. Petition of Freelove Scott, n.d., *Felt Collection,* vol. 226, p. 228, MA.

64. Resolve on the Petition of Freelove Scott, 17 March 1770, ch. 817, *Acts and Resolves,* vol. 21, p. 375.

65. Petition of Freelove Scott, October 1777, *Felt Collection,* vol. 183, pp. 241–42, MA.

66. Resolve on the Petition of Freelove Scott, 18 October 1777, ch. 454, *Acts and Resolves,* vol. 20, p. 177.

67. Petition of Freelove Scott, October 1777, *Felt Collection,* vol. 183, pp. 241–42, MA.

68. Resolve on the Petition of Freelove Scott, 25 February 1778, ch. 811, *Acts and Resolves,* vol. 20, pp. 304–5.

69. Resolve on the Petition of Freelove Scott, 18 October 1777, ch. 454, *Acts and Resolves,* vol. 20, p. 177.

70. Petition of Freelove Scott, September 1779, *Felt Collection,* vol. 185, p. 267, MA.

71. Resolve on the Petition of Freelove Scott, 17 March 1780, ch. 817, *Acts and Resolves,* vol. 21, pp. 375–76.

72. Resolve on the Petition of Elizabeth Pierpont, 5 March 1810, ch. 167, *Resolves of the General Court of the Commonwealth of Massachusetts* (Boston: Adams and Rhoades, n.d.), pp. 454–55.

73. Petition of Elizabeth Pierpont, n.d. (between 1784 and 1809), GCM, MA.

74. Petition of Elizabeth Pierpont, 28 January 1812, GCM, MA.

75. Elizabeth noted that at the time of her petition, the legislature had only paid out half of the total sum. Petition of Elizabeth Pierpont, 28 January 1812, GCM, MA.

76. Petition of Elizabeth Pierpont, 28 January 1812, GCM, MA.

77. Resolve on the Petition of Elizabeth Peirpont [misspelled in text], 29 February 1812, ch. 171, *Resolves of the General Court of the Commonwealth of Massachusetts* (Boston: Adams, Rhoades & Co., 1810), p. 386.

78. John Howard Smith, "'Sober Dissent' and 'Spirited Conduct': The Sandemanians and the American Revolution, 1765–1781." *Historical Journal of Massachusetts* 28, 2 (Summer 2000): 142–43.

79. Hopestill Capen, "To the Court of Inquiry," *Library of Congress American Memory* (Boston, 1776), accessed September 4, 2020. Available at www.loc.gov.

80. Petition of Patience Capen, n.d., *Felt Collection*, vol. 183, pp. 422–26, MA.

81. Petition of Patience Capen, n.d., *Felt Collection*, vol. 183, pp. 422–26, MA.

82. Report on the Committee of the Petition of Patience Capen, 10 March 1778, *Felt Collection*, vol. 183, pp. 422–26, MA.

83. Linda K. Kerber, *No Constitutional Right to Be Ladies: Women and the Obligations of Citizenship* (New York: Hill and Wang, 1998), 4.

84. Emphasis added. Petition of Martha Moore, 5 July 1779, RG27, E17, PSA.

85. Letter, John Gibson to Supreme Executive Council of Pennsylvania, 6 July 1779, RG27, E17, PSA.

86. Martha Moore pass granted, 8 July 1779, RG27, E17, PSA.

87. Petition of Mary Weeks, n.d., *Felt Collection*, vol. 180, pp. 280–81, MA.

Chapter 2. Independence in Dependence

1. Libel of Jane Houston, 5 March 1805, Houston divorce, RG33, A41, PSA.

2. Merril D. Smith, *Breaking the Bonds: Marital Discord in Pennsylvania, 1730–1830* (New York: NYU Press, 1991), 21.

3. Libel of Jane Houston, 5 March 1805, Houston divorce, RG33, A41, PSA.

4. On divorce in early American history, see, for example, Norma Basch, *In the Eyes of the Law: Women, Marriage, and Property in Nineteenth-Century New York* (Ithaca, NY: Cornell University Press, 1982); Basch, *Framing American Divorce*; Buckley, *The Great Catastrophe of my Life*; Chused, *Private Acts in Public Places*; and Cott, *Public Vows.*

Divorce itself was relatively rare in the revolutionary era—especially prior to the early republic—so many early Americans employed extralegal practices to effectively end their marriages. Abandonment, absconding, and self-divorce was a relatively common practice in the period. We see evidence of abandonment and absconding not just in the divorce cases studied here but also in elopement notices and in the records of local aid societies (the latter of which will be evaluated in chapter 5). On elopement notices and self-divorce practices, see especially Lyons, *Sex among the Rabble*; Mary Beth Sievens, *Stray Wives: Marital Conflict in Early National New England* (New York: NYU Press, 2005); and Sword, *Wives Not Slaves*.

5. Massachusetts allowed for divorce from 1692, from which point the governor and council heard pleas from men and women requesting marital separations. In 1780, the new Massachusetts state constitution transferred this power to county courts. While Pennsylvania allowed divorce from 1682, the law required its inhabitants to petition the governor or the legislature, which was both costly and time-consuming. In 1773, this power was transferred to colonial legislatures; from that point until 1785, the state granted just eleven divorces. The Pennsylvania legislature had attempted to pass a new divorce law prior to 1785, though the Privy Council quickly dismissed the bill. After the Revolution, though, Pennsylvania lawmakers redoubled their efforts and jumped on the opportunity to exercise their newly gained independence. In 1785, however, the wake of revolutionary fervor compelled the Pennsylvania state legislature to pass a liberalized divorce law, by which citizens of the state would request divorces through their county court system, just as their Massachusetts counterparts did. See Cott, "Divorce and the Changing Status of Women in Eighteenth-Century Massachusetts," *William and Mary Quarterly* 33, 4 (October 1976): 587; and Kerber, *Women of the Republic*, 181.

6. Before 1785, the Pennsylvania legislature had only permitted divorce in cases involving acts designated as sexual transgressions, such as adultery, bigamy, sodomy, fornication, incest, bestiality, and consanguinity. The new law, while conceding that it was naturally preferable for a marriage to continue as long as both spouses were living, acknowledged, "Where the one party is under natural or legal incapacities of faithfully discharging the matrimonial vow, the laws of every well regulated society ought to give relief to the innocent and injured person." The new law recognized that divorce, under certain circumstances, could actually promote the social order, and indeed, a "well regulated society" ought to afford this opportunity for its "innocent" and "injured" citizens. Pennsylvania's new, extensive divorce law emphasized the preservation of the social order through individual happiness. The new statute declared impotence and "wilful and malicious desertion and absence without a reasonable cause for and during the term and space of four years" in its justifications for a Pennsylvanian to seek a legal divorce. Though not necessarily based in an understanding of marriage as a civil contract, Pennsylvania law did allow opportunity for redress for women whose husbands neglected to fulfill their mutual marital duties. See Cott, "Divorce and the Changing Status of Women"; Kerber, *Women of the Republic*, 159; and James T. Mitchell and Henry Flanders, *The Statutes at Large of Pennsylvania from 1682 to 1801*, vol. 12 (Harrisburg, PA: Harrisburg Publishing Co./State Printer, 1906), 94. Kirsten Sword provides a contrary opinion regarding the impetus for the change in Pennsylvania's divorce law: "In the context of the long-term transatlantic conversation over households . . . the revolutionary politics of divorce seem less a rupture than a replay of previous conflicts." Sword, *Wives Not Slaves*, 246.

7. Cott, "Divorce and the Changing Status of Women"; and James T. Johnson, "The Covenant Idea and the Puritan View of Marriage," *Journal of the History of Ideas* 32, 1 (January–March 1971): 107–18.

8. Few examples of Philadelphia women's petitions exist in which they referred to their husband's violation of the marriage "contract" explicitly. Subpoenas issued to their husbands made reference to marriages "contracted" between the petitioner and her husband, but this was hardly regular, and does not seem to have been influenced by the words of the petitioner or her legal advocate.

9. The state required that a "next friend"—a surrogate representing those with legal disabilities—sponsor and cosign petitions of married women seeking separations from their husbands. This "next friend," was, more often than not, a man, but there are several instances in which female petitioners sought the assistance of other women, primarily their widowed mothers, to act as their legal representative in these cases. Of the extant divorce case files in the collection of the Pennsylvania State Archives, only five women between 1785 and 1815 represented other women as a "next friend." See the Attimus, Moore, Scott, Whatson, and White divorces, RG33, A41, PSA. James Foot's answer to his wife's libel underscored the importance of this legal intercessor; he complained that his wife Mary's petition was "not conformable to law" because she signed only her own name to the document, "without assigning any Friend." See Answer of James Foot, 5 October 1787, Foot divorce, RG33, A41, PSA. Massachusetts, however, required no such assistance; women were free to petition the court in their own names, without any outside representation aside from legal counsel.

Each Pennsylvania woman seeking a divorce was also required to swear an oath to the court, promising that the details of her petition were true, and that her decision was "not made out of levity," nor influenced by any collusion with her husband. Each Pennsylvania woman's divorce file included this oath, which immediately followed the text of her petition. The oath was sworn and often signed or marked by the petitioner's hand, or in some cases, by her "next friend," as well as the representative of the court. Massachusetts, however, did not demand this oath of its citizens. The stipulations that Pennsylvania's county courts required of women demonstrate the reticence of the state—its lawmakers and citizens—to allow for divorce in the first place, the seriousness with which they took the matter, and their understanding of women as helpless in terms of their comprehension and execution of the law. See Thomas R. Meehan, "'Not Made out of Levity': Evolution of Divorce in Early Pennsylvania," *Pennsylvania Magazine of History and Biography* 92, 4 (October 1968): 441–64; and Smith, *Breaking the Bonds*.

10. While some early Boston women's divorce files contain witness testimony, they were not nearly as prevalent nor as numerous as they were in their Philadelphian counterparts' files.

11. On gendered expectations in marriage present in various forms of conduct literature, see Margaret Beetham, *A Magazine of Her Own? Domesticity and Desire in the Woman's Magazine, 1800–1914* (New York: Routledge, 1996); Cathy N. Davidson, *Revolution and the Word: The Rise of the Novel in America* (New York: Oxford University Press, 2004); Kevin J. Hayes, *A Colonial Woman's Bookshelf* (Knoxville: University of Tennessee Press, 1996); Catherine Kerrison, *Claiming the Pen: Women and Intellectual Life in the Early American South* (Ithaca, NY: Cornell University Press, 2005); E. Jennifer Monaghan, *Learning to Read and Write in Colonial America* (Amherst: University of Massachusetts Press, 2007); Frank Luther Mott, *A History of American Magazines.* Volume 1, *1741–1850* (Cambridge, MA: Harvard University Press, 1939); and Kathryn Shevelow, *Women and Print Culture: The Construction of Femininity in the Early Periodical* (New York: Routledge, 1989).

12. Cott, "Divorce and the Changing Status of Women," 589.

13. See, for example, Jan Lewis, "The Republican Wife: Virtue and Seduction in the Early Republic," *William and Mary Quarterly* 44, 4 (October 1987): 689–721; and

Rosemarie Zagarri, "The Rights of Man and Woman in Post-Revolutionary America," *William and Mary Quarterly* 55, 2 (April 1998): 203–30.

14. See, for example, Petition of Elizabeth Alexander, 28 March 1800, Alexander divorce, RG33, A41, PSA. See also Petition of Sarah Gore, 30 November 1786, Gore Divorce, RG33, A41, PSA.

15. See, for example, Petition of Deborah Bellot, 3 August 1796, Bellot Divorce, RG33, A41, PSA.

16. See, for example, Petition of Elizabeth Cannon, 25 July 1796, Cannon divorce, RG33, A41, PSA.

17. Petition of Catherine Rogers, 2 November 1811, Rogers divorce, Docket #424, March 1812 Term, JA, MA.

18. Petition of Mary Hamilton, 21 November 1754, Hamilton divorce, #129733, vol. 793, *Suffolk Files*, SJC, JA, MA.

19. Petition of Susanna Moses, 27 April 1795, Moses divorce, #106953, Record Book, *Suffolk Files*, SJC, JA, MA.

20. Lewis, "The Republican Wife."

21. Petition of Jane Everly, 15 July 1801, Everly divorce, RG33, A41, PSA.

22. See, for example, Petition of Ann Bickerton, 17 December 1802, Bickerton divorce, RG33, A41, PSA; Petition of Susanna Brauer, 27 April 1786, Brauer divorce, RG33, A41, PSA; Petition of Isabella Smith, 29 July 1801, Smith divorce, RG33, A41, PSA.

23. Petition of Sarah Lloyd, 19 November 1801, Lloyd divorce, RG33, A41, PSA.

24. Petition of Elizabeth Martin, 9 September 1805, Martin divorce, RG33, A41, PSA.

25. Thomas A. Foster, *Sex and the Eighteenth-Century Man: Massachusetts and the History of Sexuality in America* (Boston: Beacon Press, 2006), 23–24.

26. Petition of Eunice Shed, 3 November 1819, Shed divorce, Docket #155, March 1820 Term, JA, MA.

27. Petition of Lucy Bates, February 14, 1812, Bates divorce, Docket #53, March Term 1812, JA, MA.

28. Petition of Catherine Ober, n.d., Ober divorce, Docket #85, August 1800 Term, JA, MA.

29. Foster, *Sex and the Eighteenth-Century Man*, 37.

30. Foster, *Sex and the Eighteenth-Century Man*, 39.

31. Foster, *Sex and the Eighteenth-Century Man*, 40.

32. Though women's petitions for divorce increased during and after the revolutionary era, they still occurred in relatively small numbers relative to the population at large. See Cott, "Divorce and the Changing Status of Women"; and Kerber, *Women of the Republic*, 158–84.

33. See, for example, Petition of Susannah Attimus, 14 November 1801, Attimus divorce, RG33, A41, PSA.

34. See, for example, Petition of Hannah Anderson, 18 June 1799, Anderson divorce, RG33, A41, PSA.

35. Petition of Mary Smith, January 6, 1800, Smith (Mary v. Stephen) divorce, Docket #141, February 1800 Term, JA, MA.

36. Petition of Mary Murphy, 9 March 1813, Murphy divorce, Docket #132, March 1813 Term, JA, MA.

37. Ruth Beals Petition, 25 July 1801, Beals divorce, Docket #26, August 1801 Term, JA, MA.

38. Petition of Catherine Ober, n.d., Ober divorce, Docket #85, August 1800 Term, JA, MA.

39. Foster, *Sex and the Eighteenth-Century Man*; and E. Anthony Rotundo, *American Manhood: Transformations in Masculinity from the Revolution to the Modern Era* (New York: Basic Books, 1994).

40. Emphasis added. Petition of Mary Foot, 5 July 1787, Foot divorce, RG33, A41, PSA.

41. Petition of Rosanna McKanacker for alimony, 1 September 1800, and divorce decree, McKanacker divorce, RG33, A41, PSA.

42. Petition of Ann Holland, Holland divorce, 23 July 1792, RG33, A41, PSA.

43. See Depositions of Gunning Bedford and Richard Guy, 26 January 1793, Holland divorce, RG33, A41, PSA.

44. Holland divorce decree, n.d., Holland divorce, RG33, A41, PSA.

45. Petition of Esther Potter, 8 March 1814, Potter divorce, Docket #127, March 1815 Term, JA, MA; Petition of Charlotte Walker, 23 November 1819, Walker divorce, Docket #21, March Term 1820, JA, MA.

46. Petition of Maria Barbara Lee, 29 December 1810, Lee Divorce, RG33, A41, PSA.

47. Petition of Sarah Goodenow, 18 January 1794, Goodenow divorce, #106622, *Suffolk Files*, SJC, JA, MA.

48. Goodenow divorce decree, n.d., Goodenow divorce, #106622, *Suffolk Files*, SJC, JA, MA.

49. "On Conjugal Affection," in *Lady's Magazine*, September 1792, 177.

50. Petition of Elizabeth Stevens, 14 July 1795, Stevens divorce, #106940, Record Book, *Suffolk Files*, SJC, JA, MA.

51. Salmon, *Women and the Law of Property*, 77. First, only women in Pennsylvania could seek divorces on the grounds of cruelty, though later Massachusetts followed suit. See Smith, *Breaking the Bonds*, 28; and Cott, "Divorce and the Changing Status of Women," 558.

52. Women had to "rely . . . on the authorities' willingness to bend and stretch the statutes in order to protect" them "from the husband whom the law defined solely as her protector." Norton, *Liberty's Daughters*, 50.

53. Lewis, "The Republican Wife."

54. Petition of Susanna Shipley, 6 November 1800, Shipley divorce, RG33, A41, PSA.

55. Emphasis in original. Petition of Ann Gardner, 17 April 1783, Gardner divorce, #129813, vol. 795, *Suffolk Files*, SJC, JA, MA.

56. Petition of Helena Bayard, 6 May 1784, Bayard divorce, #129834, vol. 796, *Suffolk Files*, SJC, JA, MA.

57. On the process of elopement notices in the revolutionary era, see Sievens, *Stray Wives*; and Sword, *Wives Not Slaves*.

58. Petition of Margaret Knodle, 14 November 1764, Knodle divorce, #129743, vol. 793, *Suffolk Files*, SJC, JA, MA.

59. Blackstone, *Commentaries*, book 1, ch. 15, p. 432, "Of Husband and Wife," available online at http://avalon.law.yale.edu.

60. Ruth H. Bloch, "The American Revolution, Wife Beating, and the Emerging Value of Privacy," *Early American Studies* 5, 2 (Fall 2007): 231.

61. Answer of Jacob Burkhart, 1 October 1785, Burkhart divorce, RG33, A41, PSA.

62. The court, however, did not think Andrew's justification reasonable, and granted Elizabeth the divorce she requested. See Andrew McBride, Answer to Libel, 7 September 1792, and Divorce Decree, McBride divorce, RG33, A41, PSA. Daniel McKanacker presented an answer to the court in response to his wife's petition using identical language, and his appeal, too, was rejected by the courts. See Answer of Daniel W. Kanacher, 12 September 1792, and Decree of Divorce, McKanacker divorce, RG33, A41, PSA.

63. Deposition of Gunning Bedford, 11 September 1792, McKanacker Divorce, RG33, A41, PSA.

64. Petition of Tabetha Hearsey, 14 July 1755, Hearsey divorce, *Felt Collection*, vol. 9, p. 383, MA.

65. Petition of Mary Pedley, 21 February 1784, Pedley Divorce, #129830, vol. 796, *Suffolk Files*, SJC, JA, MA.

66. Petition of Mary Arthur alias Hamilton, 21 November 1754, Arthur divorce, #129733, vols. 793–96, *Suffolk Files*, SJC, JA, MA.

67. Women often did come to the aid of female plaintiffs in divorce cases, discussed in greater length in chapter 4.

68. Deposition of Henry Parker, 13 March 1812, Bates divorce, Docket #53, March Term 1812, JA, MA.

69. Deposition of John Taylor, 9 March 1820, Coombs divorce, Docket #49, March Term 1820, JA, MA.

70. Deposition of Samuel Mann, 16 March 1820, Coombs divorce, Docket #49, March Term 1820, JA, MA.

71. Deposition of Jacob Screiner, 24 August 1797, Griscom divorce, RG33, A41, PSA.

72. Deposition of David Christie, 20 December 1804, Tallman divorce, RG33, A41, PSA.

73. Response of James Tiffin, 8 January 1803, Tiffin divorce, RG33, A41, PSA.

74. Notably, three men testified for Patrick Howley. Michael Doogan held that he did not know anything regarding the questions put forth by Patrick's lawyers, except that the two "seemed to be happily together; the Respondent appearing to be an honest and diligent man." Neil McGinnis claimed to have "often" heard Mary call her husband a "drunken rascal" and heard her threaten to withhold meals from him. Israel Roberts insisted that Mary refused to feed Patrick if he did not bring home money. Each of these three men was a friend of Patrick's, while the seven others who testified on Mary's behalf were either boarders in their home or knew both of the parties in the lawsuit. See Depositions of Michael Doogan, Neil McGinnis, and Israel Roberts, 22 January 1795, Howley divorce, RG33, A41, PSA.

75. Lawrence O'Neil deposition, 20 January 1795, Howley divorce, RG33, A41, PSA.

76. William Whitby deposition, 20 January 1795, Howley divorce, RG33, A41, PSA.

77. Deposition of Edward Talbot, 20 January 1795, Howley divorce, RG33, A41, PSA.

78. Howley divorce file, RG33, A41, PSA.

79. Deposition of Jacob Graff, 4 September 1791, Black divorce (Elizabeth v. James), RG33, A41, PSA.

80. Deposition of Henry Graff, 4 September 1791, Black divorce (Elizabeth v. James), RG33, A41, PSA.

81. Deposition of John Barber Frost, n.d., Ober divorce, Docket #85, August 1800 Term, JA, MA.

Chapter 3. Sole and Separate

1. Hereafter, Elizabeth Pinckney Bellinger will be referred to as Pinckney, to distinguish her from both her first husband, William Bellinger Jr., and her second husband, Dr. John Townsend. Marriage settlements were intended to keep money and property in the family, to protect a woman from husbands' creditors. In these cases, however, equity suits filed by women were often intended to protect wives from their husbands. For more on South Carolina's marriage settlement law and practice, see Marylynn Salmon, "Women and Property in South Carolina: The Evidence from Marriage Settlements, 1730 to 1830," *William and Mary Quarterly* 39, 4 (October 1982): 655–85.

2. Mabel L. Webber, "The Thomas Pinckney Family of South Carolina," *South Carolina Historical and Genealogical Magazine* 39, 1 (January 1938): 31, 15. Several Pinckneys had married Bellingers over the course of the families' long histories in America, demonstrating the clear concern of both groups for keeping their valuable assets in the hands of an exclusive few across generations.

3. Elizabeth Townsend Bill of Complaint, 22 March 1797, #15, Equity Bills 1791–1870, Court of Equity (Charleston District), L10090, SCDAH.

4. Significantly, too, this was not Elizabeth's first foray into petitioning the state for redress. In 1795, she submitted a plea to South Carolina's legislature for compensation for her late husband's cattle, which had been impressed by the local militia during the Revolution. Her petition was not granted, as the deadline for such applications had passed. Petition of Elizabeth Townsend, 22 November 1795, *Petitions to the General Assembly*, SCDAH.

5. One particularly contentious example that revealed the tensions inherent in such agreements was in the context of James Henry Hammond's marriage to Catherine Fitzsimons. The Fitzsimonses wanted to ensure that their considerable wealth and property remained secure, and, because Catherine was a minor, her brother would retain Catherine's property in a trust. This angered Hammond, who felt it was a slight to his manhood and who was frustrated at attempts to block his ownership of a substantial plantation. Eventually, Catherine's mother would suggest dropping the matter of a settlement at her daughter's urging, but tensions remained between the Fitzsimonses and Hammond. Eventually, two impartial arbitrators were consulted, who decided against the use of a marriage settlement. Drew Gilpin Faust, *James Henry Hammond and the Old South: A Design for Mastery* (Baton Rouge: Louisiana State University Press, 1982), 61–65.

6. Elizabeth Townsend Bill of Complaint, 22 March 1797, #15, Equity Bills 1791–1870, Court of Equity (Charleston District), L10090, SCDAH.

7. Elizabeth Townsend Bill of Complaint.

8. During Reconstruction, the 1868 state constitution opened up the opportunity for South Carolinians to petition the legislature for divorce, though the issue continued to be debated until 1872. Between 1872 and 1878, a total of 157 divorces were granted under the court of common pleas. The divorce bill was repealed in 1878. In 1895, the state formally prohibited divorce. Janet Hudson, "From Constitution to Constitution, 1868–1895: South Carolina's Unique Stance on Divorce," *South Carolina Historical Magazine* 98, 1 (January 1997): 75–96.

9. Hudson, "From Constitution to Constitution," 76.

10. Although this project functioned well for the patriarchal state for generations, in the case of the Confederacy, the goal of creating an explicitly exclusionary republic eventually sowed the seeds of its own undoing. See Stephanie McCurry, *Confederate Reckoning: Power and Politics in the Civil War South* (Cambridge, MA: Harvard University Press, 2012).

11. Salmon, *Women and the Law of Property*, 207 n. 26.

12. Salmon, *Women and the Law of Property*, 46. While Pennsylvania and Massachusetts both allowed for women to obtain *femes sole* trader status, these states permitted only women whose husbands were mariners or frequently away from home to engage in business in their own name, or would apply these rulings to deserted women only, rather than women whose husbands seemed otherwise fully capable of providing for them, as was the case in South Carolina. Pennsylvania allowed deserted wives or wives of husbands who were frequently at sea to obtain *feme sole* trader designation under the law from 1718. Massachusetts replicated Pennsylvania's statute, yet did not do so until 1787. See Salmon, *Women and the Law of Property*, 44–53.

13. Mary Roberts Parramore, "'For Her Sole and Separate Use': Feme Sole Trader Status in Early South Carolina" (master's thesis, University of South Carolina, 1991), 9–10.

14. South Carolina law, deriving from English precedent, automatically considered deserted wives as *feme sole*. Parramore, "'For Her Sole and Separate Use,'" 47–49; Cynthia M. Kennedy, *Braided Relations, Entwined Lives: The Women of Charleston's Urban Slave Society* (Bloomington: Indiana University Press, 2005), 153.

15. Rather than examining a representative sampling of women in South Carolina, this chapter instead focuses on women who owned property or did business in Charleston. In urban centers, women were more likely to have the opportunity to do business in their own name, having access to a growing, transatlantic marketplace, and were central players in the growing market economy. See Ellen Hartigan-O'Connor, *The Ties That Buy: Women and Commerce in Revolutionary America* (Philadelphia: University of Pennsylvania Press, 2009).

16. On the Courts of Chancery and Equity in South Carolina, see Kennedy, *Braided Relations*, 87–89; and Salmon, "Women and Property in South Carolina."

17. Elizabeth was born into the prominent Peronneau family, descended from the Huguenot Henri Peronneau, one of the original four hundred Huguenot settlers who arrived in Carolina in 1685. Edward's occupation as a merchant would have prompted Elizabeth's family to move to protect the family wealth through the use of a marriage settlement. Horry Frost Prioleau and Edward Lining Manigault, eds., *Register of Carolina Huguenots*. Vol. 3, *Marion-Villepontoux* (CreateSpace Independent Publishing Platform, 2007), 1358.

18. Elizabeth Lightwood Bill of Complaint, 24 May 1797, #14, Equity Bills 1791–1870, Court of Equity (Charleston District), L10090, SCDAH.

19. By the time of her marriage, Elizabeth's father, Samuel, was deceased. William Webb, married to Samuel's sister, would have filled in to the role of patriarch to protect the Peronneau family wealth. A. S. Salley Jr., ed., *Marriage Notices in the South-Carolina Gazette and Its Successors* (Albany, NY: Joel Munsell's Sons, 1902), 41; and Prioleau and Manigault, eds., *Register of Carolina Huguenots*, 1358.

20. Elizabeth Lightwood Bill of Complaint, 24 May 1797, #14, Equity Bills 1791–1870, Court of Equity (Charleston District), L10090, SCDAH.

21. It is worth noting here that Edward himself understood the importance of performing the consummate position of masculine provider and head of household. Like his wife, he would cite his obligations as a husband and father, and how his actions were his attempt at fulfilling that vital familial role.

22. Elizabeth Lightwood Bill of Complaint, 24 May 1797, #14, Equity Bills 1791–1870, Court of Equity (Charleston District), L10090, SCDAH.

23. Elizabeth Lightwood Bill of Complaint.

24. Answer of Edward Lightwood, 30 August 1797, #14, Equity Bills 1791–1870, Court of Equity (Charleston District), L10090, SCDAH.

25. "Elizabeth Lightwood," 1800 United States Federal Census, Charleston, South Carolina, Series: M32; Roll: 48; Page: 123; Image: 184; Family History Library Film: 181423, Ancestry.com. Accessed May 10, 2018.

26. "Lightwood," *People and Professions of Charleston, South Carolina, 1782–1802* online database (Provo, UT: Ancestry.com, 2006), 88, 109; and "Lightwood," *City Directories for Charleston, South Carolina for the Years 1803, 1806, 1807, and 1813* online database (Provo, UT: Ancestry.com, 2006), 20.

27. "Lightwood," *City Directories*, 49; and Record of Death of Edward C. Lightwood on October 5, 1808, published in the *Columbian Centinel, U.S., Newspaper Extractions from the Northeast, 1704-1930* online database (Provo, UT: Ancestry.com, 2014).

28. "Lightwood," *City Directories*, 123.

29. Maria Beaury Bill of Complaint, 23 December 1812, #16, CH184, Equity Bills 1791–1870, Court of Equity (Charleston District), L10090, SCDAH.

30. Maria Beaury Bill of Complaint. Despite assumptions about women's work, particularly after the American Revolution, women were central participants in the public, economic sphere and contributed greatly to the market economy of the revolutionary era. See Hartigan-O'Connor, *The Ties That Buy*.

31. Exhibit A, Copy of Articles of Copartnership, 18 October 1810, #16, CH184, Equity Bills 1791–1870, Court of Equity (Charleston District), L10090, SCDAH.

32. Maria Beaury Bill of Complaint, 23 December 1812, #16, CH184, Equity Bills 1791–1870, Court of Equity (Charleston District), L10090, SCDAH.

33. Maria Beaury Bill of Complaint.

34. Decree of Henry Wm. DeSaussure, 29 December 1813, #16, CH184, Equity Bills 1791–1870, Court of Equity (Charleston District), L10090, SCDAH.

35. Some scholars have drawn attention to the performative nature of women's engagement with the law by exploiting their roles as mothers. Recent work by Michael Blaakman in part highlights the fine line that one woman—Martha Bradstreet—had to tread when advocating for herself in court, and the significant labor she exerted to craft her image in such a way that the court might rule in her favor. The situation necessitated a defense of her actions as properly "feminine" while she simultaneously and expressly transgressed those standards. Bradstreet had to account for all of her "unwomanly" behavior by reframing it as an extension of her role as a mother (544–85). Her "creative and tactical relationship to normative gender ideology" made her situation tenuous and constantly subjected her to ridicule and scorn by the courts and men in her community (546). While this argument holds true in some small ways for my subjects, these South Carolina women did not transgress the standards of "proper femininity," as it were. Blaakman's sharp analysis does recognize a careful strategy that nineteenth-century women could employ, and certainly, other historians have

examined such exceptional cases (see 549 n. 8). But, in order to define a larger pattern of women's behavior, we must recognize that more women accepted—at least superficially or tacitly—the terms of normative gender roles prescribed to them, and performed these tropes in their interactions with the court. These women knew the very power inherent in language meant to keep them in submission, and used it to their benefit. See Blaakman, "Martha Bradstreet and the 'Epithet of *Woman*': A Story of Land, Libel, Litigation, and Legitimating 'Unwomanly' Behavior in the Early Republic," *Early American Studies: An Interdisciplinary Journal* 13, 3 (Summer 2015): 544–85.

36. Jane Hedderley Bill of Complaint, 3 January 1800, #5, CH174, Equity Bills 1791–1870, Court of Equity (Charleston District), L10090, SCDAH.

37. Jane Hedderley Bill of Complaint, 3 January 1800, #5, CH174, Equity Bills 1791–1870, Court of Equity (Charleston District), L10090, SCDAH.

38. A Mrs. Patton sent word to Jane Hedderley about her husband's deception. See Jane Hedderley Bill of Complaint, 3 January 1800, #5, CH174, Equity Bills 1791–1870, Court of Equity (Charleston District), L10090, SCDAH.

39. Jane Hedderley Bill of Complaint.

40. Jane Hedderley Bill of Complaint.

41. For more on separate maintenances in South Carolina, see Kennedy, *Braided Relations*, 87; Salmon, *Women and the Law of Property*, 74–77.

42. Jane Hedderley Bill of Complaint, 3 January 1800, #5, CH174, Equity Bills 1791–1870, Court of Equity (Charleston District), L10090, SCDAH.

43. Mary Roberts Parramore found over six hundred cases from 1754—when the first extant deed was recorded—through 1824—when South Carolina began tightening restrictions on *feme sole* traders. Of this six hundred, Parramore found 357 deeds, 53 of which occurred before the Revolution. She admits that because contracts or deeds were not required by the state during her period of study and thus many women acted as de facto sole traders, the exact number of *feme sole* traders in Charleston can never be known. Parramore, "'For Her Sole and Separate Use,'" 5–6, 7–9.

44. Parramore, "'For Her Sole and Separate Use,'" 33–38.

45. See Contract between Dr. John and Anne Mackie, 1786, *Misc. Records*, Book WW, p. 408, SCDAH.

46. Indenture of Thomas and Mary Langley, 13 January 1761, *Misc. Records*, Book MM, pp. 30–35, SCDAH.

47. Indenture of Christopher and Susannah Sheets, 1763, *Misc. Records*, Book MM, p. 6, SCDAH.

48. Contract between Peter and Elizabeth Horn, 26 August 1766, *Misc. Records*, Book MM, p. 490, SCDAH.

49. Contract between James and Mary Farrell, 20 May 1768, *Misc. Records*, Book NN, p. 289, SCDAH.

50. Contract between James and Rachel Clark, 23 February 1764, *Misc. Records*, Book MM, p. 308, SCDAH.

51. Indenture of Edward and Sarah Johnston, 12 April 1771, *Misc. Records*, Book OO, p. 547, SCDAH. Job St. Julien Marion attempted to do the same when he designated his wife, Elizabeth, as a *feme sole* trader, claiming he did so "for and in Consideration of the Love good Will & concern that I have for my loving wife." Contract between Job St. Julien and Elizabeth Marion, 1799, *Misc. Records*, Book 3E, p. 445, SCDAH.

52. Contract between Robert and Mary Howard, 9 April 1771, *Misc. Records*, Book OO, p. 553, SCDAH.

53. Indenture of George and Jane Thomson, 30 July 1773, *Misc. Records*, Book SS, p. 92, SCDAH.

Chapter 4. Matriarchal Allies and Advocates

1. Libel of Mary Hopps, 11 December 1799, Hopps divorce, RG33, A41, PSA.

2. Deposition of Ann Dennis, 22 November 1800, Hopps divorce, RG33, A41, PSA.

3. Hopps divorce decreed, date unknown, Hopps divorce, RG33, A41, PSA.

4. My use of the term "allies" and "alliances" in this context is informed by Kelly Ryan's analysis of the ways in which servants, white women, and enslaved and free Blacks solicited assistance from those within and outside of their own communities to challenge and defend themselves from social violence in early America. See Kelly A. Ryan, *Everyday Crimes: Social Violence and Civil Rights in Early America* (New York: NYU Press, 2019).

5. "Matriarch, n.," *OED Online* (Oxford University Press, June 2021), accessed July 30, 2021. Available at www.oed.com.

6. The notion that these matriarchal allies and advocates might supplant the role of patriarch, at least temporarily, is informed by Lorri Glover's work. In a June 2019 paper at the Sons of the American Revolution Annual Conference, Glover characterized Eliza Lucas Pinckney as a "planter-patriarch" in her own right. From this presentation, conversation among attendees followed, highlighting the significance of Glover's queering of the term "patriarch" and the ways in which this analysis undermines our conception of a term generally seen as concretely and absolutely masculine. My subjects, for the most part, do not achieve the same level of economic status (or prowess) as Pinckney, but the women described in this chapter took advantage of the malleability of constructions of gender during wartime to help each other survive, and in so doing, occasionally fulfilled, often willingly, the traditional masculine role of protector-patriarch. Lorri Glover, "Eliza Lucas Pinckney, Female Fortitude, and the Home Front/Front Lines of the Revolutionary War" (paper presented at 2019 Sons of the American Revolution [SAR] Annual Conference on the American Revolution, "Women Waging War in the American Revolution," Philadelphia, Pennsylvania, June 14–16, 2019). Since this conversation, Glover has published this work in her biography of Pinckney. See Glover, *Eliza Lucas Pinckney: An Independent Woman in the Age of Revolution* (New Haven, CT: Yale University Press, 2020).

7. This understanding of "interdependence" builds on Barbara Clark Smith's *Freedoms We Lost*. Smith notes that before the Revolution, colonists' lives centered around "neighboring" and "mutual interdependence," rather than individualistic autonomy and self-reliance. The Declaration of Independence, however, changed both the war's purpose and American attitudes about collective dependence. See Smith, *The Freedoms We Lost: Consent and Resistance in Revolutionary America* (New York: New Press, 2010). On female-centered relationships in this period, see Caroll Smith-Rosenberg, "The Female World of Love and Ritual: Relations between Women in Nineteenth-Century America," *Signs* 1, 1 (Autumn 1975): 1–29; and Norton, *Liberty's Daughters*, 102–9.

8. Petition of Mary Pedley, 21 February 1784, Pedley Divorce, #129830, v. 796, *Suffolk Files*, SJC, JA, MA.

9. Petition of Mary Cooper, 29 January 1779, RG27, E17, PSA.

10. Petition of Mary Cumming, 23 February 1788, no. 65, *PGA*, SCDAH.

11. Petition of Mary Fraser, et al., 11 November 1795, no. 7, *PGA*, SCDAH.

12. Petition of Mary Fraser, et al.

13. Petition of Mary Fraser, et al.

14. Emphasis in original.

15. Petition of Margarett Brisbane, 22 February 1783, no. 261, *PGA*, SCDAH.

16. Petition of Margarett Brisbane.

17. Kierner, *Southern Women in Revolution*, 174.

18. Petition of Mary Booth, n.d., *Felt Collection*, vol. 66, p. 114, MA. Resolve on the Petition of Mary Booth, 15 January 1761, ch. 245, *The Acts and Resolves, Public and Private, of the Province of the Massachusetts Bay*, vol. 16 (Boston: Wright & Potter Printing Co., 1909), p. 679.

19. Petition of Hannah Horner, n.d., *Felt Collection*, vol. 66, p. 80, MA. Resolve on the Petition of Hannah Horner, 19 January 1761, ch. 246, *Acts and Resolves*, vol. 16, p. 680.

20. Petition of Ann Saunders, n.d., *Felt Collection*, vol. 66, p. 114, MA. Resolve on the Petition of Ann Saunders, 19 January 1761, ch. 244, *Acts and Resolves*, vol. 16, p. 679.

21. Petition of Isabella Whaland, n.d., *Felt Collection*, vol. 66, p. 112, MA. Resolve on the Petition of Isabella Whaland, 16 January 1761, ch. 230, *Acts and Resolves*, vol. 16, p. 672.

22. Petition of Mary Casey, n.d., *Felt Collection*, vol. 66, p. 120, MA. Resolve on the Petition of Mary Casey, 2 April 1761, ch. 345, *Acts and Resolves*, vol. 16, p. 717.

23. Petition of Ann and Elizabeth Johnson, n.d., *Felt Collection*, vol. 66, p. 122, MA. Resolve on the Petition of Ann and Elizabeth Johnson, 1 April 1761, ch. 348, *Acts and Resolves*, vol. 16, p. 718.

24. Petition of Heziah Holman and Sarah Simpson, n.d., *Felt Collection*, vol. 78, p. 430, MA. Order on the Petition of Heziah Holman and Sarah Simpson, 24 April 1759, ch. 361, *Acts and Resolves*, vol. 16, p. 359.

25. Petition of Sarah Rust, 16 January 1784, Rust Divorce, #129833, vol. 796, *Suffolk Files*, SJC, JA, MA.

26. Petition of Francis Rust, 18 March 1784, Rust Divorce, #129833, vol. 796, *Suffolk Files*, SJC, JA, MA.

27. Petition of Sarah Rust, 8 June 1784, Rust Divorce, #129836, vol. 796, *Suffolk Files*, SJC, JA, MA.

28. Petition of Sarah Rust, 8 June 1784, Rust Divorce, #129836, vol. 796, *Suffolk Files*, SJC, JA, MA.

29. See Bayard Divorce file, decreed 10 May 1784, #129834, vol. 796, *Suffolk Files*, SJC, JA, MA.

30. Rust Divorce, #129836, vol. 796, *Suffolk Files*, SJC, JA, MA.

31. Petition of Ellinor Gaillard, 15 February 1783, no. 256, *PGA*, SCDAH; Petition of Judith Gaillard, 15 February 1783, no. 257, *PGA*, SCDAH.

32. Kierner, *Southern Women in Revolution*, 126; and Thompson and Lumpkin, eds., *House Journals, 1783–1784*, 551–52.

33. Petition of Mary Coughran and Mary Rone, n.d., RG27, E28, PSA.

34. Petition of Mary Sneff and Catherine Winkeler, 27 March 1787, RG 27, E28, PSA.

35. For examples of recent scholarship on life in British-occupied cities during the American Revolution, see Lauren Duval, "Mastering Charleston: Property and Patriarchy in British-Occupied Charleston, 1780–1782," *William and Mary Quarterly* 75, 4 (October 2018): 589–622; and Donald F. Johnson, "Ambiguous Allegiances: Urban Loyalties during the American Revolution," *Journal of American History* 104, 3 (December 2017): 610–31.

36. Wives of alleged or avowed loyalists often sought to leave cities that had come under Whig control, many requesting permission from the state to depart for Halifax, Nova Scotia, or other cities occupied by the British, such as New York.

37. The *Acts and Resolves* identifies the petitioner as Mercy Graves, but the petitioner herself identifies as Mary Graves, so I have chosen to retain the petitioner's original spelling. Petition of Mary Graves, 7 April 1779, GCM, MA. Resolve on the Petition of Mercy Graves, 9 April 1779, ch. 151, *Acts and Resolves*, vol. 21, p. 81.

38. Petition of Rachel Lehr, n.d., GCM, MA. Resolve on the Petition of Rachel Lehr, 23 April 1778, ch. 994, *Acts and Resolves*, vol. 20, p. 384.

39. Petition of Ann Calvert, n.d., granted 31 May 1779, RG27, E17, PSA.

40. Petition of Sarah Johonnot, 12 September 1780, GCM, MA. Resolve on the Petition of Sarah Johonnot, 18 September 1780, ch. 160, *Acts and Resolves*, vol. 21, p. 602.

41. The most in-depth analysis of women's testimonies comes from Sharon Block's *Rape and Sexual Power in Early America* and Cornelia Hughes Dayton's *Women before the Bar*; yet, the diverging perspectives these authors present dictate that the legitimacy and power of women's testimonies, especially in cases in which they were defending female plaintiffs, depended significantly on place, time, and cause of the suit, along with the legal structure of these jurisdictions. Witness testimony landed differently depending on whether a defendant stood accused of rape, fornication, adultery, or cruelty, while the law and practice varied depending on colonial or state law, among other factors. Block notes cases in which single female victims of sexual assault often turned to other women first, disclosing the details of the assault because these matters fell under "women's purview"; their married counterparts, however, often told their husbands about the details of their rape rather than divulging this information to other women. Women were often called upon in cases that required "reading" women's bodies. In cases involving sex or sexual misconduct, courts often heard testimonies of women witnesses, which proved beneficial to female plaintiffs. Block stops shy of acknowledging a supportive community of women; evidence in rape cases suggests that witnesses—both male and female—often questioned the veracity of women's claims of sexual assault. See Block, *Rape and Sexual Power in Early America* (Chapel Hill: University of North Carolina Press, 2006), 108–13.

Dayton's study suggests that women's participation in New Haven's and Connecticut's courtrooms diminished over time from the early colonial period through the late eighteenth century. Women were an integral part of the courtroom in the seventeenth-century New Haven colony. Puritan authorities were apt to take women's word as truth in cases related to rape or sexual misconduct; these women, therefore, "had reason to believe that their voices would not be ignored." See Dayton, *Women before the Bar*, 32. Unfortunately, however, Dayton's gendered analysis of women's testimony is limited, because early New Haven and Connecticut courtrooms did not transcribe oral testimonies; instead, the only extant depositions are those presented by witnesses who lived more than twenty miles from the court or those given by deponents too sickly to come to court, and therefore there are no records of women who gave oral testimonies during this period. Dayton argues that as the eighteenth century wore on, women's roles in the courtroom became less pronounced. Women's words began to be doubted, their presence in civil litigation waned as a result of changes in the economy, and female midwives' birth testimonies were relied upon less and less. Dayton, *Women before the Bar*, 5, 53, 162, 260 n. 45. Elaine Forman Crane's work on New England women asserts the declension model as well, extending her thesis beyond the law to religion and the economy. Similarly, Mary Beth Norton's work on the Salem witch trials of the late seventeenth century presented a unique moment in which women played significant roles as accusers, victims, and witnesses. Crane, *Ebb Tide in New England: Women, Seaports, and Social Change, 1630–1800* (Boston: Northeastern University Press, 1998) and Norton, *In the Devil's Snare: The Salem Witchcraft Crisis of 1692* (New York: First Vintage Books, 2002).

42. Deposition of Lydia Shaw, 26 April 1805, Hawke divorce, RG33, A41, PSA.

43. Deposition of Mary Knider, 23 August 1797, Griscom divorce, RG33, A41, PSA.

44. Deposition of Elizabeth Martin, 27 December 1805, Martin divorce, RG33, A41, PSA.

45. Deposition of Jemma Brown, 19 November 1799, Moore divorce, RG33, A41, PSA.

46. Depositions of Mary Angel and Abigail Galloway, n.d., Air divorce, #129779, Record Book, *Suffolk Files*, SJC, JA, MA.

47. Deposition of Mary Brown, 14 April 1820, Coombs divorce, Docket #49, March 1820 Term, JA, MA.

48. Deposition of Mary Learned, 8 December 1806, Scales divorce, Docket #349, March Term 1807, JA, MA.

49. Deposition of Dr. John Jeffries, 13 March 1807, Scales, docket #349, March Term 1807, JA, MA.

50. Divorce decree, n.d., Scales divorce, Record Book, March Term 1807, pp. 199–200, JA, MA.

51. Deposition of Love Woodman, 13 March 1807, Cross divorce, Docket #348, March Term 1807, JA, MA.

52. Deposition of Daniel Woodman, 4 November 1806, Cross divorce, Docket #348, March Term 1807, JA, MA.

53. Petition of Margaret Cross, n.d., Cross divorce, Record Book, March Term 1807, p. 198, JA, MA.

54. Divorce decree, n.d., Cross divorce, Record Book, March Term 1807, p. 198, JA, MA.

55. Deposition of Robert Correy, 29 August 1791, Kinsey divorce, RG33, A41, PSA.

56. Deposition of Sibilla Bickham, 29 August 1791, Kinsey divorce, RG33, A41, PSA.

57. Deposition of William Snyder, 11 September 1792, McKanacker divorce, RG33, A41, PSA.

58. Deposition of Jedediah Snowden, 11 September 1792, McKanacker divorce, RG33, A41, PSA.

59. Elizabeth Hughes deposition, 27 March 1798, Murray divorce, RG33, A41, PSA.

60. Deposition of William Barry, 9 April 1795, Henderson divorce, RG33, A41, PSA. Robert Nelson confirmed the details of Barry's account in his own deposition. Deposition of Robert Nelson, 9 April 1795, Henderson divorce, RG33, A41, PSA.

61. Deposition of Lucy Brown, 9 April 1795, Henderson divorce, RG33, A41, PSA.

62. Deposition of Hester Fisher, 9 April 1795, Henderson divorce, RG33, A41, PSA.

63. Sarah was likely related, and perhaps married, to Robert Nelson, the man mentioned in William Barry's deposition. Deposition of Sarah Nelson, 9 April 1795, Henderson divorce, RG33, A41, PSA.

64. Deposition of Henry Armbruster, 22 March 1804, France divorce, RG33, A41, PSA.

65. Deposition of Mary Armbruster, 22 March 1804, France divorce, RG33, A41, PSA.

Chapter 5. The Problem of Dependence

1. Petition of Elizabeth Browne, 17 June 1755, *Felt Collection*, vol. 105, ch. 77, MA.

2. Emphasis in original. Resolve on the Petition of Elizabeth Browne, 19 June 1755, The *Acts and Resolves, Public and Private, of the Province of the Massachusetts Bay*, vol. 15 (Boston: Wright & Potter Printing Co., 1908), p. 360.

3. Poverty and class status were complex statuses of identity in the revolutionary era. To clarify for the purposes of this chapter, the poor women (and in some cases, men) whom I discuss were, for the most part, devoid of the ability to subsist on their own without the intervention of the patriarchal state or their local community. Some of these early Americans may have been members of the "laboring poor," who took up manual trades that were oftentimes contingent, unstable, or insufficient for a proper maintenance; they could have also been incapable of work and thus of providing for themselves. Generally, these women lived on the extreme margins of society, as evidenced by their need to rely on local institutions for basic survival, the indignities and challenges of which will be examined in this chapter. See Simon Middleton and Billy G. Smith, "Class and Early America: An Introduction," *William and Mary Quarterly* 63, no. 2 (April 2006): 211–20.

4. Martha Clark (Curator, Massachusetts State Archives), conversation with author, August 26, 2016.

5. Petition of Ann Swift, 31 March 1779, *Felt Collection*, vol. 182, p. 292, MA.

6. Petition of Mary Freeman, 6 July 1784, #1364, House Unpassed Legislation, p. 66, MA.

7. Petition of Ann Dunkin, 11 May 1780, RG27, E17, PSA.

8. Petition of Ann Williams, 15 February 1783, no. 241, *PGA*, SCDAH.

9. Thomas Cooper, ed., *The Statutes at Large of South Carolina: Acts from 1752 to 1786* (Columbia, SC: A.S. Johnston, 1838), 556.

10. Petition of Ann Williams, 15 February 1783, no. 241, *PGA*, SCDAH.

11. Kierner, *Southern Women in Revolution*, 118.

12. Arguably the most significant early works that study the urban poor in the long eighteenth century are Gary B. Nash, *The Urban Crucible: Social Change, Political Consciousness, and the Origins of the American Revolution* (Cambridge, MA: Harvard University Press, 1979) and Billy G. Smith, *The "Lower Sort": Philadelphia's Laboring People, 1750–1800* (Ithaca, NY: Cornell University Press, 1990).

13. Monique Bourque, "Women and Work in the Philadelphia Almshouse, 1790–1840," *Journal of the Early Republic* 32, 3 (Fall 2012): 383–413; Elaine Forman Crane, *Ebb Tide in New England: Women, Seaports, and Social Change, 1630–1800* (Boston:

Northeastern University Press, 1998); Ruth Wallis Herndon, *Unwelcome Americans: Living on the Margin in Early New England* (Philadelphia: University of Pennsylvania Press, 2001) and "Poor Women and the Boston Almshouse in the Early Republic," *Journal of the Early Republic*, 32, 2 (Fall 2012): 349–81; Susan Klepp, "Malthusian Miseries and the Working Poor in Philadelphia, 1780–1830: Gender and Infant Mortality," in Billy G. Smith, ed., *Down and Out in Early America* (University Park: Pennsylvania State University Press, 2004), 63–92; Clare Lyons, *Sex among the Rabble: An Intimate History of Gender and Power in the Age of Revolution, Philadelphia, 1730–1830* (Chapel Hill: University of North Carolina Press, 2006); Gary B. Nash, "Poverty and Poor Relief in Pre-Revolutionary Philadelphia," *William and Mary Quarterly* 33, 1 (January 1976): 3–30; Simon Newman, *Embodied History: The Lives of the Poor in Early Philadelphia* (Philadelphia: University of Pennsylvania Press, 2003); Seth Rockman, *Scraping By: Wage Labor, Slavery, and Survival in Early Baltimore* (Baltimore, MD: Johns Hopkins University Press, 2009); Smith, ed., *Down and Out in Early America*; Stephen Edward Wiberley Jr., "Four Cities: Public Poor Relief in Urban America, 1700–1775" (PhD diss., Yale University, 1975); and Karin Wulf, "Gender and the Political Economy of Poor Relief," in Smith, ed., *Down and Out in Early America*, 163–89.

14. See, for example, Crane, *Ebb Tide*, 118–19.

15. Eric G. Nellis and Anne Decker Cecere, eds., *The Eighteenth-Century Records of the Boston Overseers of the Poor* (Charlottesville: University of Virginia Press, 2007), 21.

16. James W. Ely Jr., "Poor Laws of the Post-Revolutionary South, 1776–1800," *Tulsa Law Review* 21, 1 (1985): 5.

17. William Penn, "Charter of the City of Philadelphia, 1701," available at www .phila.gov.

18. Finding Aid, Magdalen Society of Philadelphia, Historical Society of Pennsylvania, Philadelphia, PA. Available at http://hsp.org.

19. Oftentimes, though, pensioners who did not meet this strict requirement received outdoor relief. Benjamin Joseph Klebaner, "Public Poor Relief in Charleston, 1800–1860," *South Carolina Historical Magazine* 55, 4 (October 1954): 213.

20. Oakum is a hemp material used to make rope that acted as caulk for the seams of wooden ships. See "oakum, n.," *OED Online* (Oxford University Press, March 2015), accessed May 15, 2015. Available at www.oed.com. Evidence of these activities appears throughout the minute books of the commissioners of the almshouse. See "Journals," *Charleston Almshouse Records*, CCPL.

21. Herndon, "Poor Women and the Boston Almshouse."

22. Records of the Charleston Commissioners of the Poor, the Philadelphia Overseers/Guardians of the Poor, and the Boston Town Selectmen Minutes reveal that these men authorized relief only to those deemed "worthy," "proper," or "deserving."

23. Quoted in Klebaner, "Public Poor Relief," 220.

24. David Rothman, *The Discovery of the Asylum: Social Order and Disorder in the New Republic* (Boston: Little, Brown, 1971), 3–29.

25. Rothman, *Discovery of the Asylum*, 30–56.

26. This happened earlier in Philadelphia, from the early to mid-1780s onward. John K. Alexander, *Render Them Submissive: Responses to Poverty in Philadelphia, 1760–1800* (Amherst: University of Massachusetts Press, 1980), 48–49.

27. Rothman, *Discovery of the Asylum*, 57–78.

28. Nellis and Cecere, eds., *Eighteenth-Century Records*, 48.

29. Rothman, *Discovery of the Asylum*, 155–79. Poor Americans in the early republic were seen as "a drag on civic enterprise," thus inhibiting the growth and success of the new and fragile nation. Nellis and Cecere, eds., *Eighteenth-Century Records*, 39.

30. Americans in the early republic began to view the poor as a collective group promoting licentiousness and engaging in criminal activity. Alexander, *Render Them Submissive*, 5.

31. Rothman, *Discovery of the Asylum*, 180–205.

32. Quoted in Billy G. Smith, "'The Best Poor Man's Country?'" in Smith, ed., *Down and Out in Early America*, xvi.

33. Nellis and Cecere, eds., *Eighteenth-Century Records*, 57, 65.

34. Quoted in Alexander, *Render Them Submissive*, 92.

35. Alexander, *Render Them Submissive*, 94.

36. The founding work of intersectionality studies is Kimberlé Williams Crenshaw, "Demarginalizing the Intersection of Race and Sex: A Black Feminist Critique of Doctrine, Feminist Theory, and Antiracist Politics," *University of Chicago Legal Forum* 1989, 1, article 8. This chapter examines poor white women in these three urban centers, as the records are insufficient to conduct a thorough and consistent comparative examination of women, race, and state institutions of poor relief in Philadelphia, Charleston, and Boston.

37. Nellis and Cecere, eds., *Eighteenth-Century Records*, 34; Wulf, "Gender and the Political Economy of Poor Relief in Colonial Philadelphia."

38. Nellis and Cecere, eds., *Eighteenth-Century Records*, 35.

39. Herndon, "Poor Women and the Boston Almshouse," 351.

40. Herndon, "Poor Women and the Boston Almshouse," 351, 372.

41. Wulf, "Gender and the Political Economy of Poor Relief," 164.

42. Wulf, "Gender and the Political Economy of Poor Relief," 172.

43. Quoted in Wulf, "Gender and the Political Economy of Poor Relief," 171.

44. Wulf, "Gender and the Political Economy of Poor Relief," 181.

45. Wulf, "Gender and the Political Economy of Poor Relief," 173–75.

46. 18 January 1819, "Journals," *Charleston Almshouse Records*, CCPL.

47. A gold coin. "Johannes | Joannes, n.," *OED Online* (Oxford University Press, June 2016), accessed August 26, 2016. Available at www.oed.com.

48. 31 May 1781, Ground Rents Due to the Overseers of the Poor, Minutes March 1774 to May 1782, RG 35, PCA.

49. In early 1805, the commissioners restricted access to outdoor rations to those who, "only as from age infirmity or from some other immediate causal circumstances may be prevented from earning a livelihood." 21 February 1805, "Journals," *Charleston Almshouse Records*, CCPL.

50. 10 May 1805, "Journals," *Charleston Almshouse Records*, CCPL.

51. 7 April 1806, "Journals," *Charleston Almshouse Records*, CCPL.

52. 28 February 1788, Guardians of the Poor, Minutes September 1787 to June 1796, vol. 24, RG 35, PCA.

53. 28 February 1774 County Tax Assessment Ledgers, Overseers of the Poor Minutes, 1768–1774, RG 35, PCA.

54. 28 July 1768, County Tax Assessment Ledgers, Overseers of the Poor Minutes, 1768–1774, RG 35, PCA.

55. November 24, 1768, County Tax Assessment Ledgers, Overseers of the Poor Minutes, 1768–1774, RG 35, PCA.

56. Kennedy, *Braided Relations*, 72.

57. 6 February 1809, "Journals," *Charleston Almshouse Records*, CCPL.

58. 25 October 1819, "Journals," *Charleston Almshouse Records*, CCPL.

59. 1 July 1820, "Journals," *Charleston Almshouse Records*, CCPL.

60. 27 March 1820 and 3 April 1820, "Journals," *Charleston Almshouse Records*, CCPL.

61. 29 May 1809, "Journals," *Charleston Almshouse Records*, CCPL.

62. Alexander, *Render Them Submissive*, 24.

63. See, for example, 23 July 1802, "Journals," *Charleston Almshouse Records*, CCPL.

64. 31 August 1807, "Journals," *Charleston Almshouse Records*, CCPL.

65. 22 November 1809, "Journals," *Charleston Almshouse Records*, CCPL.

66. 1 February 1808, "Journals," *Charleston Almshouse Records*, CCPL.

67. Warning-out procedures dictated that those whom officials deemed to be "strangers" were required to leave the city or town within a certain number of days or weeks, so that the local community would not be responsible for providing them with aid. Just as in Charleston, women made up the majority of Boston's almshouse residents and the majority of those receiving other forms of relief from the city. Nellis and Cecere, eds., *Eighteenth-Century Records*, 35.

68. Nellis and Cecere, eds., *Eighteenth-Century Records*, 53; quoted on 70.

69. Nellis and Cecere, eds., *Eighteenth-Century Records*, 53.

70. See, for example, 14 July 1768, County Tax Assessment Ledgers, Overseers of the Poor Minutes, 1768–1774, RG 35, PCA.

71. 25 May 1769, County Tax Assessment Ledgers, Overseers of the Poor Minutes, 1768–1774, RG 35, PCA.

72. 8 September 1768, County Tax Assessment Ledgers, Overseers of the Poor Minutes, 1768–1774, RG 35, PCA.

73. 11 August 1802, "Journals," *Charleston Almshouse Records*, CCPL.

74. 4 August 1768, County Tax Assessment Ledgers, Overseers of the Poor Minutes, 1768–1774, RG 35, PCA.

75. 10 August 1813, Guardians of the Poor Minutes, May 1816–November 1818, vol. 31, RG35, PCA. N.b.: This volume is mislabeled, and actually contains the Minutes from May 24, 1813, to May 27, 1816.

76. 15 April 1805, "Journals," *Charleston Almshouse Records*, CCPL.

77. 20 March 1815, "Journals," *Charleston Almshouse Records*, CCPL.

78. 23 March 1812, "Journals," *Charleston Almshouse Records*, CCPL.

79. 16 February 1776, County Tax Assessment Ledgers, Overseers of the Poor Minutes, 1768–1774, RG 35, PCA.

80. Nellis and Cecere, eds., *Eighteenth-Century Records*, 21.

81. 16 February 1776, County Tax Assessment Ledgers, Overseers of the Poor Minutes, 1768–1774, RG 35, PCA.

82. Alexander, *Render Them Submissive*, 121.

83. 11 August 1806, "Journals," *Charleston Almshouse Records*, CCPL.

84. 27 November 1806, "Journals," *Charleston Almshouse Records*, CCPL.

85. 22 December 1806, "Journals," *Charleston Almshouse Records*, CCPL.

86. 16 July 1770, County Tax Assessment Ledgers, Overseers of the Poor Minutes, 1768–1774, RG 35, PCA.

87. 4 January 1781, Ground Rents Due to the Overseers of the Poor, Minutes March 1774 to May 1782, RG 35, PCA.

88. 15 February 1781, Ground Rents Due to the Overseers of the Poor, Minutes March 1774 to May 1782, RG 35, PCA.

89. 12 May 1807, Guardians of the Poor Minutes, November 1806 to June 1810, vol. 28, RG 35, PCA.

90. The applications of almshouse residents and outdoor pensioners for the Charleston Almshouse do not survive; the journals of the commissioners of the almshouse, however, do reveal the contents of some of these applications in their minute books.

91. See, for example, 14 June 1802, "Journals," *Charleston Almshouse Records*, CCPL.

92. 15 April 1805, "Journals," *Charleston Almshouse Records*, CCPL. As a result of this particular inquiry, four people were discharged from the house, including one woman.

93. 9 August 1802, "Journals," *Charleston Almshouse Records*, CCPL.

94. 30 July 1804, "Journals," *Charleston Almshouse Records*, CCPL.

95. February 16, 1776, Ground Rents due to the Overseers of the Poor, Minutes March 1774 to May 1782, RG 35, PCA; see also 21 November 1815, Guardians of the Poor Minutes, May 1816–November 1818, vol. 31, RG 35, PCA. N.b.: This volume is mislabeled, and actually contains the minutes from May 24, 1813, to May 27, 1816.

96. Elizabeth Griscomb, for example, could not obtain security from her child's father and was compelled to reside and work in the House of Employment until she could repay the cost both of her lying-in and of her confinement. 10 February 1780, Ground Rents Due to the Overseers of the Poor, Minutes March 1774 to May 1782, RG 35, PCA.

97. Wulf, "Gender and the Political Economy of Poor Relief," 163.

98. 4 September 1810, Guardians of the Poor Minutes, 3 July 1810 to 24 May 1813, vol. 29, RG 35, PCA.

99. See, for example, 28 May 1811, Guardians of the Poor Minutes, 3 July 1810 to 24 May 1813, vol. 29, RG 35, PCA.

100. On the Magdalen Society, see Lyons, *Sex among the Rabble*, 323–35.

101. Magdalen Society Minutes, HSP, p. 1.

102. Magdalen Society Minutes, HSP, p. 21,

103. Lyons, *Sex among the Rabble*, 323–35.

104. 26 May 1801, Magdalen Society Minutes, HSP, p. 27.

105. Emphasis in original. 9 February 1808, Magdalen Society Minutes, HSP, pp. 93–94.

106. 8 February 1800, Magdalen Society Minutes, HSP, p. 11.

107. Emphasis in original. 5 May 1807, Magdalen Society Minutes, HSP, pp. 91–92.

108. 5 May 1807, Magdalen Society Minutes, HSP, pp. 91–92.

109. 13 February 1810, Magdalen Society Minutes, HSP, pp. 131–32.

110. Emphasis in original. 5 May 1807, Magdalen Society Minutes, HSP, pp. 91–92.

111. 13 February 1810, Magdalen Society Minutes, HSP, p. 137.

112. 9 February 1819, Magdalen Society Minutes, HSP, p. 243.

113. 12 February 1805, Magdalen Society Minutes, HSP, p. 61.

Chapter 6. To Have and to Hold Herself

1. On manumission practices in eighteenth- and early-nineteenth-century Charleston, see Amrita Chakrabarti Myers, *Forging Freedom: Black Women and the Pursuit of Liberty in Antebellum Charleston* (Chapel Hill: University of North Carolina Press, 2011), 39–76; and Robert Olwell, "Becoming Free: Manumission and the Genesis of a Free Black Community in South Carolina, 1740–1790," *Slavery and Abolition* 17, 1 (1996): 1–19.

2. Manumission Deed of Jane, purchased and freed by Carolina Lamboll from Rachel Caw, 19 January 1779, vol. RR, 586, Misc. Records, SCDAH.

3. I am grateful to John Garrison Marks, who shared his database of Charleston manumissions, which facilitated my search for these records between 1776 and 1800. John Garrison Marks to author, Twitter direct message, July 10–12, 2019.

4. Manumission Deed of Jane, purchased and freed by Carolina Lamboll from Rachel Caw, 19 January 1779, vol. RR, 586, Misc. Records, SCDAH.

5. On gender and patriarchal power in African Americans' experiences of slavery and freedom, see, for example, Adams and Pleck, *Love of Freedom*.

6. Numerous scholars have thought critically and creatively about the power dynamics and limitations of slavery's archive. See, for example, Marisa J. Fuentes, *Dispossessed Lives: Enslaved Women, Violence, and the Archive* (Philadelphia: University of Pennsylvania Press, 2016); Saidiya Hartman, "Venus in Two Acts," *Small Axe* 12, 2 (2008): 1–14; Jessica Marie Johnson, *Wicked Flesh: Black Women, Intimacy, and Freedom in the Atlantic World* (Philadelphia: University of Pennsylvania Press, 2020); Tiya Miles, *All That She Carried: The Journey of Ashley's Sack, a Black Family Keepsake* (New York: Penguin Random House, 2021); and Sasha Turner, *Contested Bodies: Pregnancy, Childrearing, and Slavery in Jamaica* (Philadelphia: University of Pennsylvania Press, 2017). The December 2015 issue of *Social Text* and the Fall 2016 issue of *History of the Present* are both timely forums grappling with the issues of slavery's archive. See Laura Helton, Justin Leroy, Max Mishler, Samantha Seeley, and Shauna Sweeney, eds., "The Question of Recovery: Slavery, Freedom, and the Archive," Special Issue, *Social Text* 33, 4 (December 2015); and Brian Connolly and Marisa Fuentes, "From Archives of Slavery to Liberated Futures?" *History of the Present* 6, 2 (Fall 2016). Two pieces in particular from these collections helped to inform this chapter: Jennifer Morgan, "Archives and Histories of Racial Capitalism," *Social Text* 33, 4 (December 2015): 153–61; and Stephanie E. Smallwood, "The Politics of the Archive and History's Accountability to the Enslaved," *History of the Present* 6, 2 (Fall 2016): 117–32.

7. On slavery's archive and freedom's archive, see Johnson, *Wicked Flesh*, 5.

8. On "female patriarchs," see Glover, *Eliza Lucas Pinckney*.

9. All scholars of enslaved women, early American law, and American patriarchal power must contend with the realities of *partus sequitur ventrum* and the centrality of Black women's reproductive capacity in defining their and their children's legal status. Recent works that engage this concept in compelling ways are Johnson, *Wicked Flesh*; Jennifer Morgan, "*Partus sequitur ventrem*: Law, Race, and Reproduction in Colonial Slavery," *Small Axe* 22, 1 (March 2018): 1–17; Brooke Newman, "Blood Fictions, Maternal Inheritance, and the Legacies of Colonial Slavery," *Women's Studies Quarterly* 48, 1 (2020): 27–44; and Turner, *Contested Bodies*. On the embodied experience of pregnancy and motherhood more broadly, see Nora Doyle, *Maternal Bodies: Redefining*

Motherhood in Early America (Chapel Hill: University of North Carolina Press, 2018). On the paradoxical role of enslaved midwives supporting the creation of both African American families and the American nation-state, see Sara Collini, "Birthing a Nation: Enslaved Women and Midwifery in Early America, 1750–1820" (PhD diss., George Mason University, 2020).

10. Jessica Millward, *Finding Charity's Folk*; Morgan, *Laboring Women*; Myers, *Forging Freedom*; and Turner, *Contested Bodies*.

11. Jennifer Morgan argues that it was enslaved people, women especially, who "best understood the theory and praxis of racial slavery." The realities and violence of enslavement meant that the legal and social structures of the institution "displace[d] maternity." In effect, enslaved women had to come to terms with the fact that "their reproductive lives would be the evidence of radicalized dispossession." Morgan, "*Partus sequitur ventrem*," 2.

12. On the "traditional archive," see Fuentes, *Dispossessed Lives*, 1.

13. Nicole Topich first shared her database, which identified antislavery and Black petitions, in June of 2015. Nicole Topich, email message to author, June 15, 2015. Since then, Topich and others have made this data public and open access. Harvard University Center for American Political Studies, *Digital Archive of Anti-Slavery and Anti-Segregation Petitions*, available at https://caps.gov.harvard.edu.

14. Resolve on the Petition of Daphne, an African Woman, Empowering *Joseph Hosmer*, Esq., To Make Provision for Her Support, 9 March 1791, ch. 127, *Acts and Resolves, Public and Private, of the Province of the Massachusetts Bay, 1790–91* (Boston: Wright & Potter Printing Co. 1895), 229.

15. Resolve on the Petition of Daphne, An African Woman, 1791.

16. Resolve on the Petition of Daphne, An African Woman, 1791.

17. Lydia's race is not specifically identified in the document, yet she is identified as "Lydia commonly called Lydia Sharp." White women would not have been deprived of their surname in such a situation. Likewise, a white woman would not have had a marriage with an enslaved man sanctioned by Samuel Mather. See Jared Hardesty, *Unfreedom*, 90–91.

18. The result of this case is unknown; the court made a number of attempts to compel Boston to bear witness to the charges, yet the extant materials show no evidence that he ever complied. Lydia Sharp v. Boston (A Black Man), 5 June 1773, Sharp divorce, #129775, *Suffolk Files*, SJC, JA, MA.

19. Notably, Black patriarchy within the household structure was not the same as white patriarchy within the household structure because the economic circumstances of Black patriarchy and white patriarchy within society were not equivalent; Black patriarchy existed within, and was less powerful than, white patriarchy. On the ways in which Black women sought the protections of patriarchy, see Adams and Pleck, *Love of Freedom*, 10, 51–79.

20. The petitioner is self-identified or identified by the state in three ways over the course of her petitioning efforts: first, simply as "Belinda" or "Belinda, an African"; later, as "Belinda Royal" or "Belinda Royall," having taken or been assigned the surname of her enslaver; and finally, as "Belinda Sutton," evidently her surname after marriage. For consistency's sake and out of respect for Belinda's life, I have primarily identified her as Belinda (rather than with the surname "Royal/Royall") until she later identifies as Belinda Sutton.

21. A number of scholars have analyzed Belinda's case. For especially relevant and more in-depth examinations of these petitions, see "Belinda: The Politics of Petitions," in Sharon M. Harris, *Executing Race: Early American Women's Narratives of Race, Society, and the Law* (Columbus: Ohio State University Press, 2005), 69–79.; and Nicole Topich, "Abolitionist Black Histories and Historians in Massachusetts Petitions," in Claire Bourhis-Mariotti, Claire Parfair, and Hélène Le Dantex-Lowry, eds., *Writing History from the Margins: African Americans and the Quest for Freedom* (New York: Taylor & Francis, 2016), 43–54.

22. Petition of Belinda, An Affrican, 14 February 1783, Royall House & Slave Quarters, accessed. July 9, 2022. Available at https://royallhouse.org.

23. Emphasis added. Petition of Belinda.

24. Petition of Belinda.

25. "Belinda Sutton and Her Petitions," Royall House & Slave Quarters, accessed August 10, 2021. Available at https://royallhouse.org.

26. Margot Minardi, "Why Was Belinda's Petition Approved?" Royall House & Slave Quarters, accessed August 10, 2021. Available at https://royallhouse.org.

27. Petition of Belinda Royall, 1785, #1707, House Unpassed Legislation, MA.

28. Petition of Belinda, An African, 23 November 1787, MA.

29. Petition of Belinda Royall, 1793, #2007, Senate Unpassed Legislation, MA.

30. Martha Clark (curator, Massachusetts State Archives), conversation with author, August 26, 2016.

31. On the effects of the warning-out process for Boston women, see Ruth Wallis Herndon, "Poor Women and the Boston Almshouse in the Early Republic," *Journal of the Early Republic* 32, 2 (Fall 2012): 349–81.

32. Dido Benson (negress) warned to leave, 17 April 1750, #66481, *Suffolk Files*, SJC, JA, MA.

33. Phillis a negro woman, Inquisition on the body of, 5 August 1770, #101666, *Suffolk Files*, SJC, JA, MA.

34. Inquisition on the body of Sarah negro servant to Mary Foster, 17 September 1750, #67145, *Suffolk Files*, SJC, JA, MA.

35. Inquisition on the body of Mergret (Negress), 10 May 1761, #81893, *Suffolk Files*, SJC, JA, MA.

36. Hartman, "Venus in Two Acts," 8.

37. Fuentes, *Dispossessed Lives*, 4–6; and Hartman, "Venus in Two Acts."

38. Johnson, *Wicked Flesh*, 230.

39. Throughout this chapter, I am choosing to designate freedom as a status formerly enslaved people earned, claimed, or seized, rather than something that was given or offered to them by enslavers or the patriarchal state. This diction highlights the active role formerly enslaved people took in their own liberation, and seeks to undermine a popular understanding of the benevolent slaveholder who bequeathed freedom to people they held in bondage.

40. Petition of Cate Ollier to the Pennsylvania Abolition Society, 25 March 1809, Book F, Reel 21, 95–96, Man. Bk., PAS Papers, HSP.

41. On the role of the Pennsylvania Abolition Society in intervening on behalf of free and enslaved Black Americans, see in particular Gary B. Nash and Jean R. Soderlund, *Freedom by Degrees: Emancipation in Pennsylvania and Its Aftermath* (New York: Oxford University Press, 1991).

42. Petition of Cate Ollier to the Pennsylvania Abolition Society, 25 March 1809, Book F, Reel 21, 95–96, Man. Bk., PAS Papers, HSP.

43. Erica Armstrong Dunbar, *A Fragile Freedom: African American Women and Emancipation in the Antebellum City* (New Haven, CT: Yale University Press, 2011), 32–33; and Nash and Soderlund, *Freedom by Degrees*, 115–18.

44. Petition of Cate Ollier to the Pennsylvania Abolition Society, 25 March 1809, Book F, Reel 21, 95–96, Man. Bk., PAS Papers, HSP.

45. Manumission Deed of Molly, formerly enslaved by George Young, 17 September 1800, vol. 3Q, 143, Misc. Records, SCDAH.

46. Manumission Deed of Sarah, formerly enslaved by John Bull, 18 April 1801, vol. 3R, 76, Misc. Records, SCDAH.

47. Myers, *Forging Freedom*, 47–48.

48. The legislature ratified a law that severely restricted the rights of free people of color, dictated standards by which enslavers ought to control the enslaved people that labored for them, and curtailed the ability of an enslaver to manumit those whom they held in bondage. The law, as it was written, intended to halt the emancipation of enslaved people who "have been of bad or depraved character, or, from age or infirmity, incapable of gaining their livelihood by honest means." In order to mitigate what patriarchal legislators saw as a significant social problem, these officials outlined a set of guidelines for emancipation going forward. Enslavers would have to present their case to a magistrate and "five indifferent freeholders" in their neighborhood, present the enslaved man or woman to this group, and attest to, essentially, their fitness for freedom. If the enslaved person could prove their worthiness of freedom, those freeholders present would attest to this fact, and provide their signatures to a deed then required by law. The law was intended, in patriarchal legislators' own words, to force enslaved and free Black South Carolinians into "due subordination." "No. 1745 An Act Respecting Slaves, Free Negroes, Mulattoes and Mestizoes; for Enforcing the More Punctual Performance of Patroll Duty; and to Impose Certain Restrictions on the Emancipation of Slaves," in David J. McCord, ed., *The Statutes at Large of South Carolina*, vol. 7 (Columbia, SC: A.S. Johnston, 1840), 440–43. See also Myers, *Forging Freedom*, 47–48, 53–54.

49. Manumission deed of Diana et al., formerly enslaved by Samuel Theus, 2–3 March 1801, vol. 3Q, 360, Misc. Records, SCDAH.

50. Marriage was, and would continue to be, associated with freedom, liberation, and civil rights throughout American history. On free and enslaved Black marriages and family life, see especially Adams and Pleck, *Love of Freedom*, 51–125; John Blassingame, *The Slave Community: Plantation Life in the Antebellum South* (New York: Oxford University Press, 1972), 149–91; Herbert Gutman, *The Black Family in Slavery and Freedom, 1750–1925* (New York: Pantheon Books, 1976); Tera Hunter, *Bound in Wedlock: Slave and Free Black Marriage in the Nineteenth Century* (Cambridge, MA: Harvard University Press, 2019); and Brenda Stevenson, *Life in Black and White: Family and Community in the Slave South* (New York: Oxford University Press, 1996), 206–319.

51. Hunter, *Bound in Wedlock*, 14.

52. Hunter, *Bound in Wedlock*.

53. Jessica Millward briefly touches on this phenomenon in her discussion of family members purchasing the freedom of their kin. Importantly, Millward, noting

this pattern, recognizes that "it does not follow that white men viewed black men as equals." Millward, *Finding Charity's Folk*, 49.

54. Emancipation Deed of Phillis, freedom purchased by John Mills from Jonas Phillips, 2 January 1793, Book B, Reel 20, 39, Man. Bk., PAS Papers, HSP.

55. Emancipation Deed of Phebe, freedom purchased by Archibald Davis, 17 February 1801, Book E, Reel 21, 199, Man. Bk., PAS Papers, HSP.

56. Manumission Deed of Dinah, formerly enslaved by Thomas Irwin, 1 October 1792, Book C, Reel 20, 41–42, Man. Bk., PAS Papers, HSP.

57. Manumission Deed of Phillis Williams, freedom purchased by Sampson Williams, 21 December 1807, Indentures and Releases: Both Parties to Contract Being Black, Reel 23, PAS Papers, HSP.

58. Indenture of Andrew to John Riddle, 24 March 1809, Indentures and Releases: Both Parties to Contract Being Black, Reel 23, PAS Papers, HSP.

59. Phillip Lairy v. William Hollingshead, 19 September–4 October 1792, Materials Concerning Problems of Individual Blacks, Reel 24, PAS Papers, HSP.

60. Deed of Purchase of Dinah by Abraham Willing, 6 April 1784, Bills of Sale, Reel 22, PAS Papers, HSP.

61. Jessica Millward notes that "purchasing kin presented . . . a paradox. By participating in these monetary transactions," she contends, African Americans "reinforced the idea of human beings as commodities." Millward, *Finding Charity's Folk*, 46.

62. Marriage, as historian Tera Hunter has observed, "was not an inviolable union between two people but an institution defined and controlled by the superior relationship of master to slave." Hunter, *Bound in Wedlock*, 6.

63. Writ of Habeas Corpus for Peggy, a negro, 16 February 1782, #102787, *Suffolk Files*, SJC, JA, MA.

64. Petition of Thomas Walker to Court of Common Pleas, 1 January 1782, #102787, *Suffolk Files*, SJC, JA, MA.

65. Petition of Thomas Walker to Court of Common Pleas, 1 January 1782, #102787, *Suffolk Files*, SJC, JA, MA. It is unclear from the extant documentation whether Roger and Peg had been enslaved prior to their run-in with Thomas; slave traders were, unfortunately, not above kidnapping free Black Americans and selling them into slavery. One of the most notable examples of these cases was the abduction and enslavement of Solomon Northup. See Northup, *Twelve Years a Slave: Narrative of Solomon Northup, a Citizen of New-York, Kidnapped in Washington City in 1841, and Rescued in 1853* in *Documenting the American South*, University of North Carolina–Chapel Hill, 1997, accessed August 11, 2021. Available at https://docsouth.unc.edu.

66. Petition of Thomas Walker to Court of Common Pleas, 1 January 1782, #102787, *Suffolk Files*, SJC, JA, MA.

67. Petition of Thomas Walker to Court of Common Pleas.

68. Petition of Thomas Walker to Court of Common Pleas.

69. Petition of Thomas Walker to Court of Common Pleas.

70. Notice to bring Peg to court, 18 February 1782, Petition of Thomas Walker to Court of Common Pleas, 1 January 1782, #102787, *Suffolk Files*, SJC, JA, MA.

71. Notice of Peg being brought to court from jail, Petition of Thomas Walker to Court of Common Pleas, 1 January 1782, #102787, *Suffolk Files*, SJC, JA, MA.

72. Numerous scholars have studied these pivotal cases. Recent studies include Emily Blanck, "Seventeen Eighty-three: The Turning Point in the Law of Slavery

and Freedom in Massachusetts," *New England Quarterly* 75, 1 (March 2002): 24–51; Chernoh Sesay Jr., "The Revolutionary Black Roots of Slavery's Abolition in Massachusetts," *New England Quarterly* 87, 1 (March 2014): 99–131; and Manisha Sinha, *The Slave's Cause: A History of Abolition* (New Haven, CT: Yale University Press, 2016), 65–96.

73. I am grateful to John Hannigan at the Massachusetts Archives for helping me work through all possible conclusions to this case and exhausting all possible source material where these conclusions may have been located.

74. Morgan, *"Partus sequitur ventrem."*

75. Emphasis added. Emancipation Deed and Indenture Agreement of Teeny, formerly enslaved by William McMurtrie, 16 August 1786, Book A, Reel 20, 8, Man. Bk., PAS Papers, HSP.

76. On indentured servitude as a tenuous position between slavery and freedom, see Dunbar, *Fragile Freedom*, 26–47.

77. Emancipation Deed of Rosetta, freedom purchased by Abigail Lee, 31 October 1800, vol. 3Q, 261, Misc. Records, SCDAH.

78. Nash and Soderlund, *Freedom by Degrees*.

79. Marcia Anne Collier Ferqueau v. Marcie and her two Children, 21–23 March 1705, Book E, Reel 21, 439–40, Man. Bk., PAS Records, HSP. See also a copy of the court's summary of the case, Papers and Related Documents Concerning Court Cases in which Slaves Were Awarded Freedom, Reel 24, PAS Papers, HSP.

80. Manumission Deed of Lise et al., formerly enslaved by Anthony Peter Provenchere, 15 February 1802, Book E, Reel 21, 276, Man. Bk., PAS Papers, HSP.

81. Emancipation Deed of Marinette and Alcindor, formerly enslaved by Elizabeth Garresché, 9 March 1807, Book F, Reel 21, 29, Man. Bk., PAS Papers, HSP.

82. Millward, *Finding Charity's Folk*, 14–26.

83. Testimony of Margaret Gough on behalf of Richard Gough, 1 September 1818, vol. 3Q, 261, Misc. Records, SCDAH.

84. Manumission Deed of Eunice, formerly enslaved by Thomas O. Elliott, 5 February 1790, vol. YY, 132, Misc. Records, SCDAH.

85. Olwell, "Becoming Free"; Myers, *Forging Freedom*, 51.

86. Testimony of Rachel Williams (senior) and Rachel Williams (junior) on behalf of Mary Anthony, 18 March 1793, Book F, Reel 21, 438, Man. Bk., PAS Papers, HSP.

87. Testimony of John Gordon on behalf of Hannah, et al., 20 May 1817, vol. 40, 9, Misc. Records, SCDAH.

88. On the idea of the republican mother, see Kerber, *Women of the Republic*, 199–200, 229–30, 235, 269.

89. One especially notable exception to this is Jessica Millward's *Finding Charity's Folk*. Millward explores motherhood as a force of agency and resistance, particularly as it relates to emancipation efforts, noting that "motherhood held the potential to be revolutionary." Likewise, she contends that "as mothers, black women tried to instill in their children a brighter vision of freedom." Millward, *Finding Charity's Folk*, 15, 18.

90. I am grateful to Catherine Kerrison for helping me to flesh out this argument. Catherine Kerrison, phone conversation with author, January 16, 2021.

91. See, for example, Karen Cook Bell, *Running from Bondage: Enslaved Women and Their Remarkable Fight for Freedom in Revolutionary America* (Cambridge: Cambridge University Press, 2021); Douglas R. Egerton, *Death or Liberty: African*

Americans and Revolutionary America (New York: Oxford University Press, 2009); Sylvia Frey, *Water from the Rock: Black Resistance in a Revolutionary Age* (Princeton, NJ: Princeton University Press, 1991); and Sesay Jr., "The Revolutionary Black Roots of Slavery's Abolition in Massachusetts."

92. Karen Cook Bell's important work reconceptualizes the American Revolution as a conflict in which enslaved Black women and girls fought for freedom for themselves and their children by escaping enslavement. This notable contribution to the historiography finds that these "founding Black mothers" were deeply motivated to escape or attempt to escape enslavement by a desire for freedom, but also by love of family and their children in particular. See Bell, *Running from Bondage*.

93. For example, see Johnson, *Wicked Flesh*; and Millward, *Finding Charity's Folk*.

94. On the concept of social death in enslavement, see Orlando Patterson, *Slavery and Social Death: A Comparative Study*, with a new preface (Cambridge, MA: Harvard University Press, 2018).

95. See especially Dunbar, *Fragile Freedom*; Johnson, *Wicked Flesh*; Millward, *Finding Charity's Folk*; and Turner, *Contested Bodies*.

96. Johnson, *Wicked Flesh*, 4.

Chapter 7. The Rights Revolution

1. Brendan McConville, *The King's Three Faces: The Rise and Fall of Royal America, 1688–1776* (Chapel Hill: University of North Carolina Press, 2007).

2. On the politicization of women as a result of the Revolution, see especially Kerber, *Women of the Republic*; Norton, *Liberty's Daughters*; and Zagarri, *Revolutionary Backlash*.

3. "Rights talk" emerged in the early years of the American Revolution and later captured the rapt attention of the American public with the publication of Thomas Paine's *Common Sense* and the composition of the Declaration of Independence in 1776. Finding its precedent in the English tradition, much of this discussion and debate was centered around American colonists' rights as British subjects. This "rights talk" first focused on issues of representation and taxation and later evolved to advocate for a separation from Great Britain and the declaration of the sovereignty of the United States of America. Even in the creation of a new nation, rights talk was a focal point of debate. At the Constitutional Convention, some participants moved to include a Bill of Rights, which aimed to protect the rights of individuals in the face of a strong, centralized government, as a necessary element of the new state. Most of the authors of these tracts and laws, which formed the ideological framework for the war and the new nation that would be born of it, were men. For more on the English rights tradition and a discussion of rights talk during and after the American Revolution, see, for example, Bernard Bailyn, *The Ideological Origins of the American Revolution* (New York: Belknap Press, 1992); Jack N. Rakove, *Declaring Rights: A Brief History with Documents* (New York: Bedford Books, 1998); John Philip Reid, *Constitutional History of the United States*, abridged edition (Madison: University of Wisconsin Press, 1995); Gordon S. Wood, *The Radicalism of the American Revolution* (New York: First Vintage Books, 1991).

4. On free and enslaved Black Americans utilizing the rhetoric of the Revolution and pushing for its ideals to become reality, see, for example, Frey, *Water from the*

Rock (Princeton, NJ: Princeton University Press, 1991); and Sesay Jr., "The Revolutionary Black Roots of Slavery's Abolition in Massachusetts."

5. On the abolition process in Pennsylvania, see for example Nash and Soderlund, *Freedom by Degrees.* In Massachusetts, see Emily Blanck, "Seventeen Eighty-three."

6. Zagarri, "Rights of Man and Woman," 203–5.

7. Zagarri, "Rights of Man and Woman," 223.

8. Zagarri, "Rights of Man and Woman," 205.

9. Scholars of the American Civil War and Reconstruction era have examined the ways in which women and enslaved people expected certain relief and protection from the state, and made assertive claims "as if they had a right" to this aid. Gregory Downs, *Declarations of Dependence: The Long Reconstruction of Popular Politics in the South, 1861–1908* (Chapel Hill: University of North Carolina Press, 2011), 2. In so doing, these dependent groups of people who experienced unequal citizenship attempted to "stretch the boundaries of legal rights." Downs, *Declarations of Dependence,* 223 n. 2; see also Laura Edwards, *A People and Their Peace: Legal Culture and the Transformation of Inequality in the Post-Revolutionary South* (Chapel Hill: University of North Carolina Press, 2009); Kate Masur, *An Example for All the Land: Emancipation and the Struggle over Equality in Washington, D.C.* (Chapel Hill: University of North Carolina Press, 2010); and Stephanie McCurry, *Confederate Reckoning: Power and Politics in the Civil War South* (Cambridge, MA: Harvard University Press, 2012).

10. In their petitions, women used the conceptions of possessing a "right" and being "entitled" to something almost interchangeably, and it is clear that they declared rights inherent to their status as dependents (i.e., protection and support) and demanded the entitlements that came with these rights.

11. For studies of women's rights and political roles during the American Revolution and in the early republic, see, for example, Carol Berkin, *Revolutionary Mothers: Women in the Struggle for America's Independence* (New York: Vintage Books, 2005); Ruth H. Bloch, "Republican Virtue: The Gendered Meanings of Virtue in Revolutionary America," in *Gender and Morality in Anglo-American Culture, 1650–1800* (Los Angeles: University of California Press, 2003), 136–53; Susan Branson, *These Fiery Frenchified Dames: Women and Political Culture in Early National Philadelphia* (Philadelphia: University of Pennsylvania Press, 2001); Linda Grant DePauw, *Founding Mothers: Women of America in the Revolutionary Era* (Boston: Houghton Mifflin, 1975); Kerber, *Women of the Republic*; Cynthia A. Kierner, *Beyond the Household: Women's Place in the Early South, 1700–1835* (Ithaca, NY: Cornell University Press, 1998); Klepp, *Revolutionary Conceptions*; Jan Lewis, "The Republican Wife: Virtue and Seduction in the Early Republic," *William and Mary Quarterly* 44, no. 4 (October 1987): 689–721; Norton, *Liberty's Daughters*; Norton, "The Evolution of White Women's Experience in Early America"; Alfred F. Young, *Masquerade: The Life and Times of Deborah Sampson, Continental Soldier* (New York: First Vintage Books, 2004); Zagarri, *Revolutionary Backlash*; and Zagarri, "Rights of Man and Woman."

12. Petition of Ann Valk, 16 November 1811, no. 59, *PGA*, SCDAH.

13. Petition of Freelove Scott, October 1777, *Felt Collection,* vol. 183, pp. 241–42, MA.

14. The Massachusetts Confiscation Act was unique from its counterparts in other states, as it "explicitly encouraged the wife of the absentee to break from her husband," essentially requiring her to assume her own political identity supportive of the

revolutionary cause—in order to win back her family's property. See Kerber, *Women of the Republic*, 124.

15. This case stands in stark contrast to that of another Massachusetts woman, Anna Gordon Martin, who escaped punishment for her husband's treason on the basis that she was not responsible for her political leanings. Instead, her case hinged upon the argument that a wife's political identity was not separate or distinct from her husband's. See Kerber, *No Constitutional Right to Be Ladies*, 3–46.

16. Joseph Scott was an absentee whom Freelove alleged had no intention of returning to Boston or caring for his family in the future. Resolve on the Petition of Freelove Scott, 18 October 1777, ch. 454, *Acts and Resolves*, vol. 20, p. 177.

17. Additionally, the state may have considered the benefit of this property being held by a woman, as opposed to a loyalist like Joseph Scott, who might use that leverage to benefit the British cause.

18. Petition of Isabella Kingsley, 28 January 1783, no. 343, *PGA*, SCDAH.

19. Petition of Judith Scott, n.d., *Felt Collection*, vol. 218, pp. 84–88, MA.

20. Resolve on the Petition of Judith Scott, 17 April 1778, ch. 962, *Acts and Resolves*, vol. 20, p. 363.

21. Petition of Elizabeth Freeman, n.d., *Felt Collection*, vol. 236, pp. 482–84, MA.

22. Resolve on the Petition of Elizabeth Freeman, 13 June 1782, ch. 30, *Acts and Laws of the Commonwealth of Massachusetts* (Boston: Wright & Potter Printing Co., 1890), p. 201.

23. Petition of Susanna Hood, 1 June 1788, GCM, MA.

24. Resolve on the Petition of Susanna Hood, 9 June 1788, ch. 12, *Acts and Laws of the Commonwealth of Massachusetts* (Boston: Wright & Potter Printing Co., 1894), p. 180.

25. Salmon, *Women and the Law of Property*, 14–40.

26. On widowhood in early America, see Kristin A. Collins, "'Petitions without Number': Widows' Petitions and the Early Nineteenth-Century Origins of Public Marriage-Based Entitlements," *Law and History Review* 31, 1 (February 2013): 1–60; Vivian Bruce Conger, *The Widow's Might: Widowhood and Gender in Early British America* (New York: NYU Press, 2009); Wilson, *Life after Death*; and Wood, *Masterful Women*.

27. Kirsten Wood demonstrates how widows of slaveholding planters benefited from their continued identification and association with their husbands. These women, because of their economic status in marriage, did not lose "all of their husbands' reflected glory," even after these men died. Similarly, the notion of their dependence did not disappear when they became widows. "Wives," she asserts, "like slaves, were not supposed to outgrow their need for manly protection." Although widows were legally independent individuals, cast outside the protections of coverture, the specter of dependence still haunted their social and economic positions. From the Revolution through the Civil War, slaveholding widows used their status as widows to demand assistance from the state and from their families. Wood, *Masterful Women*, 1, 3–4, 82.

28. Wood, *Masterful Women*, 216 n. 4.

29. Kirsten Wood argues that widows took advantage of their often pitiable positions by demanding the care, protection, and support of mostly male family members. They framed these claims in terms of "familial reciprocity" owed to them on the basis of the roles they had played as wives and mothers. Wood's subjects essentially

employed guilt as a mechanism in their quarrels with family, a particularly "powerful ethical weapon." Wood, *Masterful Women*, 13.

30. Wood, *Masterful Women*, 62–63.

31. Wood, *Masterful Women*, 82.

32. Committee Report on the Petition of Major Brown, 4 December 1800, File of Joseph Chandler Brown, no. 817A, *Revolutionary Accounts Audited*, SCDAH.

33. Christiana Davis, for instance, cited her entitlement to "the annuity allowed by Law to widows Left under distressing Circumstances." Petition of Christiana Davis, 2 December 1794, no. 1779A, *Revolutionary Accounts Audited*, SCDAH. See also Petition of Ava Cuilliat, 8 December 1800, File of Adam Culliat, no. 1676A, *Revolutionary Accounts Audited*, SCDAH.

34. Petition of Ann Tatnall, 10 April 1779, granted 15 April 1779, RG27, E28, PSA.

35. Emphasis added.

36. Petition of Hannah Ellis, 18 November 1779, RG27, E28, PSA.

37. Petition of Mary Booth, n.d., *Felt Collection*, vol. 66, p. 78, MA. Several other women in the same circumstances petitioned for support using similar language. See chapter 4.

38. Emphasis added. Petition of Elizabeth Shelton, n.d., *Felt Collection*, vol. 184, p. 232, MA.

39. Petition of Sarah Tucker Simons, 15 November 1819, File of James Simons, no. 7007, *Revolutionary Accounts Audited*, SCDAH.

40. This woman's name was alternatively spelled "Clendining."

41. Under the Confederation government, the Continental Congress lacked any meaningful financial authority, and thus increasingly printed paper money to fund the costs of the war. Inflation rose exponentially and the body devalued its currency in 1780, which Clendening seems to reference here. See Benjamin Irvin, *Clothed in the Robes of Sovereignty: The Continental Congress and the People out of Doors* (New York: Oxford University Press, 2011), 205.

42. Petition of Margaret Clendening, December 1792, File of John Barnet, no. 296, *Revolutionary Accounts Audited*, SCDAH. Margret's petition was denied by the committee because she did not submit the petition by the required deadline. See Kierner, *Southern Women in Revolution*, 85.

43. Committee Report on the Petition of Mary Bell, 13 December 1813, and Letter to the State of South Carolina from Joseph McJenkins, 21 November 1813, File of James Bell, no. 417, *Revolutionary Accounts Audited*, SCDAH.

44. Committee Report on the Petition of Mary Bell, 13 December 1813, and Letter to the State of South Carolina from Joseph McJenkins, 21 November 1813, File of James Bell, no. 417, *Revolutionary Accounts Audited*, SCDAH.

45. Petition of Mary Avery, n.d., GCM, MA.

46. Petition of Elizabeth Chatham, 23 November 1785, RG27, E28, PSA.

47. Petition of Anna Christiana Labar, 9 December 1797, File of John Labar, no. 4389B.5, *Revolutionary Accounts Audited*, SCDAH.

48. Report on the Petition of Anna Christiana Labar, 23 December 1797, File of John Labar, no. 4389B.5, *Revolutionary Accounts Audited*, SCDAH.

49. Linda Kerber's study of women's petitioning in the revolutionary era found that "deference" was a necessary component of these pleas, and that overall, "this hesitancy of American women to become political actors would persist." Kerber, *Women of the*

Republic, 285. Other scholars, especially Susan Branson and Rosemarie Zagarri, have not been as tentative in their analysis of women's political roles, demonstrating that instead, women purposefully occupied political roles (though a backlash did follow in the Jacksonian era). See Branson, *These Fiery Frenchified Dames*; and Zagarri, *Revolutionary Backlash*. Here, I would like to argue that women exploited the terms of their dependence not in a deferential way but instead these petitioners identified themselves as bearers of rights in that dependence who were owed protection and assistance from the state on the basis of those rights.

50. Massachusetts Office of the Secretary of State, *Massachusetts Soldiers and Sailors of the Revolutionary War: A Compilation from the Archives*, vol. 5 (Boston: Wright & Potter Printing Co., 1899), 79–80. Available at https://archive.org.

51. Petition of Hannah Durant, n.d., GCM, MA.

52. Petition of Catherine Tolley, 23 December 1778, RG27, E28, PSA.

53. Petition of Sally Jones Wilson, n.d., Wilson divorce, Docket #112, November Term 1803, JA, MA. Emphasis added.

54. Petition of Nancy Robinson, 3 August 1807, Robinson Divorce, Docket #348, Record Book, March Term 1808, JA, MA.

55. Petition of Elizabeth Winneck, 15 August 1797, Winneck Divorce, #107512, *Suffolk Files*, SJC, JA, MA.

56. Petition of Sarah Dix, 16 April 1818, Dix Divorce, Docket #112, November 1818 Term, JA, MA.

57. Decree of Divorce, Dix Divorce, Docket #112, November 1818 Term, JA, MA.

58. Salmon, *Women and the Law of Property*, 76–77.

59. On alimony, see Salmon, *Women and the Law of Property*, 63, 66–71, 76, 212–13.

60. Salmon, *Women and the Law of Property*, 212.

61. Salmon, *Women and the Law of Property*, 68.

62. "An Act Concerning Divorces and Alimony," in Pennsylvania, *The Statutes at Large of Pennsylvania from 1682–1801: Compiled under the Authority of the Act of May 19, 1887*, vol. 12 (Harrisburg, PA: State Printer, 1906), 99.

63. Patrick M. Coyne, "The History of Alimony in Pennsylvania: A Need for Further Change," *Duquesne Law Review* 28, 4 (1989–1990): 711.

64. Salmon, *Women and the Law of Property*, 67; and Merril D. Smith, *Breaking the Bonds*, 12.

65. Marylynn Salmon uncovered a divorce case in New York in which a judge was quick to judge a wronged wife, despite her husband's adultery; he insisted that "if the wife had been perfectly discreet, prudent, and submissive to her husband, I should have allowed her half of this property." Women were required, then, to present their continued dependence on and submission to their husband's authority, even when their husbands themselves had not remained faithful to their marriage vows. See Salmon, *Women and the Law of Property*, 66.

66. Petition of Eliza Morgan, n.d., Morgan Divorce, Docket #235, March 1814 Term, JA, MA.

67. Petition of Elizabeth Orrock, 26 February 1805, Orrock Divorce, Docket #38, March Term 1805, JA, MA.

68. Depositions of Henry Armbruster, Mary Armbruster, and William Cummins, 22 March 1804, and Petition of Catherine France, 9 December 1803, France divorce, RG33, A41, PSA.

69. Beyond the record of her petitions, the records of the case have been lost. See Blake Divorce, November 1809 Term, SJC, JSA, MA; and Petition of Mary Blake, n.d., Blake Divorce File, Docket #136, March 1810 Term, JA, MA.

70. Petition of Ann Gardner, 17 April 1783, Gardner divorce, #129813, vol. 795, *Suffolk Files*, SJC, JA, MA.

71. Petition of Elizabeth Finney, 19 November 1782, Finney Divorce, #129808, vol. 795, *Suffolk Files*, SJC, JA, MA.

72. Petition of Mary Lobb, n.d., Lobb divorce, #129800, vol. 795, *Suffolk Files*, SJC, JA, MA.

73. Petition of Sarah Parker, 23 February 1781, #129798, vol. 795, *Suffolk Files*, SJC, JA, MA.

74. Petition of Katherine Mayhew, n.d., GCM, MA.

75. Petition of Susannah Mitchell, 7 September 1795, Mitchell Divorce, #107072, *Suffolk Files*, SJC, JA, MA.

Conclusion

1. Historian Linda Kerber mused that "to ask what they might have done had they lived instead in a world that allowed political concerns to be women's concerns is to ask an unanswerable question. To criticize them for not acting as if they lived in such a world is pointless." Kerber, *Women of the Republic*, 85.

2. "Collaborator, n.," *OED Online* (Oxford University Press, June 2020), accessed August 11, 2020. Available at www.oed.com.

3. My thinking on women's participation in their own subjugation has evolved a great deal from the time I finished my first draft of this book—in which I argued that women might be *complicit* in this project—to its final version, in which I see this process less as any woman's or women's *fault*, but more a feature of the larger patriarchal power structure. Especially useful was a summer 2020 article in the *Atlantic* by Anne Applebaum, in which she cites Harvard professor Stanley Hoffmann and his analysis of French citizens who collaborated with Nazi occupiers during World War II. Hoffman suggested that "a careful historian would have—almost—to write a huge series of case histories; for there seem to have been almost as many collaborationists as there were proponents or practitioners of collaboration." Quoted in Anne Applebaum, "History Will Judge the Complicit," *Atlantic*, June 2, 2020, available at www.theatlantic.com.

4. In the first draft of this conclusion, I wrote the following: "In their collaboration, however, they neglected the suppression of their sex by men in favor of attaining the more feasible goal of expressing power over their own individual lives." Thanks to the careful eyes of members of my writing group—Kristen Beales, Lauren Duval, and Shira Lurie—I came to the conclusion that I myself had fallen victim to the very trap that I critiqued in this book's introduction. Patriarchy is a powerful force, an intoxicating one, an all-encompassing one; it permeates culture, society, economics, politics, language, and knowledge. Even for a scholar who studies and evaluates the pervasiveness of patriarchal power as I do, it is difficult to escape its structures.

5. See, in particular, Catherine Clinton, *The Plantation Mistress: Women's World in the Old South* (New York: Pantheon Books, 1982); Thavolia Glymph, *Out of the House of Bondage: The Transformation of the Plantation Household* (New York: Cambridge

University Press, 2008); and Stephanie Jones-Rogers, *They Were Her Property: White Women as Slave Owners in the American South* (New Haven, CT: Yale University Press, 2019).

6. Ellen Carol DuBois, *Woman Suffrage and Women's Rights* (New York: NYU Press, 1998), 9–10.

7. Donald T. Critchlow, *Phillis Schlafly and Grassroots Conservativism: A Woman's Crusade* (Princeton, NJ: Princeton University Press, 2005).

8. Dobbs v. Jackson Women's Health Organization, No. 19-1392, slip. op. (U.S. June 24, 2022), https://www.supremecourt.gov/opinions/21pdf/19-1392_6j37.pdf.

A Note on Sources

1. Martha Clark (Curator, Massachusetts State Archives), conversation with author, August 26, 2016.

2. Aaron McWilliams posits that some of these petitions *may* have survived, and extant copies *may* be in some individual legislators' personal papers. The original minutes of the Colonial Assembly do not exist; they were copied in the eighteenth century and Benjamin Franklin printed them. Copies of those copies have been published in the *Pennsylvania Archives* 8th series (votes and proceedings), which can be accessed online. Aaron McWilliams (Reference Archivist, Pennsylvania State Archives), phone conversation with author, July 9, 2021.

3. Nellis and Cecere, eds., *Eighteenth-Century Records*. This volume also addresses the limitations of the source material.

4. Another reflection on the particular challenges of locating Black women in the archive and in telling stories of their experiences is in Adams and Pleck, *Love of Freedom*, 20–25.

5. Marisa J. Fuentes, *Dispossessed Lives*, 7.

Index

Page numbers in italics indicate Figures

ABOUT THE AUTHOR

Jacqueline Beatty is Assistant Professor of History at York College of Pennsylvania. She holds a PhD from George Mason University. Her work has appeared in *The South Carolina Historical Magazine* and the edited volume *Women Waging War in the American Revolution* (2022). She was a finalist for the 2017 SHEAR Manuscript Prize.

www.ingramcontent.com/pod-product-compliance
Ingram Content Group UK Ltd.
Pitfield, Milton Keynes, MK11 3LW, UK
UKHW041008090325
455861UK00013B/107/J